EDITED BY F. JAY TAYLOR

D1328470

The Secret

Diary of

Robert Patrick

1861–1865

LOUISIANA STATE UNIVERSITY PRESS
Baton Rouge and London

Louisiana Paperback Edition, 1996
ISBN 0-8071-2072-3 (pbk.)
05 04 03 02 01 00 99 98 97 96   5 4 3 2 1

The Library of Congress has cataloged this book as follows:

Patrick, Robert, 1835–1866.

   Reluctant rebel; the secret diary of Robert Patrick, 1861–1865
Edited by F. Jay Taylor. [Baton Rouge] Louisiana State University
Press [1959]

   260 p. illus. 24 cm.

   1. U. S.—Hist.—Civil War—Personal narratives—Confederate side.
2. U. S.—Hist.—Civil War—Regimental histories—Louisiana Infantry—4th. 3. Louisiana Infantry. 4th Regt., 1861–1865.   I.
Taylor, F. Jay, ed. II. Title.

                    Full name: Robert Draughon Patrick.

E605.P3   973.782   59–9083 ‡

Library of Congress

FOR

Adele Nash Ethridge

AND FOR

Evelyn AND *Terry*

Preface

Several years ago I was invited to examine a private collection of Indian artifacts at the home of Mrs. Adele Ethridge in Colfax, Louisiana. Although the Indian relics proved to be of great interest, my attention was diverted when Mrs. Ethridge remarked that her uncle had fought in the Civil War and had kept a journal of his experiences. Moreover, this manuscript had been treasured and preserved. Within a few moments I was curiously reading the yellow pages of this historic document and marveling at the penmanship of Robert Draughon Patrick. Mrs. Ethridge also produced photographs of " Uncle Robert " as well as several notebooks and letters written by him while serving in the Confederate army. It was soon agreed that I would take the manuscript and make a careful study with a view toward publication.

The original diary, now in my possession, exists in a large ledger of 223 pages. Patrick, a well-educated man with many talents, wrote the journal in small notebooks using Benn Pitman shorthand. At his leisure the author would transcribe the shorthand into the ledger. These notebooks, which are also in the possession of the editor, were sent to the Phonographic Institute of Greenville, Ohio, for a professional transcription. In comparing the two accounts only a few discrepancies were noted. Mrs. Ethridge has also generously placed at my disposal several letters written by Patrick during the conflict. With the exception of a few pages, the diary, notebooks, and letters are in an excellent state of preservation.

The diary has been reproduced as nearly as possible in the form in which it was originally written. Dates of entries were verified and corrected in rare instances. In several chapters paragraphs were broken when they ran too long for good reading.

Several omissions from the manuscript were made to sustain the reader's interest. For example, Patrick's detailed descriptions of the weather and frequent comments on the difficulties of learning shorthand seriously impair the movement of the narrative and were deleted. All parentheses in the work are those of the author while brackets indicate additions or changes made by the editor. No attempt has been made to correct errors in spelling and all misspelled words are repeated faithfully as they were written and are not labeled [sic]. Fortunately, Patrick was gifted with an uncommon ability to express himself and usually did so in an accepted form.

I have tried to identify most persons mentioned in the diary, especially those in Patrick's regiment, and friends living near his home in Clinton, Louisiana. These names appear in the appendix and can be readily located by reference to the index. The spelling of names in various sources did not always agree, and in cases where verification was impossible the most frequent spelling was used. Obscure nicknames and first names without surnames which had no direct connection with the narrative were generally ignored.

Notes have been provided to assist in identifying little known places or things as well as dates, lesser battles, strategy, events, and rumors of events. Certain other matters are explained for the serious reader. Whenever possible the most important source or secondary work has been cited.

This research was made possible in part by a grant received from the Southern Fellowships Fund. I also make grateful acknowledgment to Deans H. M. Weathersby and John R. Timmerman and the Louisiana College Faculty Research Fund. Without such generous assistance this book would not have been realized.

I am indebted for their friendly interest and assistance to President G. Earl Guinn, Librarian Sammy A. Dyson, Dr. and Mrs. E. Frank Masingill, Mr. Grady Welch, Miss Paula Halbert, Miss Jerry Lowery, Miss Wyn-Nelle Lee, Mr. Penrose St. Amant, and Mr. Abraham Attrep, all of Louisiana College; to Judge H. H. Kilbourne, Mr. and Mrs. Ventress J. Woodside, and Mrs. Mary A.

Norwood of Clinton; to Mr. and Mrs. L. F. Taylor of Gibsland; to Mrs. Ethel Holloman and Mr. Tommy Kohara of the Alexandria *Daily Town Talk*; to Mr. James M. Robinson, editor of the St. Francisville *Democrat*; to Dean John R. Hubbard of Newcomb College, Tulane University; and to Miss Elsie M. Hahn of Greenville, Ohio, who is one of the few persons able to transcribe Pitman shorthand today. The editor is deeply grateful to Mr. V. L. Bedsole and Miss Marcelle F. Schertz of the Department of Archives, Louisiana State University, for their assistance in locating important manuscript material, particularly one of Patrick's lost notebooks.

For their extensive and helpful suggestions I wish to express my appreciation to Professors Bell I. Wiley of Emory University, Frank E. Vandiver of The Rice Institute, T. Harry Williams of Louisiana State University, Louis Rubin of Hollins College, Bennett H. Wall of the University of Kentucky, Mr. Stephen E. Ambrose of the University of Wisconsin, and particularly to Dr. Edwin Adams Davis, editor, Source Studies in Southern History, also of Louisiana State University.

A note of gratitude is likewise due Professor Raymond D. Nichols of Louisiana College who lent his artistic talent to the maps and line drawings.

My special thanks are due Mrs. Ethridge for permitting me to prepare her uncle's diary for publication. Those who love history and treasure historical documents as does Mrs. Ethridge, help to assure future generations of a more careful understanding of their nation's past.

Finally comes love and thanks to my son Terry and to my wife Evelyn who endured so much and typed such long hours.

F. JAY TAYLOR

Louisiana College
Pineville, Louisiana
January, 1959

Table of contents

Maps and illustrations

Reluctant Rebel

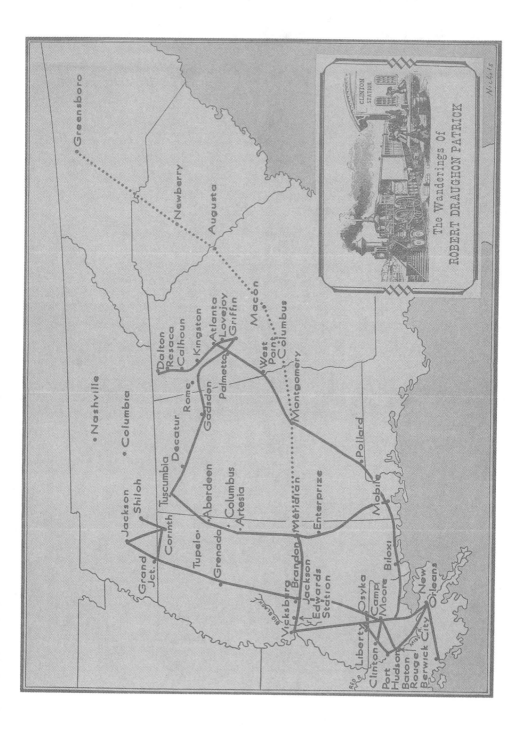

The Wanderings Of
ROBERT DRAUGHON PATRICK

Introduction

The fighting phase of Confederate army history has been more than covered in numerous personal narratives. But the problems of logistics and supply—what went on behind the shooting and marching of the soldiers—is a relatively unknown quantity in Confederate history. Robert Patrick's diary throws much light on this obscure area of activity.

Comments on the quality of Confederate supply officers are especially revealing. Combatant soldiers habitually disparaged the commissary and quartermaster officers. Patrick's first-hand, undoctored observations indicate that Johnny Reb's low esteem had abundant justification.

Especially valuable also are Patrick's comments on civilian conditions in areas near army camps and along the route of march. Because of his location in the rear, and the nature of his duties, Patrick saw much more of the people and the country in the no-man's-land bordering the fighting zones than did the ordinary soldier. His observations on destitution and dissolution in the environs of Johnston's army in Georgia in 1864 are particularly revealing. He shows that Southerners suffered about as much from Confederate as from Yankee depredation.

Patrick's honesty, literary craftsmanship, and lack of inhibitions in expression give his narrative unusual realism. He is much franker about the evils that accompany war than are most diarists and correspondents of this orthodox and romantic age. He was a keen observer who had a flair for descriptive writing. His diary helps to recapture the spirit of what has been described as America's most dramatic conflict—"the last war between gentlemen." The journal abounds in humor and numerous anecdotes which contribute much to its liveliness. "Poor Clarence,"

Patrick wrote, "I never knew before that he was so much addicted to drinking. If he had been as fond of his mother's milk as he is of whiskey, he would have been awful hard to wean." Even when he suffered, Patrick's humor was irrepressible. He blamed his troubles on the treatment of "ignorant, sap-headed physicians" who through doses of calomel and quinine "injudiciously administered" either "kill the individual or ruin his constitution for life."

The Patrick journal is also a contribution to the history of the state of Louisiana. It vividly describes his hometown of Clinton and serves, in part, as a wartime history of this then small village located in the southeastern section of the state. Other descriptions of Port Hudson, Greensburg, New Orleans, and Berwick City are recorded. The difficulties of communication and travel, the attitudes and plight of the people, as well as the state of public morale are likewise revealed by the diarist.

Nor does Patrick neglect the military because, after all, he was first a soldier, serving most of the war in one of the state's best-known regiments—the Fourth Louisiana Infantry. This regiment has a particular claim to be remembered in Louisiana because its second colonel was Henry Watkins Allen, afterwards brigadier general in the Confederate service and wartime governor of the state. Patrick was a particular friend of Colonel Allen and he gives us a splendid portrait of this gallant officer. The diary is also one of the best contemporary records of the Fourth Regiment as it marched through Louisiana, Mississippi, Alabama, and Georgia. When the end came this group was but a ragged, hungry, war-torn remnant listing one of the highest records for casualties in the entire Confederate army.

The pages of Robert Patrick's diary also reveal an intimate portrait of this young Southerner. He had an alert mind and was usually far superior to his comrades in intellectual ability and achievements. His formal education began at the age of five and continued in private schools until his seventeenth birthday. His observations give the reader a careful look into his life as a young-man-about-town in the prewar era and as a talented clerk in the Commissary and Quartermaster departments of the Confederate army.

4

Robert was a worthy representative of a well-established, highly respected upper middle class Louisiana family. He was accepted in the best social circles in the village of Clinton. He was interested in politics, music, and literature. His favorite author was Shakespeare although he enjoyed the writings of Scott, Moore, Thackeray, Pope, and Byron as well as the novels of such popular writers as Eugene Sue, Wilkie Collins, William Gilmore Simms, Charles A. Murray, Samuel Warren, and Charles J. Lever. His journal indicates a profound respect for the Bible and religion although he dwelt very little on spiritual matters.

Patrick was a firm believer in Southern rights and there can never be any doubt concerning his loyalty to the Confederacy. He always regretted, however, that " we are not engaged in a holier cause." Patrick was in full agreement with the school of historical thought which holds that fanatical agitation of small groups on both sides caused the Civil War. Although many contemporary historians still hold to the primacy of the slavery issue in evaluating the causes of the struggle, Patrick blamed the radicals on both sides of the Potomac and Ohio rivers. He wrote, " If I only had the fanatics of the North and the fire eaters of the South in equal numbers in a pen together, I'd make ' dog eat dog.' I'd ' make Rome howl ' for once."

Yet his fierce hatred of the Yankee invaders was almost boundless. Upon passing the grave of a Union soldier he once commented that this small plot of earth was a " just reward " for those who " must come to the South to murder our citizens, burn our houses, desolate our homes and lay waste to our country; to make war upon women and children turning them out to die of cold and want, without the slightest compunctions of conscience." He longed for the days when peace would be restored to the unhappy Southland and, by some miracle, the Confederate states could enjoy their independence. Even then he exhibited skepticism, as he predicted that Texas would not be satisfied and would soon seek to disrupt the new nation.

Robert never ceased to hope for victory but he had little faith that Southern independence could be achieved on the battlefield. After the defeats at Vicksburg and Gettysburg his comments indicated a growing anxiety and a realization that the South would eventually lose the war unless England and France intervened or the North quit the struggle. During the Atlanta campaign he began to consider seriously his postwar plans. His earlier graphic descriptions of an optimistic South thrilled with the prospect of a quick and glorious victory soon faded into tragedies of defeat, devastation, refugees, incompetence, shortages, and death. Even so, Patrick declared that he was " not in favor of stopping the war until we are united."

Viewed critically as a reliable account of the contemporary scene, the Patrick diary is not without deficiencies. Some of the material is reminiscent rather than a day-by-day record; the detail is frequently excessive; and there are gaps in the narrative resulting from Patrick's losing his notebook on several occasions. This sometimes gives the journal a lack of cohesion and movement. He often digressed in his writings, and continuous comment on certain subjects such as his health was almost a mania. This was especially true during long, cold months in camp when relatively little action was taking place. He was usually careful, nonetheless, to distinguish fact from rumor and much of the narrative is corroborated by other reliable data.

In addition to his wartime narrative, Robert Patrick left a detailed account of his life in the antebellum South.[1] In this biographical sketch Patrick recalled that

> Mother [Emeline Draughon Patrick, 1811–1869] says, and she ought to know, that I was born on the 24th day of December 1835. My earliest recollections were of being at my grandfather Robert Draughon's plantation, near old man Shropshire's place, a distance of two or three miles from Hebsibah [Hepzibah] Church.[2] That has been a long time ago, but

[1] As a preface to his diary Patrick filled thirty-seven pages of the ledger with recollections of his youth. He stated that "I have decided to write a brief sketch of my whole history. It will not fill many pages and as I have nothing to do, it will be as well to employ my time and amuse myself this way as any other." Unless otherwise indicated, all quotations in the Introduction are from Patrick's journal and letters and are not footnoted.

[2] The only remaining trace of the old church is its almost abandoned cemetery where Patrick was buried beside the grave of his father on December 9, 1866. Robert Patrick's mother and his Uncle Robert Draughon were also buried in Hepzibah cemetery.

although I was very young at the time, I still remember how everything looked. I remember the house, which was a *double* one, with a hall or passage between and a gallery in front. The horse lots and stables stood rather in fronting the dwelling, and a little on the right of the house as you approached it. I remember the cross-barred gate before the door, with a huge rose bush growing beside it, and on the left of the walk running from the gate to the house there was a wide spreading beech tree, under whose grateful shade I have spent many a childish hour, and in the cool, pleasant and melancholy autumnel days, I gathered many a pocketful of the rich, brown mast that the breeze had blown upon the ground. I remember the smokehouse, the kitchen, and the old sweetgum tree that stood near. The gum balls were always a kind of mystery to me, and I always considered them the most wonderful production of nature.

About this time being nearly five years old, and being able to repeat the alphabet both forwards and backwards very rapidly, which was more than most of the larger children could do, I was sent to school, along with the other children, my aunts and uncles. The old schoolmaster's name was Gas, a great, big bellied old fellow, who was very good natured and kind. He boarded at my grandfather's and took a very great fancy to me, on account of my aptitude at learning.

Although Robert could not recall additional details of his life at Grandfather Draughon's plantation, he did describe the serious financial reverses suffered by his family in 1841. Patrick's father, Reuben Woodworth Patrick (1798–1855), and his father's brother, Palmer Patrick (1796–1865), formed a partnership and attempted to operate a trading boat on the Red River. Robert remembered that " everything went on swimmingly for a time, until one morning Palmer came up among the missing, with a considerable amount of ready money belonging to the firm." Other irregularities were traced to Palmer Patrick and soon the firm was forced into bankruptcy. Reuben Patrick was burdened with heavy debts which were not wholly cancelled until 1854.

After this ill-fated venture Reuben Patrick borrowed a small sum of money and moved his family, including Robert's baby sister Mary Adelia (1840–1923),[3] to Greensburg, Louisiana.

[3] On December 6, 1866, just two days before her brother Robert's sudden death, Mary Adelia Patrick married James E. Nash. On April 7, 1877, they became the

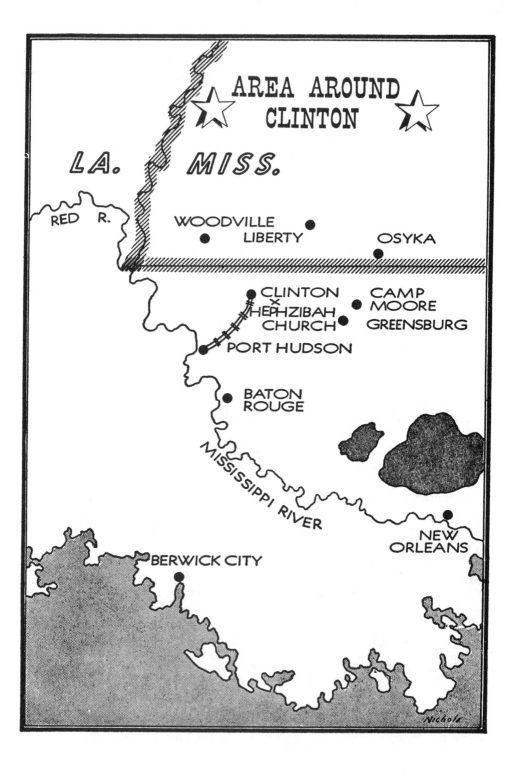

There he opened a small store, but because of his many debts the business had to be carried in the name of Harrison McKie, a relative of the family.

Once again Robert returned to school. His teacher was the Reverend D. B. Roberts, whom Patrick described as a " simple, childish old man, with little or no education, though as a matter of course he could have taught all such chaps as I was for years to come." Patrick complained that " there was no society about Greensburg at that time, and nearly all who lived there were ignorant, vulgar, low flung people and my family had blessed little to do with them." He also observed that

> The country all around Greensburg is very poor and the citizens, as a class, poor and ignorant, and they seem to think more of a little money, *cash*, than they do of any amount of education. We had a garden spot attached to our premises, and the ground was so poor that my father used to say that the vegetables would grow up until they could see themselves, become ashamed of their appearance, and hide themselves in the earth again.

> There was very little business done in Greensburg and all the goods were brought there from New Orleans, across the lake via Springfield. From Springfield they were transported in wagons. The principal business was done in the whiskey and card playing line. All the youth of the surrounding country took to whiskey and gambling like ducks do to water. Any boy who could play cards and drink whiskey—I don't think they ever had any other kind of liquor—was looked up to by the balance of us. How I longed for the time to come when I could walk up to the bar and take my drink, or sit down to the card table and have a four handed game of *seven up*. What an admiration I had for a fellow who would stand up and curse another, and if he resented it, knock him down, and give him the devil generally. After I had left these scenes however, I came to have a perfect fear and horror of a drunken man.

> They would have a general muster every month, and that was the grand day for drinking. The military was composed entirely of cavalry, and a grand display they made on their thin, grass gutted, piney woods poneys,

---

parents of a daughter, Esther Adele Nash, who married James W. Ethridge on February 9, 1914. Mrs. Adele Nash Ethridge is currently residing in Alexandria, Louisiana, and it is through her kindness and understanding that this diary, written by her Uncle Robert, has been made available for publication.

with their manes and tales filled with cuckleburs, and looking as though they had never had a curry comb or horse brush upon their shaggy, woolly hides.

Every now and then during the parade they would draw up in front of a groggery and the commanding officer would order a bucket of whiskey to be brought out, and carried down the line.

The Patrick family resided in Greensburg for almost a year and then moved to Clinton in 1842. Clinton was an aristocratic community with a population of one thousand which served as the center of a vast cotton growing area in the Feliciana country of southeastern Louisiana. This region differs from most of southern Louisiana in that its early settlers were largely of Anglo-Saxon rather than of Latin origin.[4] The predominance of this stock, particularly English, is reflected in its culture and architecture. The classic tradition may still be observed in the courthouse and in a score of homes.

Clinton was a very prosperous community prior to the hostilities of the sixties. Versatile leadership had favored the area. Its rich plantation economy, its banking institutions, and even its commerce and industry, were well-established. It was the terminus for the Clinton and Port Hudson, one of the first railroads built in the state. The village was a cultured one and the social life was brilliant and gay. The educational institutions of the parish had achieved a reputation by 1850 which was not surpassed by any other parish in the state for several decades.

Reuben Patrick secured employment as deputy clerk under Franklin Hardesty,[5] who was at the time Clerk of the District Court in Clinton. Young Robert resumed his studies as a student of Miss Eliza Mills—" a strict disciplinarian and very exacting." He lamented that " my powers were always taxed to the utmost . . . to memorise the long lessons she gave me. Instead of being in bed asleep, where a child my age should have been, I was sitting

---

[4] The Patricks migrated into the Feliciana area from upper New York and the Draughons had moved from the Edgefield district of South Carolina.

[5] In tribute to this close friend Reuben Patrick named his second son Franklin Hardesty Patrick (1851-1907). In the diary Robert refers to his brother as " Little Frank."

The Courthouse at Clinton

up poring over my long lessons, thus depriving me of my natural and needful rest and undermining my constitution." Robert stated that he received many thrashings from Miss Eliza but admitted "learning more than I ever did at any other school in the same length of time."

Among the childhood events recalled by Patrick was the Presidential election of 1844 when Henry Clay and James K. Polk were candidates. Robert declared that he was a Whig—" a strong, tremendous Whig, and I thought that the fate of old Clay depended upon the *vim* which I would sing the electioneering songs, and the number of times I would shout ' Hurra! for Clay and Frelinghuysen.' " [6] But the Whigs lost the election and Patrick blamed Clay for the defeat. "I do not believe old Clay was a Southern man at heart," Patrick wrote, " because he didn't wish to see the South strengthened by the annexation of Texas."

In 1845 young Robert enrolled in a new school kept by Martin Townsend, whom he described as " a Yankee by birth, but a well educated man and a good teacher." School days continued until 1851. Holidays were passed in hunting and fishing but were marred on several occasions by hard spells of sickness. That he was growing up was evidenced by his increased romantic interest in the young ladies. One lively affair, which he erroneously described as my " first and last love scrape," involved a young Clinton belle by the name of Josephine Rich. " Great Caesar! how I loved her. I thought she was the prettiest and the smartest creature that I ever saw." But his ardent love for " darling Josephine " soon cooled and the romance ended. Although there were several other occasions when Robert was entranced by the company of certain young ladies, particularly " Maggie," he never seriously considered marriage and died a bachelor.

In the spring of 1851 Robert Patrick was taken into the firm of his uncle, R. H. Draughon, to learn bookkeeping. This arrangement lasted only a few months when Reuben Patrick decided that his son should study medicine. Accordingly, Robert was sent to the local office of Dr. A. J. Ranaldson to serve as an apprentice.

[6] Theodore Frelinghuysen, Whig candidate for Vice-President on the ticket with Henry Clay.

Patrick explained that he got along very well until one night the doctor was called upon to amputate the arm of a Negro which had been mangled in a gin. "I had to hold the arm, which smelled worse than a dead horse, while he performed the operation. After it was through with the Doctor proposed to have an oyster supper, but I had no appetite for anything of the kind. The next morning I informed him that I thought the profession would not suit me and that was the last of my studying medicine."

Once again Robert assumed the position of bookkeeper for R. H. Draughon. It was in his uncle's store, he sadly related, that "I learned to drink. In the backroom . . . where he kept almost every variety of wines and liquors and secure from observation, was where the tempting ruinous draught first passed my lips." Robert's addiction to drinking was a serious problem that he was never quite able to solve. Although freely acknowledging his love for drink, Patrick declared that he had never had any disposition to gamble and "never played for anything except on one or two occasions."

In late 1854 Reuben Patrick established himself as an independent businessman in Clinton and Robert became his chief assistant. The partnership was cut short, however, by Reuben Patrick's sudden death in the spring of 1855. He had traveled to Iowa to purchase stores and on the return trip he died of cholera in St. Louis.

Robert was not content to remain in business without his father, and in the winter of 1855 he was appointed local agent for the Clinton and Port Hudson Railroad. Patrick explained that he "got along tolerably well, though I continued to drink a good deal." But he was restless in this position and soon returned to work for his uncle as bookkeeper, a position he held until the summer of 1860. At that time he was appointed deputy sheriff. "This was an easy job," Robert wrote, "for I had never more than two hours work a day, because I was office deputy and had no riding to do. . . . I liked this situation first rate, and I remained in it until the breaking out of the war." When hostilities began Robert Patrick enlisted in Major Samuel E. Hunter's company of volunteers, the first unit organized in East Feliciana Parish.

On the 28th day of April, 1861, the Hunter Rifles, nearly one hundred and fifty strong, climbed aboard the train at the Clinton depot and amid many tears and sad farewells were off to Port Hudson. Shortly after arriving the soldiers embarked aboard the transport *J. A. Cotton* and were soon steaming down the Mississippi for New Orleans. Robert described the boys as " all in a high glee and as we had some violins aboard, they were fiddling and dancing all the way down." After several days of " frolicing " around the Crescent City, the troops were assembled at the old Metairie race course. This site proved to be unsuitable for a military encampment and the troops were transferred to Camp Moore, located some seventy-eight miles north of New Orleans in the higher climate of St. Helena Parish. There on May 25, 1861, the Fourth Louisiana Infantry Regiment was mustered into service.

Patrick was detailed as a clerk in the Commissary Department but fearing criticism that he might be shirking duty, he resigned this position, took up his rifle, and went into the ranks. The Fourth Regiment was soon dispatched to the Gulf Coast along the Mississippi Sound to protect this region against invasion. Life was pleasant at the regimental encampment in Biloxi. Robert commented that his tent was " right on the beach, where we could bathe as much as we wished, and had any amount of fish, crabs, and oysters."

Patrick complained, however, " that staying in the ranks didn't pay. That everyone was looking out for an easy place, and that no one thought any more of me, nor gave me any credit for giving up an easy position and going into the ranks. I therefore resolved to get through the war as easy as I could. But I didn't intend to use any dishonorable means to attain this end." Thus when the regimental quartermaster offered Robert a position as clerk, he accepted and noted that " from this time on, I carried a gun during the war only when I saw proper to do so, and that was only on one or two occasions."

The Commissary and Quartermaster were two divisions of the Confederate War Department charged with the responsibility of food and subsistence and with seeing that these materials reached the army. The Commissary provided the soldiers with food and the Quartermaster was concerned with blankets, tents, uniforms, shoes, cooking utensils, and certain hospital supplies. The Quartermaster was also charged with army transportation, with providing feed for all livestock, and with the payment of troops. Because of the nature of their duties these divisions worked very closely together.

Robert Patrick served as a clerk in both the Commissary and Quartermaster divisions, assuming responsibility wherever his services were ordered. Although he occasionally assisted the paymaster and scoured the countryside for commissary stores, most of his time was spent in various regimental and brigade offices keeping books and making quarterly returns.

Perhaps there was some tinge of conscience that he was not fighting in the front lines, for Patrick found it necessary to explain that

> I did not seek nor desire the " bubble reputation," nor did I have any particular desire to make myself " food for powder." In short I had no military aspirations whatever, and I only entered the army from a sense of duty alone, for I conceive it to be the bounden duty of every man to serve his country, in some capacity, when called upon to do so. No man's too good to serve his country. I soon found however that there were easy places in the army as well as elsewhere, and that they were to be filled by someone. At first I declined all offers of easy positions, because I thought it looked better and that it was my duty to bear my part of the labors, the hardships and the dangers incidental to the life of a soldier, but I soon saw that every man was laboring hard to better his condition, and every one who had any capacity and a great many who didn't, were striving with might and main for office.

> I made no efforts in this way because as I said before I had no military aspirations whatever, but after watching the workings of the wires in all their various little ramifications, I came to the following conclusion: That I would take the comfort and accord to others the glory, or I would give them the glory and I would take the comfort.

> *Apropos*, this reminds me of a passage in the First part of Henry Fourth. It is part of a conversation between Prince Hal and Jack Falstaff just before the battle, when old Jack has sad misgivings as to how he will come out in the fracas. Prince Hal remarks, " Why, thou owest God a death." Falstaff, " Tis not due yet; I would be loath to pay

him before his day. Why need I be so forward with him that calls not on me? Well 'tis no matter. Honor pricks me on. Yea, but how if honor prick me off when I come on? How then? Can honor set to a leg? No. Or an arm? No. Or take away the grief of a wound? No. Honor hath no skill in surgery then? No. What is honor? A word. What is that honor? Air. A trim reckoning! Who hath it? He that died o' Wednesday. Doth he feel it? No. Doth he hear it? No. Is it insensible then? Yea, to the dead. But will it not live with the living? No. Why? Detraction will not suffer it therefore I'll none of it! Honor is a mere scutcheon and so ends my catechism."

I do not mean to imply that I ignore honor. Quite the contrary. I resolved from the first to do my duty and my whole duty wherever I might be placed, and when I enlisted, I mentally repeated the words of Feeble, old Falstaff's recruit. "By my troth I care not; a man can die but once; we owe God a death; I'll ne'er bear a base mind; an't by my destiny, so: an't be not, so; and let it go which way it will, he that dies this year is quit for the next."

After I had been in the service about three months, I saw that no one thanked me nor cared anything more for me because I worked hard, or drilled hard, and stood my guard regularly. I resolved to accept the very first position that was offered me which would render my soldier life—disagreeable enough at best—more pleasant and easier.

In the autumn of 1861 the various detachments of the Fourth were assembled and sent to Berwick City, Louisiana, located seventy miles southwest of New Orleans at the mouth of the Atchafalaya River. This region served as a terminal point for the Texas trade and was also an important center for blockade runners. Robert remained in Berwick City until the middle of February, 1862, when the regiment was ordered to Jackson, Tennessee, to join the Confederate army commanded by Albert Sidney Johnston.

Shortly after arriving in Jackson, Patrick was detailed as a clerk in the office of General Braxton Bragg, a position he maintained until the Fourth moved to Corinth, Mississippi, a few weeks later. Patrick related that he did not have much to do with Bragg as "he always had his head working on something that the balance of us didn't know anything about." He described the General as a "tall, fine looking man and very stern." Later, he was much more critical, commenting that " Bragg is not fit for a general . . . the most he is fit for is the command of a brigade and he would make a damned poor brigadier. . . . If Jeff Davis will just let old Bragg alone, I think he will do us more damage than the enemy."

Efforts were made to have Patrick remain in Bragg's office but when the Fourth Regiment entrained for Corinth on March 21 he managed to get aboard. This trip was a miserable one for, " The weather was dreadful . . . it was cold and the rain poured down in torents." After this toilsome journey, the regiment went into camp near Corinth. Robert declared that he was amazed at the vast assemblage of men: " As far as the eye could reach over the hills and vales, the earth was thickly studded with the white tents of the soldiers. Men, horses, wagons and mules were crowding in every direction. A slow, cold rain mingled with sleet fell all day long. . . . Long trains of cars passed up and down the road every hour of the day and night, and the shrieking of the locomotive made the most dismal sounds imaginable. . . ."

The Fourth remained near Corinth for several weeks. Patrick, displaying an optimism that was characteristic throughout the war, wrote his sister, " The enemy are reported thirty thousand strong, encamped on the bank of the Tennessee. I do not know whether they meditate an attack on us or not, but I will vouch for one thing, and that is if they leave the river they will be the worst whipped set of men that ever started out to fight or we will be entirely cut to pieces. They cannot march through Mississippi and they had as well ' subside.' "

The Union army under Grant, however, was even larger than Patrick surmised. Instead of " subsiding " they fought and eventually won the battle of Shiloh, April 6-7, 1862, the first great battle of the war in the West. Although primarily concerned with caring for the quartermaster stores, Patrick found himself in the thick of the fighting: " About sunrise on Sunday morning, April 6, 1862, before we had fired a gun, Bob McKie was killed on one side of me and Jim Depriest on the other. I began to think it pretty warm to be so early in the action. This sort of work was kept up all day and the Regiment lost very heavily. How I escaped unhurt is a mystery. But so it was." Robert wearily recorded that " I toughed it through . . . but I resolved that if I could honorably keep out of it that I would never go into another."

Upon returning to Corinth with the retreating Confederate army, Patrick was detailed to the office of Brigadier General Daniel Ruggles to serve as the general's private secretary. Although he held an important position, Patrick was not satisfied working for " this bull headed old brute " and at the earliest opportune moment he slipped away to rejoin his regiment which had evacuated Corinth on May 30, 1862, with General P. G. T. Beauregard's army.

Robert found a portion of the Fourth Louisiana at Edward's Station, Mississippi, while the remaining companies were in Vicksburg constructing fortifications. A short time later the regiment was ordered back to Louisiana to assist in driving Federal troops out of Baton Rouge and possibly New Orleans. In October, 1862, Patrick moved into Port Hudson with the troops assigned to build the works at that point. He modestly exclaimed that " my Regiment was the first to fortify Vicksburg and now were the first to fortify Port Hudson." It was expected that the completion of these fortifications would make Port Hudson a second Gibralter.

It was at this point that Robert began to make regular daily entries in his diary, commencing with the date of October 21, 1862.[7] Robert explained that he had nothing better to do and

> this nice blank book having been presented to me by a friend, I have determined to jot down a few memoranda of my doings and thoughts during the war, not that I expect it to interest anyone else, for I do not intend that any other person besides myself shall ever read it, but I write it, *first*, for amusement, *secondly*, because in after years it may afford me some pleasure to peruse it.
>
> There are a great many unpleasant passages in this part of my life which I shall either leave untouched or merely revert to them incidentally, because it will not afford me any pleasure to recall my misdoings. I

---

[7] Since Patrick did not begin the daily entries in his diary until this date, his account of events prior to October 21, 1862, (Chapter I) is a reminiscence and not a part of the diary proper.

18

intend however to " stick pretty closely to my text," that is, I shall record things very nearly as they happened as well as I can remember.

I should never have kept the diary, if it hadn't been that I desired to learn Phonography.[8] I accidentally came in possession of a little work on Phonography, published in Cincinnati by Elias Longley, and as I had so much idle time on my hands while in camp, I concluded to devote my leisure moments, to the study of this brief and easy mode of writing.

Having obtained a pretty good idea of the rudiments, the next thing was to practice it until I became proficient. I copied from books and newspapers until I got tired of that plan, and I thought it better to write original matter entirely. As I know no one who understood, I could not open a correspondence in that style, and being thus left entirely to the resources of my own mind I resolved to keep a diary, wherein I would record such little things as should occur around me, with an occasional comment upon the same. . . .

Patrick's resourcefulness soon manifested itself in a series of glowing descriptions and valuable detail depicting his stay at Port Hudson. Although not particularly happy with his situation there, Robert liked it because he could visit his home in Clinton at least once a week. Because of the nature of his duties he had many long, boring hours to while away sitting around the fire " telling long yarns and eating roasted potatoes." He promised his mother that he would stop drinking but he found this pledge a very difficult one to keep. Other days were spent studying phonography, reading, writing in his journal, acting as recorder in court martials, trying to find salt and tallow to send to his mother, and, of course, keeping books in the supply organization.

Frequently Patrick and his friends would saunter down to the bluffs of the river to view the Yankee gunboats as they steamed up from the south to shell the works. On one occasion he commented that they seemed to be " firing on some sugar houses on the other side of the river this morning which they are very good at considering the houses cannot fire back, and is a very safe way of carrying on a war." Full of confidence, he wrote, " If they

---

[8] An earlier form of shorthand.

get this place, it strikes me that they will have to fight a little first."

Robert was never in robust health. Sometimes his troubles were of his own making, such as the day his stomach was " a little deranged from drinking corn beer that Andrew made." In other instances, however, he described his sufferings as neuralgia, diarrhea, pains in the top of the head, affections of the spine, and numerous other unnamed ailments. Once he stated that his health was so bad that he was afraid he would not be able to enjoy it " after our independence is gained." Patrick had little confidence in Confederate doctors and he cynically observed, " It is astonishing what an amount of ignorance there is amongst the Medical fraternity."

According to Patrick's narrative, the grandest scene witnessed by him during the war occurred the night of March 14, 1863, when the Yankee fleet, commanded by Admiral David G. Farragut, attempted to run the batteries at Port Hudson: " About 11 o'clock we heard a heavy gun, and then the shell, then another and another, and finally the whole of the fleet let loose on us. . . . It was not long however before every one of our batteries cut loose, and of all the noises that ever I heard, this beat it. The very earth trembled." Robert had a splendid view and he vividly described the action. The most beautiful sight of all, he related, occurred when the Federal frigate *Mississippi* exploded, caught fire, and floated down the river, lighting the sky with a lurid glare.

Patrick was spared the long siege at Port Hudson when early in April, 1863, he was temporarily detached from the Fourth Regiment and ordered northward with General Abraham Buford's brigade to join General Joseph E. Johnston at Jackson, Mississippi, and co-operate in his attempt to relieve the beleaguered fortress of Vicksburg. After a long, arduous journey Patrick and his comrades arrived in Jackson where orders were awaiting to harrass the rear of Grant's army. The next few weeks were spent in performing this duty, marching and countermarching, and suffering greatly from the heat and thirst. The command expected every day to receive orders to break out of the Big Black swamp and attack Grant's rear, but the chance never came. Before contact could be made with the enemy, Patrick hastily recorded that " astounding intelligence has reached us that Vicksburg has fallen. Pemberton has surrendered. We are in full retreat."

Leaving the heart of the Big Black swamp at dawn on July 6, 1863, and in grave danger of being captured by General William T. Sherman and units of the Federal army, the Fourth Louisiana marched thirty-five miles to their destination without a halt. This was a bitter experience for Patrick: " *No water*—dust, dust, dust. My God it is awful. . . . I didn't get any sleep last night, nor have I had anything to eat for twenty-four hours and I feel pretty well worn out. I never want to be on another retreat." The morale of the men sank. Robert commented that the troops were " low spirited. . . . Desertions are frequent [and] the men and horses fall by the wayside every few hundred yards." The memories of this catastrophe remained with Patrick throughout the course of the war.

After a diversion to Enterprise, Mississippi, to prevent an advance of Federal cavalry which threatened in that direction, Robert and the Fourth Regiment were ordered into Mobile for garrison duty. Quarters were assigned to Patrick on Government Street and there he prepared to spend a pleasant winter.

In late November, 1863, Robert received a furlough and returned to his home in Louisiana. " I found Clinton very much changed in appearance," he related. " The long row of stores on the east side of the square known as ' Brick Row ' had been destroyed by fire, as also had all the buildings on each side of ' St. Helena Street.' I also found a very great change in the ideas and sentiments of the people. They were trading liberally with the Yankees, and hauling cotton to them all the time. This illicit trade was carried on to an astonishing extent. . . . I also heard a great deal of complaint against our cavalry serving in this vicinity. . . I heard the citizens denouncing the cavalry and many of them told me that they would prefer seeing the Yankees to seeing our cavalry. . . ." Like many other loyal Confederates Patrick viewed such activities with dismay. When his furlough ended Patrick seemed almost glad to leave, commenting that

" everything looked so gloomy that there was little or no pleasure in remaining, outside of the gratification of being with my family."

Upon returning to Mobile, Robert discovered that his regiment had been ordered to Dalton, Georgia, to reinforce the Army of Tennessee under General Joe Johnston. Accumulating various records and stores, Patrick boarded a train and, after a long, painful journey through Montgomery and Atlanta, he arrived in Dalton on December 31, 1863. Not altogether happy with his new assignment and somewhat distraught, Patrick recorded that " in the distance on all sides, the prospect was anything but cheerful. All looked ' naked, brown, and sear ' and the background of this uninviting picture was formed by a chain of dark and gloomy looking hills, which seemed with their frowning rugged sides to preside over this apparently God-forsaken district."

The tour of duty in Dalton was short, however, for the regiment had arrived too late to be of any service. In early February, 1864, word reached Johnston that Federal troops were moving eastward from Vicksburg, presumably headed for Meridian and then Mobile. At the urging of President Davis, Johnston ordered several regiments back to Alabama. This included Patrick and the Fourth Louisiana.

Soon after reaching Mobile, Robert endured a siege of pneumonia that almost cost him his life. Even after reporting back to active duty his health continued in such poor state that a Medical Examining Board pronounced him unfit for field service. At Patrick's request he was detailed to duty with the quartermaster of General James Cantey's brigade, the general supposition being that this unit would remain in Mobile for the duration of the war. But the quiet, serene garrison life on the Gulf Coast was suddenly interrupted in April, 1864, when Cantey's brigade was ordered to Dalton as reinforcements for Joe Johnston's Army of Tennessee. Sherman soon moved out from his fortified position near Rocky Face Ridge, Georgia, to open the Atlanta campaign, one of the decisive actions of the war. Robert Patrick and many other Confederate soldiers were rushed to the front to help stem the tide of Sherman's advance.

In early May Patrick arrived at Resaca, Georgia, a large

quartermaster depôt on the Western and Atlantic Railroad several miles south of Dalton. Even then Johnston's army was retiring and from this date until the occupation of Atlanta in September, Patrick records a long, steady, bitter retreat which saw the heroic Confederate army, fighting an enemy greatly superior in numbers and equipment, repeatedly outflanked and beaten back. Robert wrote that " the prospects are very gloomy for us. . . . I cannot place much confidence in what I hear, though I have not the slightest doubt that Johnston is retreating." A few days later he admitted that " Johnston is in full retreat and there is no doubt that we have received a good thrashing from the Yankees."

The diary reveals the effects of this retreat on the helpless civilian population. Patrick wrote, " They talk about the ravages of the enemy in their marches through the country, but I do not think that the Yankees are any worse than our own army." He described Marietta, Georgia, as " the prettiest place that I have seen anywhere in my travels." He sadly related, however, that " The whole town was in an uproar and confusion . . . citizens were standing about in little groups as if undecided what to do; the female portion of the community were at their gates looking anxiously up and down the streets; the railroad was filled with cars and the locomotives were puffing and shrieking up and down the track. All was confusion, worse confounded." Despite these reverses, Robert wrote that the " Confederacy still holds up its head and presents a bold front. . . . Our army is in good spirits and have an abiding faith in Johnston."

But President Davis had no such faith in " Old Joe," and on July 18, 1864, Patrick recorded that " an unexpected and startling announcement " had been received: " Gen. Johnston has been removed and Gen. [John B.] Hood takes command." Robert was very dissatisfied with this change in commanders. For the first time he indicated a fear that Atlanta would fall, " for the enemy is too heavy for us, and they have taken ' Old Joe ' away from the helm."

Almost every inch of ground in the long retreat to Atlanta was disputed. The Confederate soldiers, Patrick wrote, by " their unexampled, desperate, fighting qualities have even won the admiration of the Yankees. . . ." All the valiant efforts of the Confederates, however, could not save Atlanta, and in early September, 1864, the city was occupied by Sherman's victorious troops.

In fleeing from Atlanta, Patrick became separated from the wagon train and for several days he straggled southward trying to escape capture. During these wanderings he witnessed the chaotic and tragic plight of a civilian population suffering from the headlong retreat of one army and horrified at the advance of another. Robert vividly describes the pillage, destitution, and the effects of the war on the morals of Confederate women.

On September 4, 1864, Patrick overtook the wagon train and resumed his duties in the supply organization of Hood's shattered army. He wrote, " This has been an awful retreat, and the army is scattered to the four winds. The country is full of stragglers, and the men are deserting by the hundreds. I don't see what delays the enemy. If they would only come on, they can capture the whole concern." But Sherman broke off the offensive and retired his troops into Atlanta. Hood retreated to Palmetto, Georgia, and sought to reorganize and reinspire his defeated army.

Robert was detailed as clerk in the commissary of General Edward C. Walthall's division and was soon back into the routine of his regular duties. The rest at Palmetto was brief, for in early October Hood turned northward to operate against Sherman's communications. It was a feeble effort and Patrick complained, " Nothing works right. The trains are all mixed pell-mell. Nobody knows where to find anything or anybody. There are no bread rations. We now miss the master hand of Gen. Johnston. Nothing worked wrong while he had command."

The Confederates struck the railroad at Big Shanty, Resaca, and Dalton. Patrick's narrative faithfully records the events and describes the route traveled. Hood contemplated drawing Sherman into battle, but upon being advised by his corps commanders that his troops were not in condition to risk a fight with an army of such vast numbers, he turned his attention to the west and planned the invasion of Tennessee.

At Gadsden, Alabama, Hood was joined by General Beauregard and after considerable deliberation Beauregard authorized the proposed Tennessee campaign. Without further delay the army moved in the direction of Guntersville. Unable to cross the Tennessee River at this point Hood moved his troops to Decatur, then to Courtland and Tuscumbia. Patrick complained that " this kind of service is enough to wear any man out. We travelled hard . . . until after night, and then we must grope around in the darkness and find wood and water and by the time we cook our supper it is 12:00 o'clock and we must be up three hours before day. . . . This . . . is a constant thing and it is using me up." He stoutly maintained, however, that " it is better to fight always than give it up."

After enduring many irritating delays at Tuscumbia, Hood finally got his army across the river and on November 21, 1864, they moved in the direction of middle Tennessee. Patrick and other noncombatants in the brigade train were ordered into Mississippi where office duties could be performed in relative safety. Leaving Tuscumbia on November 9 and traveling via Frankfort, Alabama, and Smithville, Mississippi, Patrick arrived at a camp near Aberdeen, Mississippi, on November 20.

The chief pleasures afforded Robert at this new location were the affections of Margaret Ross whom he described as " passably good looking and tolerably intelligent." He explained that he was making love to Maggie " right heavy " and that she allowed him " to take a great many liberties . . . which I do not think she would allow anyone else to take."

Such pleasures were short lived, however, for on December 27 Patrick's unit was ordered into Columbus, Mississippi. With a tinge of sadness he recorded that " Maggie let me hug her and kiss her for perhaps the last time. [She] says that she will never forget me and I do not believe that she will for I never talked to any woman in my life as I did to her. . . . She gave me a lock of her hair before we parted."

After arriving in Columbus on December 28 Patrick established an office and was soon back into the routine of his responsibilities. He sent Maggie a " paper of snuff which I ascertained she was in the habit of using " and wrote her many long letters. On December 30 he learned of Hood's disaster in Tennessee.

" Taken all together," he wrote, " the aspect of affairs is anything but encouraging. . . . If the government allows Hood full swing, he will soon terminate his army."

After the shattered remnants of the Army of Tennessee retreated to its base at Tupelo, Mississippi, Robert received orders to report to his old commander, Major Mulherin, at West Point, Mississippi. The final entry in Patrick's diary, dated January 30, 1865, notes that he would " leave in the morning at daylight if I can get all things ready. I am glad to get away though I would like to have received a letter from Maggie before I left."

Considering Patrick's meticulosity it is hard to believe that he did not continue his journal until the end of the war. Since the final entry was written on the last page of the ledger, it is probable that Robert continued writing in another book which has unfortunately been destroyed or lost.

But what happened to Robert Patrick during the remaining months of the war? Certain facts have definitely been established: (1) He left Columbus, Mississippi, to join Stewart's corps, which was bound for the Carolinas. (2) He wrote a letter from Newberry, South Carolina, dated April 24, 1865. (3) His name appeared on a list of Confederates paroled at Greensboro, North Carolina, "————, 1865." (4) He was back home in Clinton by July 27, 1865.[9]

The tired, battered Army of Tennessee, reduced to less than twenty thousand, was summoned to the Carolinas to join their " Old Joe " Johnston in attempting to stop Sherman's march from the South.[10] Newberry was on the route traveled by the army in its efforts to join Johnston. Also, this village served as a supply depot for the Confederates. So it is probable, then, that Patrick

---

[9] Andrew B. Booth, *Records of Louisiana Confederate Soldiers and Louisiana Confederate Commands*, Vol. III, Bk. II (New Orleans, 1920), 81. A notation in Patrick's handwriting on the back of the original manuscript indicates that he had returned to Clinton at least by July 27, 1865.

[10] Hood had resigned from his command and after a few weeks under the leadership of General Richard Taylor, the army, upon reaching the Carolinas, was once again placed under the command of their beloved Johnston. Stanley F. Horn, *The Army of Tennessee* (Norman, Oklahoma, 1953), 422-23.

went to South Carolina with the Army of Tennessee and remained in Newberry with the commissary stores.

The pitifully small Confederate army under Johnston was no match for Sherman's 110,000 troops and, after the surrender of Lee on April 9, Grant's unoccupied army of 180,000. Johnston sadly realized that the end was at hand and with the permission of President Davis, negotiations were opened with Sherman to discuss terms of capitulation. Patrick describes these last days in a letter to his friend Bill:

I sit down to write you though I fear that you will never receive it because it is such a difficult matter to get letters through just now. I presume you have heard all the news, but I will give you a recapitulation of the whole of it. I have my doubts about the *whole* of it being true, though it is all believed to be true. General Lee and his army surrendered to Grant on the 16th [9th] inst. All the captured men have been paroled and Gen. Lee himself is on parole in Richmond. This is true because the soldiers are passing through this place by hundreds everyday, and one of Lee's army, a Louisianian, promises to take this letter through.

There is no doubt that an armistice has been declared for it has been officially announced everywhere and Gen. Johnston has sent couriers all over the country stopping the enemy, where ever he can send the intelligence to them, and we are now sending supplies to the Yankee Gen'l Stoneman's forces, which are only some 30 or 40 miles from Chester, and were making their way to Johnston's rear.

All this I know to be true, but the following needs confirmation. " That Abe Lincoln was assassinated at the theatre in Washington City. That Seward and his son were both mortally wounded at their residences by another assasin at the same time that Lincoln was slain in the theatre. That the Confederacy has been recognized by England and France. That they have had a fight with the Federal vessels off the Balize. That the port of Charleston has been blockaded by the French fleet." [11]

President Davis in a speech at Greensboro said that everything would come out right and that an honorable peace would soon be secured to us. A wagon train laden with bullion passed through this place last week. This was the coin contained in the Banks at Richmond. Everyone

---

[11] Seward's wound was, of course, not fatal. Rumors of foreign intervention kept alive Confederate hopes to the very end.

thinks we will have peace shortly and I think so myself. Johnston's army is said to be in the finest kind of spirits with a large amount of supplies on hand. Everything remains in *status quo* for the present. The armistice is *said* to be for sixty days, but I cannot say for how long a time it is. Confederate money is said to be worth dollar for dollar in greenbacks in Richmond—this I don't believe.

My health continues very good, and I hope that matters will soon be arranged so that I can return home.

Two days after Patrick wrote this letter, Sherman and Johnston agreed to the final terms of surrender and the activities of the Army of Tennessee came to a close. According to these provisions the men were not arrested as prisoners of war but were immediately paroled and allowed to return home.

Patrick returned to a devastated homeland and tried to reconstruct the life that had given him many fond memories prior to the war. He was reappointed to his old post of deputy sheriff and served in that capacity until his death on December 8, 1866.

"Away we went down the old rickety railroad"

On the 28th day of April 1861 our company numbering nearly one hundred and fifty got upon the cars at the Clinton depôt. There was a large crowd assembled at the depôt to see us off. I had a sweetheart then and with tearful eyes we bid each other farewell. There were many tears shed and many sad partings on that bright spring morning. Away we went down the old rickety railroad to Port Hudson. We found a large crowd assembled there to see us off, and here was another parting for a great many of our company lived in this part of the Parish.

We got aboard the good steamer " J. A. Cotton," and were soon under way for New Orleans. The boys were all in a high glee and as we had some violins aboard, they were fiddling and dancing all the way down. At one time so many had crowded the upper deck that it threatened to give way, and in fact it would have gone down in a few minutes if the crowd had not gone back towards the cabin. One fellow, I don't remember who he was, taking it for granted that everything was lost, jumped overboard, but as we happened to be close to shore, he managed to get out, minus his hat and coat.

We arrived at New Orleans about 4 a. m. the next day. I didn't sleep any as there was such a noise and confusion, that I found it impossible. We were crossed and piled all about in the cabin, on chairs and sofas and under the tables. As soon as we reached the levee, I went out to the market and had a cup of good strong coffee, which refreshed me considerably.

The next day we were marched off the boat and drawn up in line, on the levee, and our names were called by a man named Grivot. I do not know what position he held, but he was a good looking man and wore a very red cap. After we had all answered to our names, we were marched up to the St. James Hotel, where we had a most miserable breakfast.

After breakfast we were marched down to the cotton rooms of Messrs. Oakey and Hawkins on Carondelet Street. We were penned up in this place, about 150 of us like cattle and as the weather was quite warm, it was a terrible place to stay in. Hunter [1] placed a guard at the door-way so that no one could leave without his permission. Tom Fiester was on guard without a gun, and Jno. Morgan took a notion that he would go down anyhow and undertook to pass Fiester. Fiester told him to halt but John insisted on going down and Fiester struck him a blow between the eyes with his fist, and made a complete star, like a pane of glass makes that has had a pebble thrown against it. Said I, " John, you remind me of the song ' We'll hoist on high the bonnie blue flag that bears a single star ' " but John didn't seem to relish my jokes. He said there was no fun in a man's getting his face bunged up after that kind of a style. It certainly couldn't be very amusing to him but it was to the balance of us.

I got permission from Hunter to pass down, and I went out into the city. I had about $40 with me, and I thought I would splurge a little. So I spent two days and nights frolicing around and then my money was gone. I hadn't a cent left. I slept at the St. Charles Hotel, and I borrowed money enough to pay my hotel bill from Hilliard. After this I went to where the troops were encamped at the Metarie Race Course.[2] This was an enclosure a mile round, and in it were spacious brick buildings, comprising the Judges stand, gambling rooms, stables, etc.

We had no very agreeable time at this place, for there was a large number of troops cooped up in a very small compass. We suffered considerably for water, as all the water we used was

[1] Samuel Eugene Hunter, major, later colonel and commander, 4th Louisiana Infantry Regiment.

[2] This was Camp Walker, under the command of Brigadier General Edward L. Tracy.

brought from the river in old pork barrels, and in addition to being warm and muddy, the old grease and salt that had been in the barrels previously gave it a very bad taste. We were almost stifled by the smoke for our cooking or mess fires were very close together. Our Regiment was then made up, and our company which was too large for one, was divided into two, and the officers were elected accordingly. Hunter was made Major of the Regiment, Allen [3] Lt. Colonel and Robt. J. Barrow [4] was Colonel.

The authorities finding the Race Course unfit for a camp decided to make a camp on the Jackson Rail Road, and we were sent to Tangipahoa where we cleared off the ground and pitched our tents. This camp has ever since been known as " Camp Moore," in honor of Thos. O. Moore, the then Governor of the State.[5] It was awful hot in our tents and extremely disagreeable on that account, but in other respects we did very well. We had excellent water and plenty to eat.

I forgot to mention that before we left New Orleans for Camp Moore that I was detailed as clerk in the Commissary department, but I wouldn't remain there because I thought the boys would think that I had come out into the service with the intention of procuring a detail of some kind, but this was not the case, because I knew so little about army matters that I was not aware that there were any such officers as Quartermaster and Commissary. For fear, as I said before, that they might have some such notions, I *resigned* my position, and took my rifle and went into the ranks. This was a voluntary thing on my part,

[3] Henry Watkins Allen. In March, 1862, Colonel Allen assumed command of the regiment. He was severely wounded leading his men across an open field in an attack on Baton Rouge, August 5, 1862. Because of these wounds he resigned from his command in January, 1863. In November, 1863, Allen was elected governor of Louisiana. See Luther E. Chandler, " The Career of Henry Watkins Allen " (Ph. D. dissertation, Louisiana State University, 1940).

[4] Robert J. Barrow, a native of Bayou Sara. The New Orleans *Daily Crescent* (May 9, 1861) remarked: " A better selection of officers could not have been made. These gentlemen are known throughout the state for their chivalrous character and military accomplishments." Barrow was an elderly man, however, and actual command soon passed into the hands of Allen.

[5] The Fourth Regiment organized with ten companies containing 850 men. It mustered into the Confederate service at Camp Moore, May 25, 1861.

because the Commissary was very anxious to have me remain with him, and came to my quarters and endeavored to induce me to go back.

All the Regiments above and below our number (4th) were sent to Virginia, except the 3rd which was sent to Missouri. My Regt. was ordered on the Coast. On our way there [we] were delayed for several days at the lake end, on account of not having transports to take us over. It rained nearly all the time we were here and we had nothing to protect us from it. The musquitoes were positively awful. I never saw the like. They came upon us in clouds. We called this " Camp Misery " and an awful camp it was. At length we got away from this place and took the Steamer for Biloxi, Miss.

Our Regiment was now divided. A part was at Pass Christian, a part at Mississippi City, a part at Biloxi, another at Ocean Springs, another at Pascagoula and another at Ship Island.[6] We were sent to Biloxi, where we had a splendid camp and good water. Our camp was right on the beach, where we could bathe as much as we wished, and had any amount of fish, crabs and oysters. There was a splendid breeze all the time, and we got along as well as we could wish, and in fact much better than we ever did anywhere else. We were ordered to Ship Island, though we didn't remain there more than a week before we were ordered back to Biloxi. We remained at Biloxi until September when the whole Regiment was ordered to Mississippi City.

I now found that staying in the ranks didn't pay. That everyone was looking out for an easy place, and that no one thought any more of me, nor gave me any credit for giving up an easy position and going into the ranks. I therefore resolved to get through the war as easy as I could. But I didn't intend to use any dishonorable means to attain this end.

Kilbourne, who was Regimental Q. M., offered me the position of Clerk, which I accepted, and the first work I ever did was to assist in paying off the troops at Mississippi City. From this time

---

[6] The Fourth Regiment was sent to the coast along the Mississippi Sound to protect this region against the possibility of invasion. Colonel Allen had his headquarters in Bay St. Louis where the largest detachment of troops was stationed.

on I carried a gun during the war only when I saw proper to do so, and that was only on one or two occasions. About this time I received a furlough to go home. During my absence the Regiment was ordered to Berwicks Bay. One half the Regiment was quartered at Berwick City,[7] and the other part under command of Major Hunter was sent higher up.

We built good quarters at Berwick City and got along very well there. We got as many oranges as we knew what to do with. They grew in the greatest abundances.

The land here is exceedingly fertile, though it is low and marshy and requires a great deal of drain'g. The soil is alluvial, and where it has not been cleared is covered with a dense growth of very heavy timber, principally cypress, which are covered with moss.

The forests have a lonely, sad and mournful aspect, with their dark green foliage and long tresses of gray moss. To walk out into the woods here is about as solitary an affair as a man could well imagine. This must certainly have been the paradise of wild beasts when the country was owned by the aborigines and even now there is plenty of large game to be found.

They make nothing but sugar here and all the planters are immensely wealthy. They do not raise a stalk of corn or cotton. They find it cheaper to make sugar, and purchase corn by the flatboat load from the West.

Our rations were not so good here as they had been, and all we received was beef, salt and flour. Beef doesn't amount to much without grease of some kind to cook it. We had sugar and coffee. It was about this time that Fort Donelson fell.[8]

We were ordered about the middle of February 1862 to Jackson, Tenn. The Regiment went on, but I remained at New Orleans

[7] Berwick City, now Berwick, Louisiana, served as a terminal point for the Texas trade and was also an important center for blockade runners. Occupation of this region would have given the Federals access to Alexandria and other important cities near the center of the state. See Robert U. Johnson and Clarence C. Buel, eds., *Battles and Leaders of the Civil War* (New York, 1884-87), III, 586, 595. Hereinafter cited *Battles and Leaders*.

[8] February 16, 1862. Fort Donelson was located on the Cumberland River in northwestern Tennessee. Its loss was a critical blow to the Confederacy. *Ibid.*, I, 398-452.

for a few days with Kilbourne to fix up some papers. I went on several days afterwards in company with Dr. Pope our surgeon, Joe Whitehead and Bill Carter.

We left New Orleans and on arriving at or near Amite City, we learned there had been a collision just ahead of us. A " soldier train " that was going up collided with a freight train that was coming down. It was an everlasting smash. The up train had the 7th Miss. Regt. on board, and that train was almost a complete wreck. I counted twenty dead bodies lying side by side and I don't know how many wounded there were. It was an awful affair.

We reached Jackson, Tenn. two or three days after, and found the Regiment encamped at the fair grounds. The weather was extremely cold and the ground remained frozen for several days. Gen. [Braxton] Bragg had his headquarters at Jackson. One day Col. Hunter (he had been made Lieut. Col. while we were here) came to me and said that Gen. Bragg had sent to the Regt. for a clerk and that he thought I would suit him. I agreed to go, and accordingly I went to his headquarters and reported to his Adjutant Geo. G. Garner for duty and went to work immediately. Major Garner I found to be a very nice man and I got along very well indeed. With Gen. Bragg I hadn't much to do, as he always had his head working on something that the balance of us didn't know anything about. Bragg was a tall, fine looking man and very stern.

I remained in Bragg's office until we were ordered down to Corinth, and then I returned to my Regiment. I didn't say anything to Garner about leaving. A young man by the name of Falconer, who was afterwards Adjutant General of the Army of Tenn., was also a clerk in the office with me. I told him that I thought I would return to my Regiment. He attempted to dissuade me from it, saying that Bragg would make four or five Generals in the course of a few weeks and that he (Falconer) would be appointed Adjutant to one of them, and that if I remained with Bragg that I could take his place in the office and that it would not be long before I would be an Adjutant General myself. I would not listen to this advice, however, and in this I was very foolish.

I returned to the Regiment and we took the train for Corinth. The weather was dreadful, for it was cold and the rain poured down in torrents. On account of some accident which occurred to a train ahead of us, we were compelled to stop, and camp in the woods near the Rail Road. This was after night and the rain still poured down. We remained in the woods all night without any protection from the weather, and it certainly was a very bad night. The next day we built up large fires and proceeded to dry our blankets and clothing as well as we could.

We remained at this camp three days without anything to eat but finally we got on down to Corinth where we obtained rations. On arriving at Corinth we found a large number of troops encamped around the town in every direction. I never saw so many men in one body before. As far as the eye could reach over the hills and vales, the earth was thickly studded with the white tents of the soldiers. Men, horses, wagons and mules were crowding in every direction. Here we found the 16th and many other Louisiana Regiments. We encamped on our arrival North of the town. I shall remember that day. A slow, cold rain mingled with sleet fell all day long. It was extremely disagreeable.

The next day we were ordered down South of the town immediately on the Rail Road. We went into the woods and cleared off a camping ground and were soon as comfortably fixed as the circumstances of the case would admit. Long trains of cars passed up and down the road every hour of the day and night, and the shrieking of the locomotives made the most dismal sounds imaginable throughout the lonely night. We remained in this camp nearly four weeks I think it was and then came on the battle of Shiloh. Kilbourne insisted upon my not going into the fight; but go I would. I toughed it through but I resolved that if I could honorably keep out of it that I would never go into another. It was not expected, occupying the position I did, that I should participate and the thing was voluntary on my part. About sunrise on Sunday morning, before we had fired a gun, Bob McKie was killed on one side of me and Jim Depriest on the other.[9] I

9 These were the first casualties suffered by the Fourth Louisiana. The Confederate army was almost cut to pieces with total losses of 10,699. Federal losses were 13,047. *Ibid.*, I, 485.

began to think it pretty warm to be so early in the action. This sort of work was kept up all day and the Regiment lost very heavily. How I escaped unhurt was a mystery. But so it was. The next day's fighting was very heavy, but nothing to compare with that of the day previous.

On Monday about 12 M. our army fell back towards Corinth the most completely disorganised and demoralized army imaginable. If the Yankee army had been in a condition to have followed us they could have captured the whole concern. But they were too badly used up to attempt anything of the kind, and all that saved them was the strong re-inforcements brought up by Gen'l [Don Carlos] Buell. It was a terrible battle. I cannot pretend to give the particulars or even the general outlines of the battle. Historians will do that.[10]

Shortly after the battle of Shiloh, Gen. Ruggles [11] being in want of a private secretary I was sent to him and recommended as a suitable man to fill the position. I called at his headquarters and had a conversation with him in regard to the matter. He told me what my duties would be, and I agreed to remain with him, provided he would consent for me to rejoin my regiment if I should at any time become dissatisfied. He said certainly.

Accordingly I packed up my knapsack and reported to him the next day for duty. His Adjutant General's name was Roy Mason Hooe—A very pale, sickly looking young man and a nephew of the General's. He was a right clever young fellow too, and he and I got along very well together. One day, a short time after I had gone on duty with Ruggles, I was sent with a message to Gen. Bragg's q'rs. The sentinel would not allow me to go in.

[10] The battle of Shiloh (Pittsburg Landing), first great battle of the war in the West, opened early Sunday morning, April 6, 1862. The issue at Shiloh did not involve any strategic point. It was a pitched battle between major armies struggling for control of the Mississippi River. Faulty execution of battle plans, the untimely death of General Johnston in combat, a depletion of reserves, plus the arrival of a fresh Union army under General Buell, resulted in a defeat for the Confederates. After the battle the Confederate army retreated to its base in Corinth, a strategic railroad center in northeast Mississippi. *Ibid.*, 465-607.

[11] The Fourth Regiment was attached to the second corps of the Army of Mississippi under the command of Bragg and was a part of the first division under the immediate command of Brigadier General Daniel Ruggles.

I told the Sargeant of the guard to announce my name. This he did, and he received an order to allow me to pass in. When I entered the first man I saw, was Major Garner, Bragg's Adjutant He met me very cordially and remarked " You have come at last." I answered that I had, but said I, you speak as though you expected me.

" Certainly " said he " I have been expecting you for several days. Didn't you receive my note? "

" No," I answered " I have never received any communication whatever from either you or Falconer since we left Jackson, Tenn."

" Why " said he " I wrote a note to you stating that Falconer had been made an Adjutant General, and that I needed your services very much, and that I wished you to report to me immediately. You could not be found in Corinth, and after midnight, I sent a courier out to Monterey where your Regiment was temporarily posted. The courier returned, reporting that he could not find you, but that he handed the missive to the Major of your Regiment who said that he would deliver it to you. This was all satisfactory, and I have been waiting very impatiently for you to make your appearance, ever since."

" I am very sorry " said I " that I did not receive your note. The Major did not give it to me—and now it is too late, for I am private secretary for Gen. Ruggles and of course I cannot do otherwise than remain with him for the present at least."

" I regret very much " said he " that you failed to get it, for I am sadly in need of some one to assist me. If anything goes wrong between Ruggles and yourself advise me of the fact, and I will order you to report to me immediately. I *can* order you away now but such a proceeding would be considered ungentlemanly. I do not think you will get along well with Ruggles for he is an old brute."

After remaining a short time with Ruggles, I found that his opinion of him was correct. He was an *old brute*. Being an old army officer and a New Englander, he had no conscience nor mercy on any one. He was very exacting and it was a difficult matter to please him. There were several other clerks there, but none of them ever did anything unless it was more than I could do.

I had to sleep upon the table where I wrote, in order to be ready to write out orders at all times of the night. Whenever Ruggles came in I had to have my hat off, and have a chair ready for him. One day I handed him a document to sign, and as I was standing by waiting to receive it from him, he turned around suddenly, and said " Haven't you any more politeness than to look over my shoulder when I am writing? "

" I was not looking over your shoulder " said I. " I was not thinking of you or what you were doing."

On another occasion I took a dispatch in to his room. When I entered, he was sitting down. Gen'l [Leroy Pope] Walker was sitting on his left and General Patton Anderson was sitting on his right. I went in with the intention of laying the document upon the table as was my custom. He reached out his hand to receive it, and I handed it to him. He rose from his chair and his face flushed with anger. " Mr. Patrick " said he " have you no more politeness, have you been so ill bred as to hand me a document between two gentlemen? "

This made me very angry, and I replied " You reached out your hand to get it and I handed it to you. If you hadn't done this, I would have laid it upon the table as I always do. If I had refused to hand it to you when you reached out your hand for it, what would you have said about it? "

" I have heard enough sir " he said " go back to the office."

" I will go back " I said to myself " but I shall not remain here much longer to be insulted and brow beaten by such an old numskull as you are."

A few days subsequent to this little episode I applied to him for leave to rejoin my regiment, but he refused, and peremptorily ordered me back to the office.

" Where there's a will, there's a way " I mentally repeated. I have the will and I'll be hanged if I don't find a way to get out of your jurisdiction. In the meantime my regiment had been ordered to Vicksburg to put up some heavy guns and to fortify the place. My officers and friends were all gone and I had no one to assist or advise me in this emergency. If Col. Allen or Col.

Hunter had been there, I could have gotten away without any difficulty, but they were at Vicksburg. I thought of appealing to Major Garner, but I was tired of staying in Corinth. I was anxious to get away from the infernal hole, with its dreadful water and miserable rations. We were crowded to death and half starved, and I wished to get to some place where I could procure a plenty of wholesome food and breathe a little pure air. Corinth, and especially Corinth with old bull headed Ruggles attached, was more than I would willingly endure.

But how to get away was the question. I could not leave on the train without a pass, and that pass must be procured from Ruggles or some other commanding officer.

I thought of Major Winens of the 19th La. Regiment. A day or two after my interview with Ruggles, Winens came to my office, and he and I had a conversation about it. He told me he would see about the matter and that he would come over next day and report progress. In the meantime Hooe had thrown all the work of the office on me. He did nothing now but sign his name, and very often he would not rise from his bed to do this and I would have to carry the document to his bed to obtain his signature. I worked like a horse. No pay and almost starved, was the compensation I received, with an occasional scowl from Old Ruggles.

When I lay down that night I came to the following determination. If Winens returns tomorrow and reports that he can do nothing for me, I am resolved to work no more for Ruggles let the consequences be what they may. If he sends me to the guard house all right. I'll go there. I will be placed in irons before I will put my hand on paper again for him. With these notions in my head I went to sleep, though I had to get up several times during the night and issue orders to the Division, in accordance with orders from Bragg's office.

The next day Winens came over. He told me to wait patiently for a few days. That Ruggles would be superceded by Gen. [Thomas C.] Hindman and that if I was smart I might manage to get away then. *Verbum sapientes.*[12] I would await further developments.

A few days afterwards, an officer came into the office. He wished to see Gen. Ruggles. I showed him into Ruggle's room. He soon returned to the office. During a conversation he had with Captain Hooe I ascertained that he was Hindman's Adjt. Gen'l, and he had come to know, now that Hindman had command of the troops formerly commanded by Ruggles, if he could obtain the house then occupied by the latter for his office.

When he came out of the office he and I had some conversation. He seemed to be a little green about his duties. He returned next day and we had a long conversation. He asked me if I would act as his clerk. I told him I couldn't answer positively then. I also told him to ask Ruggles for his old books and papers to see how his business had been managed. He did so but Ruggles refused to let him have them. He told me about it. I then remarked that he (Ruggles) couldn't refuse to allow him to look at his books and to demand it of him as a right. This he did and Ruggles placed his books at his disposal for a few hours.

I sat down and wrote off a copy of all the forms I knew and when he went away I handed them to him. He thanked me for my kindness. The next morning I went down to Hindman's headq'rs where I found the Adjutant sitting at a desk writing. I bid him good morning and stated to him, that I was tired of my present occupation, and as my friend General Ruggles, was now out of command I would be obliged to him if he would write an order for me to report to my regiment at Vicksburg, without delay. " Just sit down " said he, " and write out such an order as you wish and I will sign it."

I wrote the order and he signed it. I folded it up very carefully and put it in my pocket book, and bidding the Captain good morning I started back to Ruggles' office. As I was passing the house occupied by Ruggles as his sleeping quarters and where he transacted all his very private business the old man called to me. " Mr. Patrick, as soon as you get breakfast come over, I have

[12] Patrick is probably referring to the Latin phrase *verbum sat sapienti* which is literally translated as, a word to the wise is sufficient.

some very important business on hand which demands immediate attention." " All right sir " was my answer.

I got my breakfast and went over. The papers I had to copy was the programme of the evacuation of Corinth and the plan of the retreat.[13]

" Now Mr. Patrick " said he " I think I can rely upon your discretion and secrecy, can't I? " I told him I *knew* he could.

" Well " he continued we are to evacuate this place, and to be accomplished successfully, it requires great secrecy, and if nothing is divulged we will be away from here in less than two weeks."

I went diligently to work at the papers marking down the routes of the different divisions etc. I had been at work about two hours, when the old fellow came in and took a seat beside me. " Mr. Patrick " said he " why is it that you are so opposed to staying with me? Do you still wish to leave me? " I told him that I was dissatisfied and that I still felt inclined to leave him.

" You are not fit " said he " for a soldier and you make a splendid clerk and secretary; the best I've ever had. You are an excellent amanuensis and I think it very foolish in you to wish to rejoin your Regiment and enter the ranks when you can get places so much easier and more genteel."

I told him that all that made no difference, and that I would never be satisfied while I remained with him.

" Well " said he " I am going to leave this place in a few days and you may prepare yourself to go with me. Do you have good rations? " I told him my rations were most wretched. " You Charles! " speaking to his servant. " Charles bring Mr. Patrick a dozen or two of those eggs that I received yesterday."

The eggs were brought, and I tied them up in my handkerchief.

" It is about dinner time now, and you had better stop work until after dinner."

[13] The evacuation of Corinth took place during the night before May 30, 1862. With the approach of a superior force of Union troops from Shiloh, Beauregard with great skill and secrecy was able to withdraw his army to Tupelo, Mississippi, fifty-two miles to the south. This was a great loss for the Confederacy. With Corinth went Fort Pillow and Memphis, all of West Tennessee and northern Mississippi, and even the river itself down to Vicksburg. See T. Harry Williams, *P. G. T. Beauregard: Napoleon in Gray* (Baton Rouge, 1955), 153-56.

I laid down my pen, put on my hat and started to my quarters. The old man went with me as far as the door. "Now Mr. Patrick hurry back, for you know that it is very important that those papers should be made up immediately."

"Oh yes! certainly sir. I am aware that this matter should meet with prompt dispatch."

I left him. I thought to myself—you infernal old doughguts, you expect to poke your finger in my eye don't you. You think you have bought me over with a few soft words and a dozen eggs, but before three days elapse you'll find out who's bought and who's sold. You'll know who is entitled to the bill of sale—you or me.

I made tracks for my domicil. Although I was very hard up for something to eat, and really wanted the eggs the worst kind, yet I hated old Ruggles so bad that I would not eat them and I gave them away to some soldiers on the way. It was now 12M and the train for Grand Junction left at one p. m. I hadn't much time to lose. I packed my knapsack, rolled up my blankets, put something to eat in my haversack, filled my canteen with water and I was ready. I saw a negro passing by and I hailed him.

"Don't you want to make a dollar?"

"Certainly, I does" said the darkey. "Well, take these things down to the depôt for me and I'll give you a dollar. Go down past that house" pointing to Ruggles' quarters "and take the left until you come to the Rail Road, and then follow it down until you reach the depôt. I am going another way, but I will be in sight of you in a few minutes."

"All right sah!" and away went the negro with my baggage.

I went down by the back way for I didn't wish old stick-in-the-mud to see me.

As I passed his quarters I saw the old fellow walking out to dinner.

I said half aloud "If you ain't a euchred General *one time*, I'll be damned."

Previous to leaving the Adjutant's office, however, I told one of the clerks that if the General should send for me—which I knew would be the case—to send back word that I had gone over to the 16th La. Regiment.

I went to the depôt, paid the negro his dollar, procured transportation tickets to Vicksburg on my order, jumped on the train, and the way I went a glimmering.

I subsequently learned the following from one of Ruggles' clerks. Ruggles sent over for me about an hour after I left. Postlewaite, the clerk alluded to above, sent back a message that I had gone over to the 16th La. Regiment. He sent over two or three times during the afternoon to know if I had returned, but he invariably received the same answer. The next morning he came over himself and not finding me there, he sent a courier over to the 16th to know if they had seen anything of me. No one had seen me. He then sent out a company of Arkansas cavalry to search all over Corinth for me with instructions to arrest me wherever they found me, and bring me into the presence of His Royal Highness. *But nary find.*

He came into the office, after the cavalry had reported their want of success, and pretended to be in a good humor about it, saying that I had played off a fine joke on him, but Postlewaite, said that it was only assumed in order to conceal his discomfiture in being outwitted by me. This was the last I saw of Ruggles except once. I saw him at a distance a few days previous to the fall of Atlanta.

After I arrived at Grand Junction I went to Jackson, Miss., thence to Edwards' Depôt, where a portion of my Regiment was recruiting, while the other part was at Vicksburg, and planted the first guns that ever frowned down from the " Hill City." [14]

At Edwards' Depôt, which is about midway between Jackson and Vicksburg I had a very pleasant time. Here I got some vegetables and milk and butter, which refreshed my whole system. I could take a bath nearly every day which I considered very

[14] While camped at Edwards' Station, the companies of the Fourth Regiment were detailed in rotation to work on the batteries being erected at Vicksburg. Finally, the entire command was ordered into the city, and remained during the so-called first siege of Vicksburg. *War of the Rebellion: A Compilation of the Official Records of the Union and Confederate Armies* (128 vols., Washington, 1880-1901), Series I, Vol. XV, 6-12. Hereinafter cited as *Official Records.*

conducive to good health. I became acquainted with quite a number of young ladies and I was invited out to dine very often and altogether I passed the time very agreeably. I thought I never would get enough milk, especially buttermilk and fruit.

Shortly afterwards we were all ordered to Vicksburg which was as mean a place as Corinth.

After my return to the Regiment Captain Wooster, the Commissary, came to me and asked me to take charge of his affairs and make up his papers. This I consented to. He told me I could take the papers anywhere I chose, and that if I wished to he would obtain a pass for me to go home. I told him I would prefer the pass to go home, and he obtained one without any specified time being mentioned in it. It was unlimited.

We made our way on down to Liberty without any trouble. Wedge assisted me in making up the papers, and in about four weeks we had them completed and started back to Vicksburg.

On driving up to Edwards' Depôt we found that our Regiment had been ordered down to Camp Moore,[15] and a few minutes after our arrival a train passed down with our Regt. on it. As Dan and I were not prepared to go just then, we remained at Edwards' Depôt and took the train next morning for Jackson, Miss. We afterwards got safely through to Camp Moore. The troops were ordered down to Baton Rouge, but I was ordered to remain at Camp Moore.

Soon after this I was taken sick with fever. I suffered very much from pains in all my limbs. I was sick for eight or ten days. I was occupying a house by myself with the exception of Mrs. Stone's negro Tom. I had him hired at the time. He waited on me, though he would go off sometimes and stay half a day at a time. One day having had fever so much and having no one to notice me, I got up and wandered away into the woods. I wrote home for a conveyance to take me to Clinton and as soon as I

---

[15] The Fourth Regiment was part of an expedition, under the command of General John C. Breckinridge, former Democratic candidate for President, sent into South Louisiana to drive the Federals out of Baton Rouge and possibly New Orleans. Breckinridge's little army, only 4,000 strong, left Vicksburg on July 27, 1862. *Ibid.*, 76-82.

was well enough I went over, though it was a full month before I recovered entirely.

We were posted for several weeks at Baton Rouge and we were afterwards sent to Port Hudson. My Regiment was the first to fortify Vicksburg and now was the first to fortify Port Hudson. We had a mean time at Port Hudson and the only reason why I liked to remain there was because I could come home once a week. It was about this time that I commenced keeping a diary in shorthand and from this time on I shall make memoranda from it, or perhaps I may confine myself to the diary entirely.

"The dark line of entrenchments"

My diary commences with the date of October 21, 1862. There are a great many things that are wholly uninteresting but nevertheless I will write down the greater portion of it.

Port Hudson, Tuesday, October 21, 1862: Weather fine and clear though very dry and dusty. The only thing in the way of excitement today was a fuss between Batchelor and a man named Dave Weathersby. Weathersby was the driver of our ambulance, and Batchelor, being half drunk, without permission got in, to which the driver objected. Harsh words were passed and finally they came to blows. The driver struck Batchelor with a stick and Batchelor stuck his knife in his head. The wound was not a dangerous one, and there was no particular damage done.

The 128 pounder came down on the cars to-day, and will soon be put up and in working order ready for the enemy when they come up the river.[1]

Morris Davis of the band is sleeping in my tent now, and I find him a very agreeable man. He is very well informed on almost any subject that is brought up in the course of conver-

---

[1] The Confederates experienced considerable difficulty in obtaining guns to mount at Port Hudson. The Federals had a large gunboat, the *Essex*, in the Mississippi above Baton Rouge, and thus the heavy guns could not be brought down by boat. The only means of acquiring them was over the little Clinton and Port Hudson railroad that led through the piney woods. The guns were cast in the foundry at Osyka, Mississippi, then hauled into Clinton by wagon and thence shipped by rail into Port Hudson.

sation. He told me that he had kept a diary ever since he has been in the army, and being a good draughtsman he has sketches of all the places we have been, together with a plan of the battlefield of Shiloh. It was looking at his diary that first induced me to keep one. It was well enough to do so I suppose, because it serves to pass away the idle hours now, and it may afford me some pleasure to read it over in after days.

Lewis Davis who is working in Port Hudson for the Gov't. made me two trestles or benches on which to lay some planks for a bed. I went up town today with a wagon and brought down an old door shutter, which I laid on top of the trestles and on top of this I laid some hay and then my blankets which made a tolerable bed, and kept me off the damp ground.

I make a fire in front of my tent every night where a few congenial spirits assemble and we while away the long hours until bedtime by telling long yarns and eating roasted potatoes.

Wednesday, October 22: Today I must collect the amounts due the Commissary from the officers. I never saw just such a man as Wooster is. If it were not for my attending to the matter he never would collect anything. He says he never refused a man a favor in his life, and I believe it. They will come here and borrow the last piece of clothing he has. I see there is a disposition to impose upon him, and here lately when they come to borrow, I speak for Wooster and tell them that he hasn't the articles to spare. Wooster stands by with his hands in his pockets and doesn't say a word. He always has his hands in his pockets, and always burns off the bottoms of his pants, standing too close to the fire. He is the best man I ever became acquainted. There never was a man with a better heart. He is a true soldier too, and a thorough fighting man. There's no discount on his courage.

The former book-keeper of the Commissary did not attend to his duties as he should have done and I have had to bring up all the books and papers since it has been a Regiment.

The last dispatches say that John Van Buren [2] has made a speech to the people of the North in which he urges them to put a stop to the war. Dispatches also say that Indiana has gone

[2] The son of former President Martin Van Buren.

for the Democrats, and Ohio too, and Pennsylvania, or in other words, they have gone against the administration of old Abe Lincoln, the reprobate.[3] This speech will probably benefit us as much as a victory.

General [Simon Bolivar] Buckner and the Honorable H. R. T. Nelson have been making speeches in Kentucky in favor of the Confederacy which (it is generally supposed) will have a very beneficial effect.

When I was at home the last time, I promised mother that I would not drink any more, and I intend to stick up to it if possible. I say "possible." I know it is possible, the question is whether I will do it or not. The last time I got on a bender, I lost all my money—about $220.00—which would have done me some good if I had only kept it. At any rate, it would have paid my debts and that would have been a great help to me.

Thursday, October 23: Weather fair and bright without any prospect of rain. Still very dusty. I cannot hear at all out of my ear that has been affected by neuralgia, and I fear that I will not be able to hear out of it at all any more.

Friday, October 24: Colonel Hunter drilled the men to-day and after the drill, he drew them up in line, and made a speech to them in regard to a charge made against him of cowardice at the battles of Shiloh and Baton Rouge. As well as I can recollect the following is the substance of his remarks:

> I would like to have your attention for a few minutes, while I make a remark or two to you. I have ascertained within the last few days that there have been evil reports flying around through the Regiment about me, and the substance of them is that there have been certain charges brought against me of cowardice and that I am about to be court-martialed for it; that this man says he has heard another man say, that he heard another say, thus and so. Now I have been to see General Beal[4] in regard to the matter and I have demanded of him, that a Court of

---

[3] Patrick is referring to the congressional elections of 1862. Five important states which Lincoln had carried in 1860 sent Democratic delegations to the House of Representatives. Only by a slender margin were the Republicans able to retain control of Congress. See J. G. Randall, *The Civil War and Reconstruction* (New York, 1937), 599-602.

[4] General William N. R. Beall, commander at Port Hudson.

Enquiry be convened immediately to investigate this case, and ascertain whether or not these charges are well founded.

I wish to meet my accusers face to face, and I wish any and every man in this Regiment, who thinks or knows that I have at any time acted in a manner unbecoming an officer and a gentleman to make his appearance before this Court, and give his testimony to that effect, and I now say to the officers and privates of this Regiment, one and all whatever you may have to say in regard to this matter, to come before this Court, convened expressly to hear you, and say it. If I know of any one who thinks or appears to think that he knows anything derogatory to my character I shall summon him, and insist upon his testimony being laid before the world. This course I shall pursue in justice to myself and in justice to you. If at any time I have acted an inglorious part, I wish to be cast aside and no more thought of, as all such men should be, but if these charges are groundless and made through malice I wish to stand like Caesar's wife above suspicion.

It seemed strange to me that he didn't find out sooner that the Regiment had been talking about him, but as is usual in such cases the individual most interested is the last one to know of it. This matter of Hunter's was brought about through malice.

I am reading a book by Wilkie Collins called "Basil." I like it very well.

Sitting musing in my tent a while ago I built a huge castle in the air. Suppose I thought, that I was the happy owner of say three or four millions, what would I do? Then came my mighty castle, and as its broad portals, massive pillars, huge domes and shining minarets came slowly into view, I became entirely lost to all external influences. What a delightful journey I had with some agreeable companions to England, France, Germany, Spain, Italy, in fact all round the world. What a magnificent residence awaited me when I returned etc. etc. etc.

I have also been thinking what business I would follow after the war is over, if I live. I have a notion to go into the grocery line which I think would be best suited to my capacity and means. But I suppose there is no use of thinking much about such things until the war is over with although there is a slight hope of peace now. There is a little cloud of dissatisfaction arising in the North that may come to be a storm before it quits, which I hope it will do.

Hunter has just been around and asked me to act as recorder in the Court of Enquiry about to be held in his case which I have consented to do. The opening of the Court is postponed until to-morrow morning.

Saturday, October 25: 8 a. m. Weather cloudy with every appearance of rain. My tent is not very well ditched around, and I think it good policy to follow the old maxim " in time of peace prepare for war " so while it is not raining I shall ditch my tent and then the storm may come. I have heard nothing of the Court of Enquiry this morning.

9 a. m. Hunter has just sent Dick Worsham over with a horse for me to ride over to " Court."

4 p. m. I have been busy all the day, taking down testimony in Hunter's case. The Court has adjourned until 9 a. m. tomorrow.

Monday, October 27: My time for a day or two has been wholly engrossed with the Court of Enquiry. Col. Hunter came to my tent this morning and told me that he wished me to go down to Mr. Pierce's where Colonel Allen was lying wounded, for the purpose of obtaining his testimony.

Thursday, October 30: I have been to see Col. Allen. I found him in bed, and he seems very cheerful. I took his testimony in the case. He had a long talk with me about my experience with Gen. Ruggles. It pleased him wonderfully. He says Ruggles is a " damned old Granny." He seems to think this affair of Hunter's will all end in smoke. As he says it is a " nine day's wonder."

Saturday, November 1: Weather fair and dry and comfortably cool. It looks like it didn't intend to rain any more and the earth is perfectly parched and the dust is flying in clouds.

Brigade inspection is going on now in camp and Colonel Hunter is calling the roll and mustering the men in. They have made it a rule now that no one shall receive pay unless he is here to answer his name. I was not present to answer to my name as I was busy writing up the record of the Court, but I was told that Hunter answered for me and put my name down as present which I suppose secures my pay.

The Court is to sit again to-day as General [J. C.] Gorham has come back and he wishes to summon more witnesses in the case. I wish it was all over with for I am getting very tired of it.

Sunday, November 2: Bill Montan has been sick for some days and I have been compelled to issue every morning. I am generally up before day and commence giving out the rations directly after daylight.

I am through with the testimony in Hunter's case and I have now only to bring up the record which will take me the better part of to-day although it is Sunday. I would be willing to bet two million, if I had it, that there will not be anything done with the case.

John Overton got drunk yesterday and kicked up the devil in general, and he was corporal of the Guard too. Last night while sitting in my tent writing, I heard John over at the guard-house swearing like blazes, and I understood this morning that he broke away from the guards and went lumbering down the hall before they caught him at the foot of the hall. I remember when John was considered a respectable man and mingled in good society, but now, alas! He is scarcely tolerated among the boys. This is all from the effects of drinking liquor that has brought all this on.

Tuesday, November 4: I have not been able to write any in my journal all day yesterday on account of having to make up the record of the proceedings of the Court, but I hope to be through with it in the course of a few days more at the furtherest. To-day we read over the testimony and compared the copy with the original and found it nearly correct.

Clay Davis came down to-day on the cars bringing me a letter from Sis in which she says for me to send up some salt if possible. I will try to do so, but the only chance is to get it out of the pork barrels, which I think I can do after the pork is taken out.[5] Clay says he will send me down all the dispatches that he receives

---

[5] The Confederacy was poorly supplied with salt. Needed not only as a seasoning but as a preservative, and with supplies restricted because of the Union blockade, every possible source of salt was sought. See Ella Lonn, *Salt as a Factor in the Confederacy* (New York, 1933).

while he remains in Clinton, which will suit me exactly if he will only do what he promises.

I shall try to go home as soon as I am through with this infernal trial. It will not do to go before it is through with for if I do, I will be apt to get caught which would not be very agreeable to me.

Wednesday, November 5: I received from Colonel [William R.] Miles this morning, the opinion of the Court which I appended to the transcript and also made a copy of Hunter's answer in the case. I have now seen the opinion of the Court and I suppose the next thing on the program is to give my opinion, which for the benefit of future reference, I shall put down why and it is as follows—that the trial was the rottenest thing in the way of a trial that I ever saw. There was no use to attempt to convince that board of the guilt of Colonel Hunter because all the testimony in Christendom would fail to do that. They have evidently made up their minds that he should be found not guilty and there was no use bringing any witnesses against him. Old Miles himself would turn and twist the testimony of the witness to suit himself and in favor of Hunter, and whenever a witness was brought upon the stand that was not favorable to the case of the accused, he was frowned down and his evidence made to read in Hunter's favor, if possible. The truth is, that it was utterly impossible to bring Hunter out guilty before such a Court because they are officers themselves and they did not wish to set a precedent before the men. Taking it altogether, I think it is the lamest thing I ever saw.

After I got through with the transcript of the record, I bundled up my dirty clothes and made for the depôt to go home, and that too, without a pass. I succeeded in getting off and remained until Friday the 7th inst.

As soon as I arrived in camp, Hunter came to my tent and told me that Colonel Miles wished to see me, and as soon as I had finished my dinner, I went over to see the old cock. All he wanted was for me to sign a certificate to the record which I did. I told him before I gave it to him there ought to be a certificate attached, but he said that the signature of the court was sufficient, but when he carried it up to General Beall, he returned it to him for the certificate of the recorder.

Saturday, November 8: I am busy to-day boiling down some brine to make salt to send to mother. The tallow I have not been able to obtain yet, but I will get it as soon as possible.

Sunday, November 9: It was quite cool last night, a very heavy frost this morning. It was so cold that ice formed a second time in the bucket of water between daylight and sun-rise.

I got through boiling my salt yesterday and I have now about half a peck of very good salt. As soon as another barrel of pork is opened, I will obtain what there is in it and send the whole of it up at the same time.

Bill Montan and I made some candles to-day which look well enough if they will only prove as good as they look.

The camp is very quiet to-day. Mr. Godfrey did not preach as usual although he was here this morning and stayed for some time.

Monday, November 10: I went out with a wagon this morning and brought in nearly a cord of wood. This I want to make a fire before my tent, by which to roast potatoes and tell lies.

Gen. [John B.] Villipique died yesterday at Gibbon's house where he was quartered, of typhoid pneumonia.

The report in camp to-day is that Lord Lyons the English Minister, has arrived in New York, or Washington, I do not remember, and that he has received instructions from his Government to offer terms of peace, or rather to mediate between the powers.[6]

Tuesday, November 12: Yesterday the weather changed a little. It turned much warmer, clouded up and began to rain lightly in the evening. It rained a slow rain nearly all night last night and the heavens this morning looked dark and lowering with a slight fall of rain.

I am reading the " Wandering Jew " by Eugene Sue, and I find it interesting.

---

[6] There was strong sentiment in some official circles in England advocating mediation. Lord Palmerston, the British Prime Minister, turned against the proposal, however, when reports arrived describing the failure of the Confederate invasion of Maryland and the drawn battle of Antietam. Frank L. Owsley, *King Cotton Diplomacy* (Chicago, 1931), 361-83.

I began the other day to write a sort of history of what has transpired since I have been out in the wars as well as I can recollect them and I now wish that I had kept a regular journal of all that transpired at the time.

The news in camp this morning is that General Lee has whipped the Yankees in Virginia, that he has routed them, in fact,[7] and that Seward [8] has said that foreign intervention is inevitable, all of which I hope is true.

I am reading a novel called, "Prairie Bird" written by the Honorable Charles Augustus Murray. I think he is an Englishman and he also wrote "Travels in North America." I read this book a long time ago, I think it was in '46 or '47, or about the time of the Mexican War. Reading this book again is almost like meeting an old friend. For some cause or other, I have frequently thought of passages of this book, especially when reading sketches of frontier life and hunting stories. It brings to mind memories of my early boyhood when everything went right, and which seem to me now the happiest of my life, for then I had no troubles nor cares upon my mind and could enjoy unalloyed happiness. Sometimes I look back upon my past life with much regret, being conscious (as I now am) of what I could have been and what I could have done if I had only pursued the right course.

I attribute all my faults and short-comings to that awful habit of drinking which has truly proved the bane of my existence and if I only had my life to live over again, how differently I would act. But there is one thing I shall try to do in the future, and that is to be benefited by past experience and when this war closes, to make a new start in the world. There are two great obstacles in the way, one is drink and the other is bad health. If I am afflicted with the first, it is my own fault, the other is beyond my power to a certain extent. I am confident that reading trashy novels has been a very great injury to me in my earlier

---

[7] As was so often the case, the rumor was false. Only a few cavalry skirmishes were fought during the month of November, 1862, in Virginia. Lincoln was trying to find a general who could smash the Confederates and take Richmond while Lee was reorganizing his forces after the indecisive Battle of Antietam. See Douglas Southall Freeman, *Lee's Lieutenants* (New York, 1946), II, 310–24.

[8] William H. Seward, Secretary of State.

years because I know that I have been influenced more or less by them ever since and even now I see the effects of it to myself at times.

I am reminded of a joke that occurred before the war. Tom Skipwith and Jimmie Doyle were Deputy Clerks and I was Deputy Sheriff under Alex Norwood. Jim Doyle had been troubled with pimples on his face and as he supposed these pimples were very detrimental to his good looks he went round to the Druggist and bought a bottle of some kind of a preparation to put on his face. One day Tom Skip came into the office with the bottle in his hand saying "Look here what I have found. Jim Doyle is trying to improve his good looks." While we were looking at the bottle and laughing over it Alex Norwood stepped in, and he had a good laugh about it. The label was unusually large and had only a few words written on the upper margin. Said I "Boys let's make a few remarks on this label, and we will astonish Jim the first time he looks at it." Alex and Tom readily agreed to this and first one and then another would make a suggestion, which was written upon it, until the label was entirely filled with something like the following. "Cure for baldness— certain remedy for diarrhoea, specially recommended for stubborn cases of the piles, affords instantaneous relief to women in the family way" and a great many other things of the same order we wrote until the label was entirely full. "Now" says Tom "I'll take this bottle and do it up in the paper and place it right back where I found it, and when Jim looks at it, I think he will open his eyes."

Tom took the bottle and placed it right back where he had found it and we thought no more about it. I suppose it must have been about two weeks after this that Jim Doyle rushed into my office, pale, breathless, and very much agitated.

"Why what on earth is the matter Jim" said I "you look as pale as a ghost."

"You would look pale too" he replied "if you had such a joke played off on you as I did. I wish I knew the man that did it. I would kill him, right now."

"Why Jim" said I "it must be something terrible. Sit down

there and compose yourself and enter into explanations. I am completely in the dark."

"Well, before I proceed to make any explanations I wish to know if you wrote anything on a label of medicine that I had in the office?"

The light began slowly to break in upon me. Seeing Jim's excited condition I thought the better plan would be to deny the thing *in toto*. This I did, answering that I had no knowledge of the existence of such a bottle as he described. This was a *whopper*, but I had said it and I stuck to it.

"Well" said he "I will tell you just how it happened. I was sitting in Mr. D'Armond's parlor last night (Jim boarded there) talking to the young ladies. Some how or other the conversation turned upon pimples on the face, and the girls remarked that they had some on their faces, and remarked that they wished they knew something that would take them off. I told them that I had a bottle of something that was prepared for the purpose and that if they wished it I would get it when I went down to the Postoffice. They told me by all means to bring it up with me. I went down to the Postoffice, and after I had taken out my mail I went over to the clerk's office to get the bottle. It was very dark in the office and I could not find the candle. Knowing exactly where the bottle was I didn't trouble myself any longer to look for the candle, but searched for the bottle in the dark and found it. I went up to the house, but there was no light in the parlor and the girls had gone to bed. I saw one of the servants, and without suspecting anything, I sent it to them.

On rising this morning, I found that identical bottle sitting on my bureau, and the label was perfectly covered with the most vulgar words and the names of the most vulgar diseases that you ever heard of. I went to breakfast, but neither Mrs. D'Armond nor the girls would speak to me and the girls wouldn't even look at me. This made me feel mighty bad, and a little while ago Mr. D'Armond called me aside and wished to know what I meant by sending such a thing as that to the young ladies. I explained the thing to him but he doesn't seem to be fully satisfied about it."

Jim went away in a terrible stew. I didn't say anything about the matter until Alex came down, and then I called Tom Skip in and told them about it. They enjoyed it immensely and so did I. I told Aleck to go over and explain the matter to D'Armond which he did and I heard no more of it.

It was a good joke on Jim but he didn't see any fun in it.

Sunday, November 16: Their gunboats are below the point firing on the batteries. I can hear the shells hissing through the air, every shot. I hope they will have a good old time of it.

The band has returned and we have music now. As it is here so seldom now, it is a fact worthy of notice.

Bill Montan, John Roe and myself went down to the river to see the gun-boats, but they had gone down the river out of sight, though I hear them firing some distance below this point, apparently about 10 or 12 miles from this place. They were firing on some sugar houses on the other side of the river this morning which they are very good at considering the houses cannot fire back, and is a very safe way of carrying on a war. If they get this place, it strikes me that they will have to fight a little first, and not only a little, but a great deal because we are, or will be, pretty well fortified and ready for any landed force that they can bring against us, although our force is inconsiderable.

Tuesday, November 18: There is no news of the gun-boats this morning. When last heard from, they were some 10 miles below Baton Rouge, firing away at nobody knows what, but I presume at sugar houses.

I saw a man bucked at the Guard House this morning and it is very humiliating to be placed in such a fix.[9]

Wednesday, November 19: The way it rained last night was a caution to little fishes. The fly of our tent got very slack which caused the tent to leak and I was put to some trouble to move my bed on which it was leaking pretty freely.

Yesterday the Orderly Sargents in the different companies were ordered to make out a list of all the men that have been detailed from each company. This is done, I suppose, to find out whether

---

[9] Bucking consisted of placing the culprit in a sitting position, tying his hands together, slipping them over his knees, and then running a stick or rifle through the space beneath the knees and over the arms.

there are any able bodied young men in the different departments of the regiment. I suppose a few days will show what it is for.

I think that I will go up town to-day and buy a newspaper. Matthews and I subscribed for the Memphis Appéal for 2 months to-day—that is, we wrote the letter and it will be mailed tomorrow.

No news from the gunboats this morning. I suppose they have gone to New Orleans.[10]

Thursday, November 20: The rumor in camp last night was that the Yankee gunboat Essex, was coming up to try our batteries, but we have heard nothing of her. If she comes along, I feel pretty sure that she will get well warmed up, even if she is iron-clad.[11]

I must go and get another load of wood today. If I don't keep a fire, I can't get any company. The boys don't like to talk in the dark.

Friday, November 21: Weather very fine indeed, being clear and cool and very bracing and invigorating.

I have a strong notion to write to Crawford at Camp Moore and see if I can obtain a situation with him as there seems to be entirely too many in the Commissary Department in this regiment and it is evident that one of us at least ought to leave it. All that keeps me from writing to Crawford is that I thought Wooster might be made Brigade Commissary under Allen and he has already told me that he will give me a place with him which would probably be better than attempting to obtain a place with Crawford.

Sunday, November 23: I wrote a letter to Crawford yesterday, but I have not sent it off yet. I wish Wooster would come back and see what he is going to do and let me know. I do not like to stay in the Commissary where there is so little to do. The men in the regiment notice it and make remarks about there being so many in the Commissary.

---

[10] New Orleans had been captured by Union forces in late April, 1862.

[11] The *Essex* was a river vessel of 1000 tons equipped with 15-inch guns. It participated in many actions along the Tennessee, Mississippi, and Red rivers. See H. Allen Gosnell, *Guns on the Western Waters* (Baton Rouge, 1949), 44–56.

Monday, November 24: We are moving our camp to-day over about where Miles' Legion is. I like the move in some respects and in some respects I do not. I like it on account of its being less exposed to the north wind from the river, and I dislike it because we will probably not have such good water as we have here and it will probably not be so dry there as it is here. The reason why we have to move is because they are going to build the breastworks right through our camp.

I took a walk yesterday to look at the breast-works they are building near the river and they look quite formidable, having a base nearly 30 feet through and a ditch about 7 or 8 feet deep which will be quite a job to get through.

Tuesday, November 25: Yesterday the regiment moved from our camp at the Gin House to the woods near Slaughter's field and not far from his dwelling house.[12] I had right hard work fixing up my tent, clearing off the ground and many other things too numerous to mention.

I read a splendid speech made by Richard Ogleman, which has been published in the Memphis Appeal of the 20th inst. He is down on the abolitionists and down on the domination of old Abe. It is a splendid speech and will have some effect. I look upon the triumphs of the Democratic Party as indications of peace. I think that it shows a diversity of opinion in the North which will be fatal to the successful prosecution of the war, and if they fail in this wondrous campaign, they might as well give it up and be willing to quit as they are almost exhausted now and one more failure will wind up the ball.

We had a great game last night in my tent. John Roe, Matthews, Haynes, and I played a game of " Smut " and our black faces presented a laughable spectacle as each one was blacked in his turn.

The weather's fair but there are light clouds floating around which indicate rain at no distant day. My tent is in a very low place and if it begins to rain before I get it ditched, it will be

[12] One and one-half miles southeast of the village of Port Hudson. See map of the battlefield in *Battles and Leaders*, III, 596.

very apt to drown me out. I like our present camp well enough if it doesn't prove to be a regular swamp in wet weather.

Wednesday, November 26: I slept very badly last night being troubled with the worst kind of dreams and nightmares.

I went to see Hunter this morning and obtained leave of absence to go home to-day. I wish to go for several reasons—1. I wish to be present at the concert. 2. I wish to have my coat cut out. 3. I wish to buy some tobacco besides several other little things of minor importance.

The latest dispatches, which arrived last night, say that France has proposed to England and Austria and Spain to recognize the Confederacy and that if they decline, that she will recognize us herself without the others. There was also some talk of armed intervention, but I do not believe a word of it.[13]

I have been troubled a great deal with sties on my eyes which causes them to be inflamed very much. Studying Phonography is a great strain on the eyes and I think studying and reading Phonography is the cause of my eyes being sore now. Last night I tried to keep a wet cloth on them to reduce the inflamation.

The report here is that New Orleans has been reinforced by 28,000 Yankees and that they meditate an early attack upon this place. If they do, all I have to say is that they will have a good old time of it.

Friday, December 5: I left for home on the 26th ult. and reached there about 9 o'clock that night. I did not return until Monday the first of December. I was detained by an accident which happened to the cars as we went up. The passenger car ran off the track while crossing a bridge, tearing up the track behind it, without leaving a vestige of the timbers on the track. We were forced to leave the passenger car on the track and pro-

---

[13] These reports received by Patrick were only partially true. France, suffering from a shortage of cotton, did attempt to obtain the aid of England in recognizing the Confederacy and breaking the blockade. This was the position with reference to the South which Napoleon III maintained until the end of the war, namely, that he would recognize the Confederate states and break the blockade, should England abandon her neutral position and join him. England was always willing to discuss the matter when distress in the cotton districts should demand it, but the British were unwilling to move in the direction of intervention. Owsley, *King Cotton Diplomacy*, 75.

ceed to town without it. There were several ladies in the car at the time the accident occurred and it is a great wonder that they all escaped without being hurt. We arrived at home about 9 o'clock that night without further delay. Every one at home had gone to the concert and as it was rather late, I did not go but made myself comfortable before the fire until they returned which was about 11 o'clock.

On account of the cars not being able to run, I remained at home until the following Monday. I saw nearly all the girls in town, Willa among others. She looks as well as ever. I never thought her very handsome although I used to make love to her and everybody thought that she and I were engaged. I think that she considered it an engagement herself and I am certain that the old folks thought so. I always liked her well enough but could not stand the family, the old man especially. I never had the most distant idea of marrying her although I cannot blame her for thinking so because my actions implied it as strong, if not stronger, than words would have done. I blame myself for not showing my hand earlier.

I attended the concert on Friday evening and liked it very much. Miss Jane Stoke devoted herself entirely to the piano, playing only accompaniments to songs. Sure it was a charming sight to see her led out by the handsome Mr. Cain of the band. How graceful she looked while sitting at the piano, her beautiful neck about as long as my arm and as large as a broom-stick; her charming auburn locks about the color of carrots; her beautiful rounded, snow-white arms, which look like the leg bones of a turkey after all the flesh has been taken off, or a well-rope with a knot tied in it; her heaving bosom and swelling bust were exhibited to the greatest advantage on this momentous occasion. Taking her altogether, she looked like the devil as she was led out to the piano and her back seemed as though it would break in two, she was so long and limber. Mrs. Hardesty looked a little seedy, like the tail end of better times. I suppose she cannot obtain the thousand and one little articles from the millionaires now that she had before the war and consequently, cannot bolster herself up and look as well as she used to when cash was more abundant than it is now.

61

Miss Hannah Roach looked tolerably well but seemed to be a little embarrassed on first coming out, but she soon recovered herself and sang a song in very good style.

Mrs. Comstock next attracted my attention. She looked as ugly as ever. She sang in opera style and piled on some of the most excruciating agonies, but she sang so much better than that of the others.

Mrs. Ball thought she sang very well and evidently appreciated her own music if no one else did.. Her mouth shut and opened like a rat-trap. Garnell Crocket made a short and appropriate speech which broke up the concern much to my satisfaction.

For the last day or two, John Roe and I have been making a chimney to my tent which makes it very pleasant in cold weather. It took fire last night and came near burning up chimney, tent and all. To-day we have had old Prince working at it, sticking more mud on it and I hope it will not be getting out of fix so often.

Monday, December 8: I have just returned from town. I went to see John Bradford, but he was not at home. I discovered that there are quite a number of troops concentrated at this place; in fact a great many more than I supposed there was here. I had a very good opportunity of seeing the breast-works that will soon be completed. They seem to be capable of serving as defences, sure enough, and no mistake. If the Yankees will only attack us here, I imagine they will think there are some here at any rate.

Nothing new from the enemy or from our own forces. I never see any papers now and cannot find out anything that is going on. The Memphis Appeal, I am told, has been removed to some other place, I do not know where, but I suppose to a place of greater safety and this is the reason why I have not received my paper. It may probably come along sometime or other.[14]

[14] To escape the invading enemy several papers moved from town to town but continued to publish under their original titles. Perhaps the most famous for its wanderings was the Memphis *Appeal*, being facetiously referred to as the " Moving Appeal." One writer has said that it moved so frequently that when last heard of it was the " Memphis-Hernando-Grenada-Vicksburg-Jackson-Atlanta-Griffin Appeal." It was finally overtaken at Columbus, Ga., at the end of the war. E. Merton Coulter, *The Confederate States of America, 1861–1865,* Vol. VII of " A History of the South " (Baton Rouge, 1950), 495–96.

Tuesday, December 9:   Weather very fine indeed. Just cool enough to be pleasant.

No news from our army as yet. We never see any papers and the telegraph brings nothing. I heard that General Bragg was at Granada with about 15,000 troops, but there is no confidence to be placed in this report. I think that we will hear startling news before a great while.

My health has not been very good for several days past. I have been troubled with a cough and a soreness in my breast which prevents my sleeping well at night. The other morning I could not sleep and I got up about 3 o'clock and remained up until daylight.

Our chimney makes my tent very comfortable, but when the fire goes out, I get quite cold, sometimes I arise and make up the fire and then go to bed again. We have splendid wood to burn. I had a large ash tree cut down and split up into wood of the right length to suit my fire-place.

Monday, December 15:   I have just returned from home. I went up last Friday to see about my clothing. I have lost all my under clothing by the inadvertency of the negro that brought them down for me. There is a great deal of sickness among the soldiers now and they are dying right fast at the hospitals in Clinton.[15]

The very evening that I left, the gun-boats came up near Port Hudson and on Saturday and Sunday, there was considerable firing heard from the direction of Port Hudson, and I have ascertained since I came down to-day, the following particulars— on Saturday, the gun-boats were lying below our batteries when some guerillas, a company of whom were on the other side, employed a negro man to hail one of the boats, which he did, and the commander sent a yawl with about 20 men ashore to bring the negro on board, as they thought, but when the boat approached the shore, a partisan fired on them, killing some five or six and

---

[15] Several buildings in Clinton were used as Confederate hospitals. These included Silliman College, Masonic Hall, and the stately Henry Marston home. The Silliman and Marston buildings are not only still standing but are in current use. See Annie Sanderson Kilbourne, "War Times In and Around Clinton, Louisiana," *Louisiana Historical Quarterly*, XIII (January, 1930), 64–66.

wounding several others, and they beat a hasty retreat. This caused the gun-boats to let fly with shells and grape in the woods for a good while. They afterwards fired at a mill, but did no damage. Yesterday (Sunday) morning, Boone's battery crossed the river and went down to where the boats were and let loose at them with light artillery and it is reported that they damaged one of the wooden boats considerably and that she had to be towed off by the iron-clad " Essex."

The news from above is that the enemy are retreating from Granada, which has been threatened for some time by the Yankees. I presume that old Bragg has given them a good fright by menacing their rear and they have taken the back-track to Corinth.[16] A fight is daily expected in Virginia about Fredericksburg; in fact, the enemy have already commenced firing on the town and that too, without giving the inhabitants any warning whatever.[17]

I came down on the train with some Arkansas troops and several of them were drunk which made it very disagreeable traveling, but suppose it was pleasant enough for them, but I am certain it was very unpleasant to me.

I am now reading " Ten Thousand a Year " by Samuel Warren. I have read this work before but it has been so long that I have nearly forgotten it and it is nearly as good as new now.

Tuesday, December 16: Weather very fine indeed after a storm we had yesterday. It is neither too cool nor too warm for comfort, and the sun shines bright and beautiful this morning.

I have just been looking at the artillery company drilling in front of my quarters. They put their horses through at double-quick occasionally, which is pretty tight on them over the ridges of the field.

I pass my time very pleasantly here now, not having much to

[16] Grant's army was forced to retire from Grenada after the Federal supply depot at Holly Springs, Miss., was destroyed in a daring raid by Confederate troops commanded by General Earl Van Dorn. *Battles and Leaders*, III, 475.

[17] Patrick is referring to the battle of Fredericksburg fought December 11–15, 1862. Counterbalancing the discouraging defeats in the West, Lee and the Army of Northern Virginia won a crucial victory. General Ambrose E. Burnside commanded the defeated Union army of 113,000 troops. *Ibid.*, III, 70–148.

do but issue every morning to the regiment which I generally do by breakfast time. I arise, generally about day-light, and sometimes a little before. The first thing I do is to make up a fire, wash my face and make myself comfortable until the men come for their rations, and after this, I have nothing more to do for the day.

The small pox is said to be in camp and for fear of taking it, I was vaccinated while I was at home but it doesn't feel like it would make a sore.

Our rations are right slim now. We have nothing but meal and beef and that is very inferior. I think that is what causes so much sickness in camp. We should have a changed diet occasionally and the water we have to drink is also very bad indeed and it stinks at that. Andrew, our cook, has some corn beer made and I drink that in preference to the water although it is almost vinegar.

Last night Captain Wooster, Captain Reed, John Roe and I made a rum punch and sat up drinking and talking until bed time. We did not get tight nor any ways under the influence of the liquor though.

The report in camp is that there has been a fight in Fredericksburg, Virginia, in which we have been victorious. The dispatches are meager. It was not exactly at Fredericksburg that the fight took place, but near there and was brought on, I suppose, by the attempt of the Yankees to cross the river, and the dispatches which were very short indeed, are saying that the battle would in all probability be resumed by daylight the next morning.

Louis Napoleon has made overtures to England and Russia to mediate between the contending parties in America to put a stop to the war, but they have both declined doing so. The Mobile Evening News, speaking of this refusal on the part of the other powers, says it is " very much like the first ' no ' of a young maiden to the wooings of her lover—they only need a little persuasion to make them say ' yes ' not that they wish to recognize us, but this proposition of France puts England and her selfish policy to a very severe test."

The Richmond Examiner pronounces General Burnsides [Ambrose E. Burnside] to be in a very bad " fix " just at the present writing. General Lee is in his front to dispute the passage of the river, while, according to the abolition program of campaign, it was his business to have been somewhere else until the Yankees had crossed the river. Meantime, the late heavy rains have rendered the roads next to impassable in his rear and in the direction of Falmouth. The single railroad from Aquia Creek, not yet finished, is inadequate to furnish his army with supplies, much less to afford it the means of a safe retreat. Yet he must move forwards or backwards. To stay where he is involves speedy starvation, to go backwards is official decapitation, and to go forward he must fight the best army in the world to disadvantage. Meantime, the Confederacy is waiting his determination. A Yankee letter to the Herald says the Rebels are holding their position with the greatest effrontery.[18]

Wednesday, December 17: The report in camp this morning is that the enemy is coming up the river with all their fleet composed of gun-boats, mortar boats and transports, all of which have passed Baton Rouge on their way up. The orders are that no man shall leave camp and to prepare for a fight. I suppose they will not be able to do anything for several days yet, although they may fire on the farm houses and sugar mills for I do not think that they will attempt to do anything with the batteries on the shore for they are too timid to come near without a very superior force. The little thrashing they received the other day has had its effect upon them and I suppose they feel somewhat exasperated by losing several of their men and having one of their boats injured by our artillery sharp-shooters. By to-morrow, we will know what they expect to do.

Thursday, December 18: Weather very fine indeed, clear and cool. The Yankees have landed about 1,200 men at Baton Rouge.[19]

---

[18] The plight of the Union army was not as desperate as Patrick believed. Burnside was relieved of his command by President Lincoln. The Union army then went into winter quarters and in April, 1863, General Joe Hooker launched his " On to Richmond " campaign.

[19] Federal troops, convoyed by a detachment of Farragut's fleet, took possession of Baton Rouge at daybreak December 17, 1862. Outnumbered Confederate forces with-

They arrived there day before yesterday. Our men were at work on the breast-works until mid-night last night and I suppose they will continue to work them both night and day until they are completed and ready for the Northern Vandals.

It was reported in camp last night that President Davis would be at Port Hudson tomorrow. I do not know whether this is true or not.[20]

I have been quite unwell to-day. I was up this morning at two o'clock and did not go to bed again. My stomach is a little deranged from drinking corn beer that Andrew made the other day.

Wade Mackey wrote to me yesterday to try and get his negroes sent home as he is afraid that they will take the smallpox. They have been working for the government at Port Hudson. I do not think that he can get them as we need all the hands that we can raise just at this moment.

I took the following from the Mobile Evening News, a strong electioneering document—

> The canvass has been a bitter one between the republicans and democrats, but the former, with the Government to back them, have not been able entirely to supress their antagonists.

The New York Caucasion publishes a " Ten-Year Record " of the Republican Party, with a boldness which is likely to consign the editor to Fort Lafayette.[21]

Friday, December 19: I have been quite sick ever since night before last. Last night I was very unwell indeed. My bowels are entirely out of fix and I was up almost the entire night. I kept a fire burning all night and slept very little.

The news in camp to-day is that we have repulsed the enemy in Virginia and that the Northern army is in a state of mutiny; that they refused to charge our batteries a second time; that our loss was about 1,800 and theirs about 8,000.[22] The enemy are

---

drew without a battle. The city was held without opposition until the war ended. *Battles and Leaders*, III, 586.

[20] The rumor was false.

[21] A prominent Federal prison.

[22] Reference is to the Confederate victory at Fredericksburg. Total Union losses

retreating from Granada, Mississippi, and are falling back to Corinth. If we can only rout them in Virginia and in northern Mississippi, the day is certainly ours without a doubt. The Yankees are reported as being pretty strong.

Tuesday, December 23: I have been sick for several days and this is the reason for my not writing regularly in my journal.

I am getting very uneasy about the Yankees paying Clinton a visit although I think they would hardly be mean enough to burn down the town.[23]

I am in hopes that I will receive some money today from the Brigade Commissary as I am entirely minus any cash whatever. I sold a pair of pants for a very fine shot gun the other day which I sent home to little Frank. I think I got it very cheap and is, in fact, a much better gun than the one I gave $35.00 for a year or two ago.

Wednesday, December 24: I spent a restless, I might almost say, a sleepless night. My head has been affected for several days with something like neuralgia and last night it was worse than usual and I am suffering from it a great deal to-day.

This is my 27th birthday. It astonishes me a little at the rapidity with which they come around now. A year once seemed to me almost like an age, but now I count time by years where I once counted it by days and even hours.

I wish this war was over so that I could be making something for old age, if I ever live long enough to be an old man. I am conscious of having mis-spent my time, it being worse than thrown away, in spending what money I made and contracting bad habits, which I find it no easy matter to get clear of. I intend, if I live next year, to lead a different life from what I have been doing for the last seven years. I shall endeavor, in the first place, to break off from as many of my bad habits as possible, and if the war breaks up, I intend to go into business on my own account, and try to lay up money for hard times. I suppose my

---

in the battle were 12,653, while the losses of Lee's army numbered 5,377. *Battles and Leaders,* III, 145, 147.

[23] Small detachments of Union troops were sent out from Baton Rouge on foraging raids. A few buildings on St. Helena Street were burned by the Federals in Clinton.

intentions are good enough if I will only carry them out. I shall try to adhere to them although they say the way to hell is paved with good intentions.

Charlie Whitman our quartermaster, asked me this morning if I would act as his clerk, that he knew nothing of the business and did not know how to make out his returns. I told him that I did not wish to leave the commissary, but that I would assist him in getting through with his papers. I have three positions offered me now. One with the Post Commissary, one with the Brigade Quarter Master, and the other with the regimental quarter master, but as I have already a very good place and one that I think will suit me better than any other, I think I had better keep it. Captain Wooster is a very fine man indeed and a man that I have no difficulty in getting along with, and besides, I have a great deal of leisure time to read and write, which I would not have, in all probability, with the others. Therefore, I think it best to remain with him as long as possible.

There is no news from our army in Virginia to-day, but I hope that everything is going well. Sometimes I wish I had remained as secretary in General Bragg's office, just to know what is going on, and then again, I know that I would have had a right hard time of it and on the whole, I am glad that I have come back to the regiment.

There is no news from the Yankees at Baton Rouge lately, but I suppose that they are still there making preparations to attack us. If they do, they will have a good old time of it, for the men we have here are fighting men certain, and they will never give up this place until they are badly whipped.

I am still reading $10,000.00 a Year. The book, taken altogether, is a very fine thing and worth the perusal by anyone.

The report in camp to-day is that Charleston, South Carolina, has been surrendered to the infernal Yankees, but I do not believe a word of it.[24]

Saturday, December 27:   I have not written any in my journal

[24] This was only a rumor. Charleston was under siege but did not surrender until the approach of Sherman's army in February, 1865.

for several days as I have been taking Christmas. There was a great deal of drinking among the men in camp.

The weather is dark and cloudy and last night it was very rainy. It is warm with every prospect of more rain to-day.

There is no news from our armies anywhere. The last dispatches that I have seen state that Burnside has resigned, that the radicals wish to put General Fremont in command and the conservatives desire to re-instate General McClellan.[25] I hope they will put Fremont in command because that will be very apt to make the Northern armies dissatisfied.

John Roe and I got hold of a little tallow to-day and we have been making some candles out of it. John stole some simple cerate over at the surgeons and we have put that in with the tallow which I am afraid will not work very well.

I pass a good portion of my time in playing cribbage with Matthews and John Roe. Matthews has taken it into his head to learn Phonography, but I am afraid that he has not the requisite determination and application to master it, because I think I have stuck to it right steadily and I have not done much at it yet, and I fear that I never will unless I have someone to help me along. I intend to devote a certain number of hours each day to the study of Phonography after the first day of January next, which is only a few days off now, by which means I hope to accomplish something.

I have just heard a gun fire and I suppose that the Yankee boats are coming up to give us a little trial.

Four in the evening. The weather is turning much cooler, and I think it ought to, for it has been almost as warm as summer for the last week.

The report is that we have captured Jackson, Tennessee, and one or two other small places together with a large number of arms and 1,500 prisoners.[26]

[25] Lively intrigues were afoot in political Washington. President Lincoln removed Burnside from his command and General Joe Hooker was selected as the fourth commander to lead the Union army against Robert E. Lee.
[26] Patrick is evidently referring to the movement of Confederate raiders into this region. Under the command of General N. B. Forrest these troops won successes at Humboldt and Trenton. They failed, however, to capture Jackson. On January 2,

to believe that the advantages gained yesterday are not at all commensurate with the loss sustained, & from the comparative silence today, I hope that Genl Hood may reconsider matters, abandon his aggressive policy and await the enemy inside our lines — His course would do well enough I think, if we had plenty of men, but this is not the case, and as a matter of course he knows it. — I am forced to the conclusion that we must either give up the place, or they will surround it, and then I know "the dog's dead."

Atlanta Geo. 22nd July 1864.

At about one o'clock this morning we were ordered to pull up stakes and move. We drove our team down in town, where we remained until after daylight. I saw a sight this morning that I never saw before and never wish to see again. A lot of cavalry, said to be the 4th Alabama Regiment, went all over the business part of the city, breaking open the doors as they came to them, and robbing every house of whatever it contained, carrying away with them such things as they desired and throwing such as they did not like into the streets. They had sacks tied to their saddles and seemed to have come prepared for the business, and all through the day cavalrymen could be seen, with their horses literally piled up and almost concealed by the plunder they had on them.

They started to enter the establishment of an old lady who kept a shop, but the old lady didn't seem disposed to submit, and she drew a pistol & threatened to shoot the first man who entered — They went in however, took her out of the house and as her hair had become dishevelled in the affray, they caught up her streaming locks, and dragged her up and down the streets by the hair of her head — They then entered the house, taking away what they wanted, and making an everlasting smash of things generally.

There was another hard fight about 2 P.M. today on the our right

A Page From Patrick's Ledger

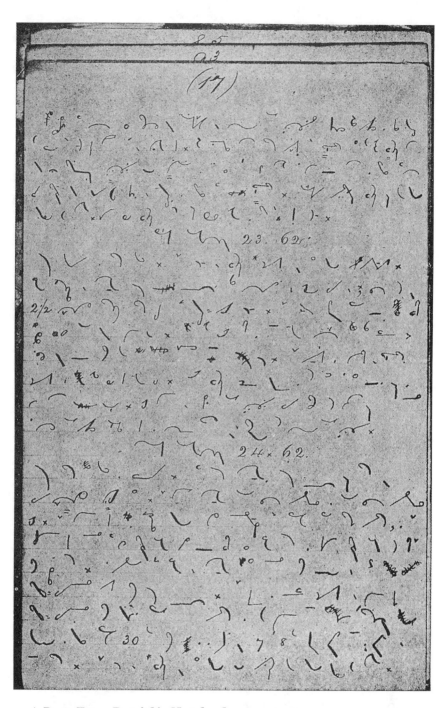

A Page From Patrick's Notebook

This is Sunday, the 28th day of December, 1862, the last Sunday in the year. It will not be '62 much longer, and the years are passing away rapidly enough. I feel a little lonesome and melancholy as I cannot help feeling at times, so I have concluded to stroll a little way from my quarters for the purpose of being alone and left to my own reflections for a short time.

To while away an hour, I have taken my " pozish," as the boys say, in good distance from my quarters on the margin of a wood over-looking a field that has been cultivated in corn this year and from which the fences are now all taken away and the field itself cut in twain by our line of breast-works which go entirely across it. The oaken fence rails have been used as barricades to hold up the earth works of the fortifications on the inside, the outside being ditched with a ditch full six feet deep. The owner of the place can rest assured of one thing and that is that he will not be under the necessity of making a ditch to drain his land for this will certainly last for all time to come.

It looks very lonely and but for the dark line of entrenchments and an occasional company or regiment out drilling, one would suppose that the Confederacy was at peace with all the world. I think if ever there was a time that ' tries mens souls,' this must be one of them, for we have to labor under the greatest difficulties in the world and have had very little clothing and very scanty fare provided for us, and for several months at a time we have not had any pork or flour issued to us. We receive half rations of rice and peas. Of salt, we did not receive full rations but we manage to get along. The sugar and molasses is of such an inferior quality that we can scarcely use it, and as for clothing, I have never received anything from the Government yet because the Government had nothing to give me. I have received, instead of clothing due me within the last two years, the sum of $50.00 which would not buy me two pair of boots to-day for they have been selling for the last twelve months at $40.00 a pair. I am not complaining of these things, but I merely mention it to

---

1863, the whole command withdrew, recrossing the Tennessee River at Clifton. *Battles and Leaders*, III, 452.

show that these are times not only to try men's souls, but it also tries their purses.

I know that if the Government were able, it would pay us off in coin. It shows the tremendous discount at which the money is now, and what it will eventually come to, no one knows. For my own part I have never had any faith in our currency, but if it will serve to carry us through the war I will be satisfied. I tell mother every time I go home to invest her Confederate money into something real, something tangible. There is the greatest field for speculation now that I ever saw, and if I were only free from the army, I verily believe that I could accumulate a wagon load of Confederate currency.

It is my firm conviction that this war will come to a close by the first day of next May, if the political aspect of things in the North betoken anything.

"The grandest scene that
ever I beheld"

CHAPTER III. JANUARY, 1863–MARCH, 1863

Port Hudson, Saturday, January 3, 1863: I have not made
any entries in my journal for several days as I have been on
another visit up home and only returned here yesterday.

Little Frank came down with me and is here to-day. He wishes
to go back to-day, but the weather is so bad that I am endeavoring to persuade him to remain until to-morrow. It rained nearly
all night last night, and there is every appearance of very bad
weather to-day. It is very dark, raining slightly with very heavy
thunder in the distance.

I do not know that I am making much headway in Phonography now, but I think I shall study a little harder this year than I
did last. If one year of pretty close study will not make a pho-
nographer of me, I shall come to the conclusion that I have not
sense enough ever to make one and that I had better give it up as
a bad job.

I did not wish little Frank to go home to-day, but he slipped off
and went home any-how. He went without his dinner and did not
take my dirty clothes with him so I shall be under the necessity of
going up town to-morrow and carrying them up myself.

The news to-day is that we have made a complete victory of it
in Tennessee which I hope is true.[1]

---

[1] Reference is to the battle of Stone's River or Murfreesboro, Tennessee fought
December 31, 1862–January 2, 1863.

Sunday, January 4: This is a very beautiful morning after a very stormy night and it is turning much cooler.

I think that the Yankees are pretty well nonplussed, and I think the end is not far off. The Yankee Army under Burnside has sustained a perfect Waterloo defeat at Fredricksburg, Virginia; they have been routed at Murfreesboro, Tennessee, and from the last accounts we have given them the worst of it at Vicksburg,[2] where they have been fighting for a week past, so that I cannot see what they are to do now to carry on the war. We will probably hear some news from Vicksburg to-day as the weather has cleared away and the lines can work.

Major General Gardner [3] is in command here now and he is a very strict disciplinarian. He says that no man shall be allowed to go outside of the lines under any pretext, and this, I suppose, puts an end to my going home for the present.

This is another lonely day in camp, but I feel a little elated at times when I think that the war is nearly over. If peace were only declared to-day, I would feel like a bird let loose from his cage.

The report is that the Yankees have left Vicksburg, and if this is the case, there is a strong probability that they have given the matter up because they had 60,000 men there and if they could not make the landing with that number, they had better give it up.

I am entirely out of anything to read now, but I think I can find something in the camp. I went down in town to-day and bought several novels from Barton, who has opened a book store. I got one called " Diana of Maridor " by [Alexandre] Dumas, " The Indies " by Mrs. [Emma D. E.] Southworth, and one of Fredrika Bremer's works.

Monday, January 5: Morris Davis and John Roe sat up until very late last night, telling long yarns about bears, panthers, etc., and I did not go to sleep until nearly 12 o'clock. John and I will be busy cutting wood to-day as we are about out of fire wood.

While I was up at home the last time, I was arrested and put

[2] The battle of Chickasaw Bluffs.
[3] Franklin Gardner. Gardner relieved Gen. Beall on December 27, 1862.

in jail and the way of it was this—Will Shropshire came to me to go with him to see the commandant of the post to endeavor to obtain a furlough to go to Vicksburg for the purpose of bringing home his brother who had been wounded in the battle up there. He wished me to go with him in order to identify him as one of the 4th Regiment, etc. I went around to Colonel Lee, who is commandant of the post. He said, during our conversation, that I spoke imprudently to him. I replied that I did not. He said I did and so one word brought on another until he said that he would send me to jail. I told him to send and be damned to him. He sent for Tom Scott, who, by the way, is a damned swell head, and had me arrested. I went down to the jail and remained five or six hours. I stayed with Caleb Gail down stairs and slept with him a part of the night, and then went up home. Tom Scott and the others thought that I remained in jail all night and locked up at that.

I shall not forget Tom Scott for the unnecessary part he took in it for there was no necessity for his being so harsh as he was. He is acting in a manner injudicious for the purpose of currying favor with the officers over him, and he is doing this at the expense of those who are his neighbors and would be his friends. Those for whose favor he is striving so hard for are all strangers to him and he will probably never see them again, but those who suffer for it are persons living in the same parish with him and I am one of them. Those men whose boots he is licking now will be gone away very soon, but I will still be there and the time may come when I will be able to repay this thing with interest.

There is to be a general inspection of the troops to-day by the Inspector General. We have had no late news from Vicksburg, Tennessee or Virginia, I suppose on account of the wires being down.

Captain Wooster told me to-day that the Post Quarter Master intended to have me detailed to write for him. I went up there a while ago to see him and he had a long talk with me about it and he talks very fair. He says that he is willing to do what is right. He wishes me to take charge of the whole thing and do my best and that he would see that I was amply paid for it and that

I should receive at least $80.00 per month, and that I should not be any loser by the transaction, so I took him at his word and I am going up there in the morning. There is only one thing that I regret by it and that is that I will be compelled to give up the study of Phonography, and that, too, at a time when I am just getting to see that I can write with something like ease. I hope that I will suit the office that I am going into as this is the first opportunity I have had to make something.

Friday, January 9: Have had no opportunity of writing in my journal until this morning and it is so dark and rainy that I can scarcely see how to write.

I am now in the office of the Post Quarter Master and I am doing very well so far. I have a great deal of work to do and I shall have very little time to practice Phonography. Captain Raphael the Quarter Master, treats me very well indeed and seems to be a very clever man, although I have been told by a great many that I should not stay with him a week.

I am trying to make up a mess as I have been boarding with an old French lady down town, and I shall send a man over to Waterloo for some dishes, etc., but as it is a very bad day, it is uncertain whether or not he will go. I am paying $10.00 a week for my board now, and I think I can live cheaper than that by having a mess. My wages will be, I think, about $100.00 or $125.00 per month which will enable me to pay off some of my debts at home if I make anything above my expenses. I have a first rate office to write in immediately on the bank of the river in Port Hudson, although I believe that I am out of range of the gun-boats.

I have no leisure time on my hands at all, but I shall do my best to keep my journal up by working at it every morning before breakfast. General Bragg is falling back from Murfreesboro, Tennessee, or in my words, he is running like the very devil.

Sunday, January 11: There is a very heavy fog upon the river this morning and the weather's quite cool.

Captain Raphael treats me very politely and in fact, he treats me very kind. Yesterday, he gave me two pairs of good, woolen socks and a pair of $50.00 boots.

I have a very nice little rough bed to sleep on and a very comfortable room for a bed-room. I am getting along very well with my work. I have a great deal to do and cannot make any very rapid headway towards my quarterly returns. My health is not very good. My bowels have been somewhat deranged.

Monday, January 12: This is a beautiful morning and looks more like spring than winter and is just cool enough to make it comfortable. My health is a little better than it has been for the last week.

I saw the old " Essex " yesterday down the river, but she was very careful not to come in range of our guns.

Tuesday, January 13: I am quite unwell this morning being afflicted with diarrhea, and having very severe pains in my stomach and bowels. This hangs on to me for a long time—so long in fact that I am afraid that it is becoming chronic.

The inspecting officer was here yesterday and told me that he would be here this morning to examine into my books and papers.

I have a great notion to send home for my violin, but I am afraid that it might get lost and I would not lose it for any consideration as my father gave it to me.

I have no work to do at night, but as my eyes are so weak and the lights I have so dim I cannot read or write at anything. This is the reason why I thought that I would have my violin brought down so that I could amuse myself during the long evenings. I am doing my best towards getting my books in shape to make my quarter returns.

I have been very unwell the greater part of the day and this evening I took my pony and went down to the regiment to see our surgeon, Charlie Lewis, to obtain some medicine, but when I got there, I did not find him at home. I received some pills from the assistant which I will take to-night.

I wrote home for my violin to-day which will be down to-morrow. I think I can spend my evenings very pleasantly here with my fiddle and a few books. I am reading " The Lady of Monacero [Monsoreau] " by Dumas, which, though very dull at the beginning, becomes very interesting as I advance. I consider him one of the best writers of the age, although Dickens, Thackeray and one or two others are certainly very fine authors.

I was lucky enough to buy thirteen yards of flannel from the Captain to-day which I sent home to mother and I know that she will be very glad to get it.

I do not think that there has been anything of importance transpiring lately and there is no news from Baton Rouge indicating anything like a forward movement from that point.

I am getting along very well thus far with the Captain and I presume that I shall continue to do so as there is nothing to prevent it that I can see at present. He is a strange sort of a genius anyway and I think that I will be able to make him out fully after a while. One thing I have ascertained beyond a doubt and that is that he is a regular toady, that is he is willing on all occasions, to kiss the feet of those above him and that is the main reason why he obtains offices and retains them after he has once got them, and another discovery I have made is that he is not a man of his word; that he slips out of his promises.

I wish to write more to-night, but the light is too dim and my eyes are too weak to write any longer.

Thursday, January 15: Last night was a very rainy and stormy night indeed, but wet and dark as it was, I had to go out several times during the night. My bowels were in a very bad way and I must certainly do something for them.

I am so hurried and have so little time to keep my journal, that it is very defective and is not a " true type of the times " for it does not show all that is going on. It is correct as far as it goes.

The weather is turning very cold and I think it will be freezing by morning unless it turns much warmer than it is now. I intended to go down to the regiment this evening, but it is so very cold and there being no one in the office except myself, I think I shall defer it until another time.

I notice a great many birds (commonly called rice birds, although they resemble the black bird more than anything else) flying and lighting on the ground in the yard, and if I only had a gun, I think I could kill about 20 at a shot. We are not having a very good time now in the way of rations and in fact, the rations we have received for 10 days are really not sufficient to last us 5, but I think that we will be able to furnish a much better table a little after we receive something from home and as Bill has gone up to-day, I presume that he will bring some eatables down with him.

Friday, January 16: I was quite unwell last night as usual, and I am scarcely fit for business to-day though I must go through with it. So far as I can learn, Raphael is well pleased with me and I like him well enough if he was not such a liar. He will make the fairest promises in the world, but he will not stick to them. He promised to give me some of his hams when I get my mess started, but since I have had the mess going, he has not said a word about hams or coffee. To-day, I think I shall try to get a ham out of him if it is possible. I have no beef at all to eat as the Commissary sent me all my meat at once and it is spoiled.

Saturday, January 17: The weather's freezing this morning. The frost looks like a young snow and the ground is frozen hard. This is pretty severe weather on the troops that are without tents, and there are a great many that have none and a great many of the men are destitute of shoes and clothing.

Bill Stone brought down some butter and eggs and we are living on that entirely, though I think that I shall try to get a ham out of Raphael to-day. He is decidedly the damnest liar I ever saw. He doesn't hesitate to tell the most unblushing lies. I get along very well with him though and so far as my work is concerned, he never troubles me and I have everything my own way, which is about the only way that I can get along with him because if he insists upon ruling me in this particular, I should be forced to quit.

Sunday, January 18: This is Sunday and I think that I shall do as little work as I possibly can to-day. I am kept very busy all the time and have just about as much as I can well attend to, though I always try to do very little on Sunday and keep it as a sort of a rest day.

Monday, January 19: It is a very dark, rainy, gloomy, cheerless morning indeed. It rained nearly all night last night and continues to rain this morning with every appearance of keeping it up until night again. The roads are almost a smooth sheet of water and where there is no water the mud is a foot deep and the roads leading out of town that are traveled much by the army wagons are almost impassable or they soon will be, so there is a great dearth of news at present. We cannot hear a word from anywhere. The old " Essex " is lying down below and fired some guns this morning at something. A plan is being laid to blow her up with something like a submarine battery as soon as they can have it fixed up. I am afraid that it will not succeed although this same man who is contriving this, managed to destroy two other boats up the Yazoo River and if he has been successful before, I do not see why he should not be able to accomplish the same feat here that he did there.

My health is improving some though my bowels are still in a very unhealthy condition.

I fear that Raphael, if he does not be very careful, will lose his position because he is narrowly watched by the officers above him and I am certain that they have no confidence in his honesty and they have already accused him of dishonesty by speculating in clothing left to be issued to the soldiers and to sell to the officers.

Tuesday, January 20: I was reading a paper of the 15th last night and I came to the conclusion from what I read there that old Bragg was very badly whipped in Tennessee. We cannot obtain any news from there which I think is ominous because if the news was good, it would not be long before we read all about it. Bragg and Breckinridge between them, got our army cut all to hell and now they are skedaddling back again to save themselves.

Bragg is not fit for a general and I have always contended for that, and the most he is fit for is the command of a brigade and he would make a damned poor brigadier. He got his name up in the Mexican War when he had command of a battery under General Taylor, and he never had anything there worthy of note. All that gave him such a reputation was that the picture makers, the getters-up of these cheap prints had a picture of a man in uniform—of an American soldier ramming away like the devil at a six pounder, with the following words under it—" A little more grape, Captain Bragg " and this same cheap print has given old Bragg his fame. If Jeff Davis will just let Bragg alone, I think he will do us more damage than the enemy, and I believe that he is cowardly too. I know one thing, that he is a perfect tyrant, and I never saw a tyrant yet but what was a coward.

Matthews stayed with us last night and played the violin until the string broke and busted up the fun.

My health is not very good, and I feel very unwell this morning. Two or three men have died within the last day or two in camp of the smallpox.

I have been kept quite busy to-day. I have so many calls that it keeps me very busy to attend to them all, besides the other work I have to do on my books, but as I have just a moment to spare, I thought that I would write a little in my journal.

Mother sent me down some light bread to-day, which is the first flour I have seen for some time, and as we have butter and new molasses to eat with it, it will go first rate.

I am not at all displeased with my position if Raphael will only stand up to his part of the agreement, which I suppose he will do as there is nothing to be lost by him in the transaction, for he can make the Government pay it, but if I had to depend upon his generosity alone, I fear that I would fare rather slim for I have ascertained beyond all doubt that he is a great liar and that his word will not do to depend upon. But it makes no difference to me how great a liar he is so he pays me. He has a sack of salt and I tried to buy half of it from him, but it was no good, he would not sell it. He also has a lot of hams and told me that as soon as I made up my mess, that he would give me some of them; but the mess has been made up for two weeks and he has never said ham to us since, and the worst of it is, I do not think he ever intends to say anything about it.

Dinner is very late to-day and I am getting extremely hungry. In fact, as the back-woodsmen say, " I am right wolfish."

No news yet from Tennessee or Virginia, but I presume that the Yankees have got the best of us there lately, though we must expect some reverses.

I notice that the Government stock looks very much under

the weather. The reason is that they have not a sufficiency of good food. The corn they have has been exposed to rain and is very much heated and is very unhealthy for stock and they get little or no fodder, and the work they are required to do is very heavy indeed, the most of it being to pull stores up the hill at the landing near the depôt.

I have not been down to the regiment for several days, but I hear that they are all getting along very well. The smallpox is creating some alarm among the soldiers, but I do not think there is much of it in camp and the most of the men have been vaccinated, so there can be but very little danger of its becoming contagious in the army. The particular reason of there being so much sickness is because the men are exposed to the weather without tents to sleep under and their food is not good. If I were compelled to live alone on the rations that I received from the Commissary, I would have a very hard time of it, certain.

Wednesday, January 21: It is very foggy this morning and I suppose it will not be many days before we have rain again and then another freeze.

The Chief of Ordnance was in the office yesterday. He called me out of the office, saying that he wished to speak to me privately. I went out and he told me that he wanted me to quit Raphael and go with him in the Ordnance Department. He argued that I could not stay long with Raphael any-how; that no clerk ever had remained with him any length of time, etc. I told him that Raphael thus far had treated me very well and that he promised very fair indeed, but that I had caught him in several lies lately and that if he did not come up to his promise at the end of the month in regard to my pay that I would report myself to him immediately.

No news from our armies or from the Yankee hordes that are swarming over the country.

I heard just now that two deserters from the Yankee army have just come over to us from Baton Rouge. I cannot hear what news they bring as to the force and purpose of the enemy in regard to Port Hudson, though I have understood that the enemy are fortifying the place and send troops off at night but bring them back again in the morning for the purpose of deceiving us. This is an old trick and I suppose that our generals are too shrewd to be duped by anything of that kind, especially when we have or ought to have so many spies in Baton Rouge, for we certainly have a great many friends there that would willingly give us all the information that we require in regard to them and their movements.

Friday, January 23: The river is rising very rapidly. It rose last night about 18 inches and is still on the rise. The work stock as well as the battery and their horses fare very badly in the way of forage, having nothing to eat except corn alone and that in a very bad condition.

Sunday, January 25: I had no opportunity of writing in my journal yesterday. I was quite busy all day, but what made the matter worse was that the inspector sent word that he wished a complete statement made out of all the receipts, issues and amount remaining on hand, which he says must be made out by 12 to-day. I went up to see him yesterday. He wears long soapy locks, shoulder straps and gold stripes down his pants. He seems to understand his business though, and explained to me what I had to do.

I saw John Bradford yesterday for the first time since last summer. He has been quite sick and looks very badly now. I think from his appearance and from what he told me that he had a case of pox on hand which will be about as much as he can well attend to for some months to come. He is coming down to see me to-day and then I will find out all about it, and, of course, I shall give him the best advice I can in the matter. There are many things I would like to say this morning, but I have too much work on hand.

Thursday, January 29: I have been hard at work all day and I feel very much fatigued—more so in fact, than I usually do. I am weary, so weary with this soldier's life that sometimes I almost wish myself over all my troubles and safe in the other world, but this, I know, is wrong and I am much better off than a great many others because I am not exposed to the inclemency of the weather as I have a good place to sleep and my work is such as I have always been accustomed to.

I heard from the regiment last night and they had a big fuss amongst them. It seems that Tom Skipwith had a sort of gathering at his tent and they had, as a matter of course, plenty of liquor, and they all got drunk. Lieutenant McCarthy, who was one of the number, got into a difficulty with Tom Skipwith, and knocked him in the top of a tree that had been cut down, and as it was dark and McCarthy drunk, he could not find him, but kept asking the by-standers where Tom was. At length Tom recovered sufficiently to answer him and as soon as he discovered Tom's where-abouts, he jumped on him and pounded him good before they could take him off. Major Pennington came over to see what was the matter and when he arrived there, he immediately called McCarthy, saying that he put him under arrest, whereupon, McCarthy proceeded to knock him down and got his head in the fire-place and beat him up considerably, which I am right glad of for he is nothing more than a grogg shop bully, having been a bar keeper in Lake Providence before he entered the service. I suppose that he will, of course, have McCarthy arrested and court martialed for it, which would be very mean in him because he pitched into him like an ordinary blackguard that he is.

My health is very bad indeed and I hope that I may be able to weather it through this storm though I am afraid that I will not be able to enjoy it after our independence is gained, although I am in a much better position than I would be if I were in the ranks, still I am heartily sick and tired of the war, but I suppose that I must make up my mind to go through with it all, and I think I see peace in the not distant future. I will hail the day with joy that brings peace over our distracted country and so will many thousands of others, for there is no pleasure in the land while this state of things lasts, but end it must and will, and that to, in a very short time for one side or the other must give it up as a bad and hopeless undertaking.

I frequently think of the happy hours of my boyhood and then I wish myself a hermit, away from the cares and ambitions, the strife, and the jarrings of the active world, with no seductions of dissipation, neither prolonged stimulants, nor the late hours of passion.

But my eyes are weak and my light so very dim that I cannot see to write so that I must close for to-night.

Saturday, January 31: This is a beautiful morning and I wish we could hear news to correspond with the weather. I have heard within the last day or two that the Yankees have been able to run the ferry boat through the channel. They have got opposite Vicksburg.

Sunday, February 1: This is the first day of February—another month and very little done by either of the armies. This is a very dark and gloomy day. It is beginning to rain already and it is not yet 8 o'clock, so I suppose that we will have a rainy day of it.

I am kept very busy now and about the only time that I can obtain to write in my journal is in the morning before breakfast, and as I very often over-sleep myself, I do not always have an opportunity to write in my journal.

Kentucky has declared herself out of the Abolition Government,[4] Illinois and Indiana have placed themselves in a very threatening attitude. The Northwest does not seem to like the idea of supporting the New England States and will evidently split the northern states wide open in spite of all that they can do to prevent it. I think that I see the day breaking and that we will have peace in a few months. The Yankees are preparing for another "On to Richmond," but there must certainly be a deep gloom over the whole army.

I have positively had two or three hours of leisure time, and I have been taking a nap, though I am afraid that it will prevent me from sleeping tonight. I was not sleeping well these long nights and I almost hate to see night come.

I am reading "Davenport Dunn" by Charles Lever, and a first-rate thing it is too. I have also Pope's works to read now, though

---

[4] The situation in Kentucky was very confused because of conflicting loyalties. The government of Kentucky refused to furnish troops for the North, and endeavored to enforce neutrality, but by the end of 1861 the legislature had declared its allegiance to the United States.

as I have commenced "Davenport Dunn," I would finish that before I undertake to read the other.

The river is rising very fast and I suppose it is as high now as the Yankees desire it. There is no news from the Yankees that I can hear other than that mentioned above.

I believe so strongly in there being peace by the first of May that I am making my calculations as though it were a foregone conclusion, and I expect to be out of the army and at home by that time if I live to see that day.

We have a very poor table now, the particular reason being that we have no cook that knows anything about cooking, and that makes the matter much worse than it has been.

Monday, February 2:   I rose early this morning after a terrible night's rest. I walked out a little to obtain some fresh air. I notice that the " Father of Waters " is rising very rapidly and is now quite high. Almost every time I look at the river, it reminds me of the song that Gus Heckler used to sing the chorus of which went as follows—

> To the South, to the South, to the home of the free
> Where the mighty Mississippi rolls down to the sea
> Where a man is a man if he is willing to toil
> And the humblest may reap the fruits of the soil.

I learned last night from a steam-boatman, that the Yankees have not been able to effect anything at Vicksburg as yet; that it is an utter impossibility for them to do anything with the ditch they have been digging; that on account of the current, at that point, or rather eddy, that they will never be able to make the water run through the ditch, and another reason, he says, is that the surface of the ground is much lower about the middle than it is at the extremeties, thereby causing the water to over-flow the canal, and thus the water would be conveyed away to the swamps and all the water would enter from each end and flows out of the middle.[5] He also stated that the Yankees were desert-

---

[5] Patrick is referring to " Grant's Canal." In June, 1862, Federal forces landed at De Soto, Louisiana, which is opposite Vicksburg, plans being to cut a canal across the mile-wide peninsula formed by a hairpin turn of the Mississippi. It was hoped that

ing by 50's and 100's; that in a skirmish the other day, we obtained papers from the body of an officer who was killed, their whole plan of attack on Vicksburg.

I have been suffering greatly from a pain in the top of my head. There was a man in the office yesterday who told me that it was an affection of the spine; that it would get in the back of my neck; then in my shoulders; then in my back; that it would finally affect all my limbs. This is not a very pleasant prospect truly, but I hope this will not be the case.

I think that I will invest some money in a newspaper again and see if I can get the money through this time. I have sent the money several times, but I have never heard of the money nor paper either.

Friday, February 6: The weather since last Tuesday has been very cold indeed and the ground has been frozen nearly all the time, and I keep big roaring fires all day and night too.

About a week ago, and a few days after his spree and fight with McCarthy, Tom Skip went to Bayou Sara to a concert on another spree and while there, he and a man by the name of Kendrick, who is our forage master, got into a fracas with some of the citizens and they mauled our two friends in good fashion. They struck Kendrick over the eye with an andiron, shot him on the top of the head and struck Tom Skip on the head with a piece of iron. All this occurred to-night one week ago and Kendrick told me a while ago that Tom Skip died last night at Jackson, Louisiana. I am inclined to think that this is not true and I hope it is not, still it is not at all improbable for a blow from a fire-dog would not be apt to come very gentle. Kendrick said that Tom had a very hard fit on the morning after the fight.

One of the Yankee gun-boats passed the batteries at Vicksburg by the negligence of the men at the guns and she was nearly by them before they saw her. Since she passed Vicksburg, she has taken three of our steamers which are now lashed together in the middle of the Mississippi at the mouth of Red River, and the

---

the river could be diverted through this channel thus by-passing Vicksburg and enabling the Federal gunboats to pass down the river without running the batteries at Vicksburg.

gun-boat has gone up Red River. There is a plan on foot now to capture her, and an expedition starts out this afternoon, or to-night, on the steamer " Dr. Beatty " for that purpose. I hope they will succeed. 10,000 Texas cavalry are in that neighborhood and I suppose they will assist in her capture if it can be done.[6]

Tuesday, February 10: Since writing last I have been up home.

I have been quite unwell lately, and I am now scarcely able to sit up. I cannot find out what is the matter with me. I have no fever that I know of yet I grow weaker every day. I have been to two or three surgeons but they do not seem to know. It is astonishing what an amount of ignorance there is amongst the Medical fraternity. The most of them will administer a large dose of calomel to the patient it doesn't matter what his disease may be, without caring how much the constitution may be in-jured. Then comes dose after dose of quinine and other strong medicines until they either kill the individual or ruin his constitu-tion for life. If a man recovers under their treatment, he is always sick afterwards from the effects of their strong medicines injudiciously administered, and they will remark " that man has no constitution; he can't stand anything." No I suppose he couldn't nor never can while life lasts, because his whole system is thoroughly filled with the very worst of mineral and vegetable poisons. I know these fellows and I am suffering now from the treatment of ignorant, sap-headed physicians.

Wednesday, February 11: I arose this morning about 4 o'clock and sat by the fire until daylight. I feel much better than I did yesterday and I hope that I will soon be well again, although I am yet very weak. The chief surgeon gave me a couple of pills night before last made, I think, of Blue Mass, which did me a great deal of good and if I could only regain my strength, I think that I would be all right again in a very short time. I have been

---

[6] Reference is to the Federal gunboat *Queen of the West* which in early February, 1863, ran past the Vicksburg batteries. The *Queen* steamed up the Old River, Atchafalaya and Red, capturing supplies and causing considerable damage. She was captured, however, by Confederate forces in the Red River, repaired and outfitted as a gunboat in the Confederate navy. Gosnell, *Guns on the Western Waters*, 177–203. See also J. Thomas Scharf, *History of the Confederate States Navy* (New York, 1887), 351–61.

living almost like a dog for the last six weeks, having had nothing to eat but beef and very bad corn bread, and this is so miserably cooked that it was almost impossible to eat it.

I have heard nothing more of the gun-boat that passed Vicksburg the other day. The last accounts, she had gone up Red River since which time I have not heard a word from her.

There is to be a transport up the river to-day, (they say) to bring up prisoners to Vicksburg for the purpose of exchanging them, and in view of the passage of this boat, the General Commandant has ordered all the batteries to be masked with brush of the branches of trees.

Saturday, February 14: My health continues very bad indeed and my head and eyes are very much affected. I suffered a great deal last night from it, which prevented me from sleeping much.

This is the 14th of February—St. Valentine's day, which brings to mind many a happy day spent with the girls at home.

Yesterday I got all my papers fixed up for my discharge which I will obtain in about 10 days. It is not my intention to leave the service, but by getting a discharge I will be able to obtain better wages.

Sunday, February 15: Yesterday was Bill Stone's birthday and I told him that his mother received a mock valentine about 22 years ago.

I have got my papers all fixed up for my discharge and all that remains to be done now is to send them on to General [John C.] Pemberton to be signed by him, and this Dr. Barnet promises to have done for me and I suppose that I will receive them in about 10 days.

From all accounts, the Yankees are preparing to make another attack on Vicksburg, though the high water has drowned them out on the peninsula opposite the city and they are moving up the river to dry land, I presume to better arrange for the attack. Two boats have already passed and I suppose that they can all pass when they see proper.

I think that there will be peace in a short time for the following reasons—

1. The Northern Government has been kept up by the capitalists

of the northern states and they are beginning to tire of the good work because they do not see when their money is coming back again, and gold is now at 167½ in New York with an upward tendency.

2. There are dissensions among them, particularly in the west, which will be certain to break up in a grand row sooner or later. Valandingham [7] has made another flaming speech in the United States Congress, which will be a terrible blow to the radicals and they acknowledge it themselves.

3. We will most certainly be recognized by some of the leading powers of Europe before many days pass over our heads for all the working classes of France and England are suffering terribly from a cotton famine and they will be very apt to take some measures to alleviate their sufferings.

For these reasons, I think that there will be a cessation of the war before a great while.

I have just finished reading Tom Moore's " Lalla Rookh " for the third or fourth time in my life and I find it prettier every time I read it. Captain Fogg has all the Waverly novels [8] here and I believe that I will read them, for strange to say that with all my reading, I have never read these. The print is so very fine that it hurts my eyes to read them.

As I write very few letters now, I have taken a notion to keep a copy of them all the more for the purpose of practicing Phonography than anything else and besides, sometimes I would like to know what and to whom I have written. If I only had a copy of all the letters that I have written since the war, I would be very glad indeed, for I have written a great many that I ought not to have written and although that is the case, I would like all the more on that account to be possessed of them. The following is the copy of a letter that I wrote to Charlie Hyde at Edwards Depôt. He is there in the hospital as steward.

PORT HUDSON
11th February, 1863

DEAR FRIEND CHARLIE,

    I have taken up my pen at least a dozen times and deliberately seated

---

[7] Clement L. Vallandigham, Democratic politician and leader of the Ohio Copperheads.
[8] Sir Walter Scott, *Waverly Novels* (25 vols., London, 1852–54).

myself to write you a long letter, but just that often have I failed in accomplishing my task. I am on the way now and if Uncle Jeff's mail is true to its trust, you will receive this one provided you are at Edwards Depôt, where, as the fellow says, " you orter be."

My health has been very bad indeed ever since Christmas, and for the last week, I have scarcely been able to go about though I have forced myself to keep up. The particular cause of my bad health I attribute to bad food we receive, being nothing more than damaged corn-meal and very tough beef.

I must say that never since I have been in the army have I fared so badly and in truth I have been almost starved. If better food is not provided for the troops we will certainly lose a great many men from this cause alone. Last week corn on the ear was issued to the troops in lieu of meal, and I call this getting pretty low down, don't you?

There is a great dearth of news about Port Hudson and there is nothing occurring of interest, and we are all at a dead-lock for the want of some little excitement. The only thing on the tapis just now is the rumor that a boat is coming up the river under a flag of truce, with prisoners to be exchanged at Vicksburg. There was a little sensation created by the passage of the gunboats past the batteries at Vicksburg which, from all accounts, they were enabled to do through the want of watchfulness on the part of our men. She has captured three of our steamers at the mouth of Red River and destroyed all of them, after which she went up Red River to commit other depredations, I suppose. I think there are some exertions being made by the General commandant at this post to capture this gun-boat by means of cotton-clad rafts, but whether or not there is any show of success I am unable to say, though the probability is that, like most of our aquatic attempts, it will prove a singular failure.

From my office I have a fine view both up and down the river which helps matters a little, though I must say, only a very little.

Charlie, I am thoroughly disgusted with a soldier's life and I so long for a little peace and quiet once more that the contemplation of the war's lasting another 12 months, makes me sick at heart and I sometimes almost wish that my hopes, my joys and my sorrows were ended.

I often think of the many happy hours we spent together in Clinton— of our balls and private parties, our evening and Sunday visits, our sweethearts, Anne May and Phyllis May—of our occasional sprees and serenades in which we were involved in sundry troubles with irate teachers and professors, of our music box in the store that played that pretty air, "What is Home without a Mother."

Ah! Those were happy days, Charlie, brighter I fear than we will ever spend together again, but my mind constantly reverts to those by-gone times, and in hours of despondency, are about my only solace. Some drown their sorrows in the glass, others seek comfort in religion, but as I have abjured the one and make no profession of the other, I must content myself with reflections and dreams of the past.

I wish you were down here. I could have obtained a good easy place for you in the office with me where you would have had little to do and no responsibility. Do you think you could get off or would you feel inclined to do so if I got you a clerkship. It would be better on one account—you would be much nearer home and you could take a trip up to Clinton occasionally. I was up at Clinton the other day, but everything presents a cheerless and gloomy appearance and even the dogs and little negroes look downcast and foresaken. The piano is never heard and of my old violin, I can only say that she lies unstrung, and

> The harp that once through Tara's halls
> The soul of music shed,
> Now hangs as mute on Tara's walls
> As if that soul were fled.

Write soon and be sure to let me have your opinion in regard to my attempting to secure you some position.

s/ROBT. D. PATRICK

Monday, February 16: I have been amusing myself this morning by reading Pope's Essays which I think are very fine.

Bill Stone went up home Saturday and will be down to-day I presume, and I hope he will bring something to eat with him. If he only brings down some butter, it will suit me for if I have good biscuits and butter, I can get along.

I have been working very hard to-day on abstract " K " which I hope to be through with by to-morrow night if I am not interrupted.[9]

Bill Stone came down to-day and brought about $40.00 worth of stuff with him. He brought two turkeys at $4.00 each, two

---

[9] Abstract " K " was a requisition for all issues except fuel, forage, straw, and stationery.

geese at $1.50 each, some lard at $1.00 a pound and eggs at $1.00 a dozen. Bacon sells at 60¢ a pound, flour at $100.00 a barrel, potatoes at $2.50 a bushel. These are pretty high prices and it is a hard matter for us to keep up our mess as the Government does not furnish us with anything but tough beef and corn meal. The Commissary pretends to issue rations of rice, but we eat up $10.00 worth of rations at two meals.

Tuesday, February 17: I was up this morning before day, I wake now about an hour or two before day nearly every morning. The nights are so long that I cannot sleep all night. One reason is because I go to bed very early and another reason is because I am not well and suffer a great deal from pains in my head and limbs and my belly is very often out of fix.

Raphael continues to treat me very kindly indeed and I am well pleased with him if it only keeps up. He says that he expects to go to Mobile and will be absent for about 20 or 30 days and that I must act as quarter master while he is away.

This has been a very rainy and unpleasant day, but I think that it will fair off by night and turn cold. I would like to see fair weather, but I do not desire to see cold weather.

Our forces have succeeded in capturing the Yankee gun-boat " Queen of the West " up Red River, and the captured boat in company with the gun-boat " Web," [10] which is one of our boats, are in pursuit of another of the Yankee concerns. This is good news and I hope we will hear more of it. Our little steamers are poking their noses out of Thompson's Creek once more. I suppose they think they are safe now that the boat has been captured.

Wednesday, February 18: Nothing new to-day. Nothing from Baton Rouge or Port Hudson. I heard, though, that the Yankees had received marching orders, but I do not believe a word of it and even if it is so, they cannot do anything to hurt us because if the deserters tell the truth, there is great demoralization amongst them and we need apprehend no danger from that source at any rate.

[10] The Confederate ram *William H. Webb*—a powerful side-wheeler which one authority describes as " quite possibly, at the time, the fastest thing afloat." Gosnell, *Guns on the Western Waters*, 193.

I received something to eat from home to-day. Some light bread, onions and mutton which is first-rate and coming in good season.

Thursday, February 19: The " Dr. Beatty " a steamboat they have fixed up with cotton to take the Yankee gun-boat that is up Red River, left this afternoon. She had three pieces of light artillery and one piece of heavy ordnance in the bow. I hope she will be successful, but I will never believe that she will do anything until I hear it is so.[11]

I went down to the regiment this evening and they told me that Scott Worthy and Sam Williams went on the gun-boat to-day. It is all right to hunt up a fight, but I am not one of that kind. If I am ordered into a fight with the regiment, I will do the best I can, but I will not put myself to any trouble to seek it, that is certain.

Friday, February 20: I was up this morning very early and made a fire. This is a beautiful day and quite cool. It is the prettiest morning I have seen for some time and everything looks as pleasant as spring only it is a little too cool.

No news from Yankees anywhere. I read a speech of Sollaceberry's [12] the other night and it is on very much the same style as Vallandigham's. Sollaceberry is from Dellaware and I think he has been placed under arrest once by the Yankee Government for his free speeches.

Saturday, February 21: I was up this morning by 3 o'clock. My head hurt me so badly that I could not sleep. Directly after daylight, I took a walk down to the boat landing and saw the steam-boat " Frolick " leaving under a flag of truce for Baton Rouge for the purpose of exchanging some prisoners.

I have succeeded in getting some tallow—25 pounds—for mother. That is, I have the order to get it at the Commissary which I will send for this morning. I shall also try to buy some salt, if it is possible.

There is no news of the motions of the enemy nor of our

[11] Reference is to the Union ironclad *Indianola* which had also successfully steamed past the Confederate batteries at Vicksburg.

[12] Willard Saulsbury, U. S. Senator (Democrat) from Delaware.

army. If anything is going on, we cannot hear it, though there is a sort of rumor afloat that there is to be an armistice, but there is nothing to confirm it.

Comrade Bill Stone and Bradford Barnets are looking on over my shoulder at my writing and keep pretending to understand what I am putting down. Comrade says—" Well, I never saw anything like that afore." There is always such a din and crowd around me in the office that I can scarcely write as a general thing.

Charlie Lewis was in the office this evening and stayed a good while. I got an order for him to have a pair of boots made at the Government shop which is now in the charge of Captain Raphael. I also procured a bottle of liquor for Captain Pullen to-day. These fellows were very kind to me in assisting to procure my discharge, which, by-the-way ought to be here in a few days.

I have all the volumes of the Waverly novels, but the print is so small that I cannot read it without hurting my eyes. I have nothing to read now, but three of Shakespeare's plays—" The Tempest," " All is Well that Ends Well," and another.

Sunday, February 22: I was up this morning by the time it was light. We had an inspection of all the wagons, mules, etc., this morning and there was quite a string of them—nearly a quarter of a mile long.

Tuesday, February 24: After dinner I went up home. I had a very pleasant time going up, all things considered. Mother has a great many boarders now—in fact, every house in town is a boarding house and still there is not enough to supply the demands.

The report in Clinton while I was there, was that the Yankees were preparing to attack us at Port Hudson, but when I returned, I heard nothing cf it.

Several young ladies came down to-day on the cars—Miss Steward, Miss Rogers, Miss Reems, Miss Dunn and some others. They said that they expected to remain in camp until day after to-morrow and I think they will have rather an unpleasant time of it.

I think myself that the Yankees will have to do something before long because it will not do to stay where they are because that will never subjugate us and it seems to me they are afraid to begin. From all accounts they are about to commence hostilities at Vicksburg. The more affairs develop themselves, the more fully I believe that the war will terminate at an early day.

Wednesday, February 25: I arose this morning at half past five and after it was light, I took a walk down to the depôt and back. The steamer " Texas " is lying at the landing and I think she is the prettiest boat that I have seen here yet. She came down yesterday but I did not hear from what point.

There is no news from our flag of truce boat which went down several weeks ago. The rumor is that the Yankees have detained it. For what reason is not known but I suppose that she will be along after a while.

Thursday, February 26: I went down to the regiment yesterday and they were expecting marching orders, and sure enough, this morning they are all on board the steamer " Red Chief " bound up the river to fight the Yankees. The Yankees are at Morganza and over on the other side of the river and the 4th Regiment, Miles Legion and Fenner's Battery are ordered up there. I hear the bell of the boat now as they are backing out from the land and their band is playing " The Marseillaise."

There is nothing new from Vicksburg. At last accounts, the enemy had commenced bombarding the city. The Yankees, I think, are trying to get above Port Hudson and cut off our communication with Red River and this force is sent up to cut them off.

This is a very gloomy, dark and dreary day, and the men who have been sent over the river will have a very bad time of it indeed for there is every appearance of a storm and a more dreary prospect than the river and opposite shore presents at the present moment could not well be imagined, at least for this portion of the country. I hope they may be successful in their expedition which I think it more than probable will be the case.

The " Dr. Beatty " returned to-day bringing the intelligence that our gun-boat " Webb " had sunk the federal iron clad " Indianola," carrying four 11-inch Columbiads. She sunk in shallow water and they are taking her guns off now. I think they will be able to raise the boat itself in a few days. It looks like the men at Vicksburg allowed them to pass one at a time intentionally for the very purpose of capturing them after they got by. At any rate, we have succeeded in making prizes of two of them if we are able to raise the last one, we will then have three which will be able to cope successfully with any single vessel they can run by our batteries at Vicksburg.[13]

I have heard nothing more from my discharge, but it ought to be here in a few days at the latest.

The boats landed the troops at the Hermitage, about three miles above Port Hudson, and they are to march from that point towards Morganza. They will certainly have a dreadful time of it to-night unless they can obtain shelter from the storm in some of the houses.

Soldiering is an awful business, sure, and I think that every one is dreadfully disgusted with it. I know I am and from all accounts, the federal soldiers are as tired of it as we are. There is no use for them to attempt to disguise the fact.

Friday, February 27: Raphael told me yesterday that he wished to send me up to Clinton with some stores for the hospital there, which will suit me very well as I have not much to do in the office just now.

We had about 30 or 40 condemned horses turned over to us from the batteries the other day and Bill Stone and I have selected one apiece which we intend to fatten up for our own use. The Captain told me that I could keep mine if he proved to be any account, and I think he will although he is very poor at present.

The troops that went off after the Yankees yesterday played hell finding them. They went up as far as Hermitage, which is not more than three miles above Port Hudson and remained there through all the rain and storm of yesterday and returned a little

---

[13] On February 24, 1863, the Union gunboat *Indianola* was overtaken near New Carthage and captured, after a fierce battle, by the Confederate rams *Queen of the West* and *William II. Webb.* Fearing recapture, the victors blew up the vessel. Later it was decided that the *Indianola* was not irretrievably destroyed and salvage operations were undertaken. Gosnell, *Guns on the Western Waters,* 194–201.

while ago to Port Hudson without doing anything, that is the way to whale the Yankees.

This kind of weather will put a stop to the notions of the enemy for a while at any rate because I know the nature of the country between this place and Baton Rouge, and it is certain they cannot advance with any show of success over the miry roads, for it is little better than a swamp all the way from Port Hudson to Baton Rouge.

It is thought that we will be able to raise the wreck of the " Indianola " without much trouble and I hope it may be so, for then with the aid of " The Queen of the West," " The Webb," and what cotton boats we can bring into the service, we can clean out the river below this point without much difficulty, I think, or if we do not clear the river, we will annoy the enemy very much.

The last news I have heard is that Brute Butler was killed in Washington City by Bouligni from New Orleans, but I do not believe a word of it.[14]

Saturday, February 28: I suffered very much from my eyes last night and this morning they hurt me considerably. Last night was a terribly stormy one. It seemed as though the flood gates of Heaven had let loose sure enough, for I never heard a harder rain fall than that last night.

I was up this morning by the time it was light and the weather to-day is almost as bad as it was last night. This will certainly prevent the Yankees from making much head-way towards an attack on Port Hudson. The country between this place and Baton Rouge is almost one continual lake after such a rain as we had since yesterday.

I saw by the papers that Governor [Claiborne F.] Jackson of Missouri is dead and [Thomas C.] Reynolds is now the Governor, and he has issued his proclamation asking all good citizens to join the Confederate army and help to whip out the Yankees.[15]

Sunday, March 1: A new month begins to-day and I hope it will be a more pleasant month than the last one was. I tried to

---

[14] Benjamin F. Butler. The rumor was, of course, false.

[15] After 1861, the Confederate governorship of Missouri was little more than a title. The Confederates, however, maintained a government in exile until the end of the war.

keep out of doing any work to-day as it is Sunday, but I have been compelled to make out my semi-monthly report in order to have it ready to send on to-morrow.

I am about to make a race with Bill Stone between two of the old bags of bones in the yard for $20.00. Bill backed out of one race that he made with me.

I employ the most of my leisure time in reading Tom Moore and Pope, though I prefer the former, not on account of its depth, but on account of its jingling along so smoothly and has so much of love in it. As I never intend to marry, it would appear that I would have no taste for such reading, but I have. In fact, I am very fond of such works and more, I presume, on account of old associations than anything else for I never read a verse of Moore's works without its reminding me of the happiest days of my life spent with the girls in dear old Clinton. A retrospective, however, brings to mind the pleasant times when I was in love with Lizzie Hardesty, Josephine Rich, Louise Rowen, and Sam Butler, who was my particular crony at that time, was deeply enamored on Anna Dunbar to whom he was afterwards married. It is really astonishing how hard I loved Josephine Rich. I almost worshipped her for about a year, but after that, some-how I never knew exactly why, I took a very violent dislike to her, and in fact, I believe it was mutual between us. In later years, I took a fancy to others, but they too have nearly slipped from my thoughts and now I have no particular regard for any of them.

I have many friends among the ladies, but I believe I am past the age for loving them. I have spent many happy hours with the girls, and I notice that I have also spent all my money and now I think that it behooves me to make a sufficient amount of money to provide for all my wants for the future, or in other words, that all my energies must be applied to money-making for a time at least. With a capital of four or five thousand dollars, I have no fears of failing to make as much as I want. I am fully satisfied that a married man is happier than an unmarried one, but still I cannot make up my mind to marry.

Monday, March 2: This is another beautiful day and the sun shines congenially and warm and it makes me feel more cheerful after having such very bad, comfortless weather as we have had for the last two months.

We have had no mails here since last Friday on account of the railroad bridges being out of repair and there has been no news by telegraph that I have heard.

Bill Stone and I took a ride yesterday up to John Bradford's where I had a long chat with John and borrowed a volume of Byron from him which I have been reading to-day. When we were coming back, Bill's horse, an old, poor looking creature that seemed as though the life was almost out of it, started off and ran away with him. This is the horse that Bill intends to run against my mustang pony. I think I will beat him though for the pony is as quick as lightning and he must start right fast if he gets off before mine. We are to run them the first day of next April.

I heard yesterday that our men had blown up the gun-boat " Indianola."

Friday, March 6: I went up home day before yesterday and I have just returned. While I was at home, I told mother as provisions were so scarce, that it would be much better for her to close our house, which she has consented to do.

As soon as I arrived here, Captain Raphael asked me to exchange over-coats with him, which I did as my coat, although a very fine one, was too large for me and his just fit me. My coat I obtained at the Battle of Shiloh, out of an officer's tent and I gave it to one of our wounded boys to lie on and he brought it on to Corinth. If it had not been for this, I would have been compelled to leave it on the field as it was out of the question for me to take care of it. Mine is the most valuable coat, but I saw that he was anxious to have it so I traded with him.

There is nothing new in camp that I can hear. The last dispatches say that Van Dorn has captured 3,000 prisoners at a little town about 15 miles this side of Nashville. There are no particulars of the affair.[16]

---

[16] The battle of Thompson's Station, Tennessee, fought March 4 and 5, 1863. Confederate cavalry under Major General Earl Van Dorn defeated a small Union force commanded by Colonel John Coburn. Some 1,300 Federal troops surrendered; the rest fled. Robert S. Henry, *The Story of the Confederacy* (New York, 1943), 288.

Sunday, March 8: I did not rise this morning until nearly 7 o'clock, lit my pipe and took a walk down to the steam-boat landing and returned to the office. My head gets no better and my eyes are very much affected by it and sometimes I am not able to see how to read or write which makes me very uneasy about it.

There must be a perfect stand still everywhere just now, but we will probably have an avalanche of news from Vicksburg before many days, for from all accounts, the Yankees are preparing for an attack. Three deserters from the Yankees at Baton Rouge—two noncommissioned officers and a private—came in yesterday and they say there is no unanimity of feeling amongst the men in Bank's command, that they are divided on the negro question. They said that the rumor is that they will attack Port Hudson at an early day, but these men say that the Yankees will not fight, that it is not much of an army anyway. This may all be very true, yet still I think it behooves us to be preparing as though it were the best organized army in the world.

The papers say that Hooker's command in Virginia is absolutely being thinned out by the desertions. The Lincoln Congress has passed the Conscript Act bringing out all between the ages of 18 and 45. This will make a tremendous army, to be sure, but the question is, will they fight after they are brought out. If not, they will only be worse off than they were before, and in truth, they already have as many men in the field now as they can maneuver well.[17]

Sir Robert Peal, Member of Parliament and Chief Secretary of Ireland, made a public speech in England, in which he recommended to Lord Palmerston [18] to recognize the South. He thinks that a split in the Union will more surely effect the extinguish-

[17] It was not until 1863 that the Federal government passed a national conscription law. By the provisions of this act (March 3, 1863) all able-bodied male citizens between the ages of twenty and forty-five were declared liable to military service. Numerous exemptions, the practice of buying a substitute, and lax enforcement caused the act to become one of the great scandals of the war. About 46,000 conscripts and 118,000 substitutes, comprising some six per cent of the Union forces, were drafted into the Federal armies. Randall, *Civil War Reconstruction*, 410–15.

[18] The British Prime Minister.

ment of slavery more than anything else. He urges it on account of the dullness of trade, the sufferings of the poor, the increase of taxes to the diminution of revenues; that the subjugation of the South is utterly impossible, and that if the reconstruction of the states is the point in view, that the only way to effect it is by reconciliation and not by force of arms. In the North, they look upon our recognition by France as a certain fact, and they are very much afraid of a general recognition in Europe.

Kendrick was telling me this morning all about the difficulty that he and Tom Skip got into at Bayou Sara, and he says that Tom would have recovered if it had not been for his own imprudence. After he was able to walk about, he got some rum and got very drunk, which caused inflamation to ensue and produce death in the course of a few days. So much for drinking liquor.

Monday, March 9: Yesterday, we heard very distant, a rapid firing in the direction of Baton Rouge, and deserters that came in yesterday reported that the Yankees are preparing to advance, but I think it will be impossible for them to make any headway if this weather continues because it will make the roads too bad for baggage trains and artillery. If the accounts we receive be true, they are very loath to come, and will endure the battle without a hope of success.

I learned this morning that we had a skirmish with the Yankees this side of Baton Rouge and that the enemy is advancing in full force.[19]

Tuesday, March 10: I have nothing to do this evening and I have taken a seat on the hand-rail of the gallery to take a view of the river and of what is going on.

The weather is cloudy with a slight rain falling and the prospect is very hazy. The fog is drifting up river in banks and the shore on the other side as far as I can see, is under water. There is a crevasse above which is submerged—the other side for miles and miles. There is no one to be seen except an occa-

---

[19] General Banks was attempting to move 12,000 men from Baton Rouge to the rear of Port Hudson in early March, 1863. This move was made in an effort to co-operate with Admiral Farragut who tried to send a part of his fleet past the Port Hudson batteries on March 14 and 15, 1863. *Battles and Leaders*, III, 590.

sional soldier with a bucket or a bundle on or under his arm, but as the rain is beginning to fall pretty heavy, my operations are cut short.

Thursday, March 12:   This is a beautiful morning and looks like spring sure enough. There is some excitement this morning. The Yankees are reported coming up with their fleet of gun-boats and mortar boats and are only about 5 or 6 miles below the point. I will believe they are coming when I see their boats in the river, and not until then because I know that they will not venture to bring up their land forces until they have their fleet in fighting trim.

Captain Fogg is sick and has gone to Clinton and this throws the forage to my hands again, which I was in hopes I had got clear of it altogether, but at the very time that I did not want anything to do with it, it comes in on me. Damn the luck, I say.

Friday, March 13:   There are 5 of the enemy's vessels in sight this morning. Four of them appear to be men of war, and the other is the " Essex." The four have masts and smoke stacks. They have landed about 150 men at Springfield which is about 10 or 12 miles below on this side of the river, but I understand that they have gone back again. I suppose that it was merely a reconnoitering party to ascertain how the land lies. I am not particularly fond of fighting, but I must say that I would like very much to see an engagement between the boats and the batteries. I have heard nothing of the main body of their army.

Sunday, March 15:   About dark last night, I saw the whole fleet drawn up in line of battle, just above the head of Prophet's Island.[20] I remarked to Bill Stone that I thought there would be the devil to pay next morning, because if I could judge by the motions of the vessels, they intended to try our batteries. I told him that we had better go to bed early for they would in all probability commence before day. Bill laughed at the idea. About 11 o'clock we heard a heavy gun, and then the shell then another and another, and finally the whole of the fleet let loose on us, though our batteries did not answer for some time. It

[20] A few miles south of Port Hudson just out of range of the Confederate heavy guns.

was not long however before every one of our batteries cut loose, and of all the noises that ever I heard, this beat it. The very earth trembled. It waked everybody up in Clinton, and was heard very distinctly high up on the Jackson Rail Road. This was kept up without the slightest intermission, until near two o'clock, when they drew off, with the loss of one of their finest vessels, the "Mississippi." She took fire, and floated away down the River. It was a grand sight to see her, as she drifted slowly down, lighting up the neighboring shores and the turbid tide of the Mississippi with a lurid glare, and the shells on her decks were exploding constantly. After she drifted below Prophet's Island her magazine exploded with a tremendous roar. Several other vessels were badly damaged.

This was the grandest scene that ever I beheld. The flag ship "Hartford" succeeded in passing the batteries and is now lying up about Waterloo. The gun-boats have steam up and I suppose that they intend to make another attack on us before night, but as I am very much fatigued, not having slept any last night, I have not time to note the particulars. One thing is certain, and that is that the crews of the boats suffered severely and there was more than a hundred lives lost on "The Mississippi" alone.[21]

Raphael ordered me to have a wagon brought to the door and put his trunk containing some $50,000 or $60,000 dollars, and my most valuable papers in it and carry it up to Maj. Bennett's quarters. I started up with them in a four mule wagon, and when we got about half way the shells began to fall so thick that the mules became frightened and ran through a panel of fence that was down, and there they were the mules through the fence in the enclosure and the wagon outside. The driver could not manage

[21] Operating with the *Queen of the West* and the *Webb*, the Confederates regained control of the waters between Port Hudson and Vicksburg. This included the Red River system which the Confederacy was dependent upon for transportation and supplies from Central and North Louisiana and Texas. Since Admiral Porter did not have any ships available to send down from his command above Vicksburg to regain supremacy, Farragut decided to come up from below and run the Port Hudson batteries with his fleet of steam sloops and gunboats. Farragut had in his fleet several large, new, screw sloops-of-war, as well as the old side-wheeler *Mississippi*, which had carried Perry to Japan in 1852. *Official Records of the Union and Confederate Navies,* I, 19, 20, 24. See also Gosnell, *Guns on the Western Waters,* 204–22.

them, and the shells were falling thicker and thicker every moment, and I soon became convinced that the mules, wagon, trunks and boxes, would soon be blown to the devil if I didn't get away from there. I saw several negroes passing, full speed and I tried in vain to get some of them to assist me. They were too badly frightened to heed anything. After a while another came along, almost out of breath.

"Stop there!" said I. "I want your assistance here a few minutes to untangle these mules." "No sah! I can't stop now" said the negro blowing like a porpoise. "Yes, but you must" I answered, and drawing a pistol I told him if he didn't help me that I would kill him on the spot. This brought him to a stand, and he very reluctantly went to work to render some assistance. I at length succeeded in disentangling the mules from the pickets and I had no further trouble. But taking the money and papers up to Bennett's was no better than leaving them where they were at first, because the shells fell just as thick or thicker there than they did at my quarters.

The negroes were dreadfully frightened. One in his terror, broke off towards the woods through the darkness, and not being able to see before him he ran over a stump and broke his neck.

There were several women who had come down to see their husbands in the camp. They tried to get away and not knowing the geography of the country, they fell into a stream of water and a woman and child were drowned. I gave an order for coffins yesterday as they succeeded in recovering the bodies. I think that the Yankees are too badly damaged to make another attack for some time.

Monday, March 16: It looks very dismal this morning and there is a very heavy fog on the river so that nothing can be seen 50 yards from the shore. General Buford [22] stayed all night with us last night, and he is "some" when it comes to size. I think that he will weigh at least 300 pounds.

All the damage that we have done to the Yankees so far as I can learn, is the loss of one of their steam-ships which was burned as mentioned above, and another was so much injured that she

---

[22] Brigadier General Abram Buford, Confederate cavalry commander.

called out to our men not to fire on her any more that they were in a sinking condition and surrendered their vessel, which drifted away with the current.

The weather is cloudy and heavy thunder is rumbling in the distance and judging from appearances, I think that we will have a rainy night of it. We all think that we will have another bombardment to-night, though if we have injured the enemy as much as we think we have, they will not be able to make the attack to-night. I believe they can pass if the night is very dark and cloudy.

I can hear nothing of the movements of the main body of their army, though I presume that it is on its way to make the attack.

A Yankee Captain, who was wounded and taken prisoner yesterday afternoon outside the breast-works, when told that one of their splendid ships was burning, exclaimed, "It is not possible, it is not possible," but they convinced him of his error by pointing out the burning vessel, which cast a lurid glare over the turbid waters of the mighty Mississippi. It was a gratifying and happy sight for our brave boys to see her timbers falling one after another, and amid the roar of artillery, could be heard the loud shouts of our men as the flames mounted higher and higher and deck and masts and yard-arms were enveloped with a firy, winding sheet. As she drifted slowly down the stream, her guns were going off as fast as they were heated by the fire and shells were exploding every few minutes, and finally about 5 o'clock, as the current took her past the point, her magazine exploded with a tremendous noise that shook the very ground.

Thursday, March 19: Banks army, which was within a few miles of Port Hudson the day after the bombardment, took fright at something and rushed pell mell back to Baton Rouge without waiting to be fired on by our troops at all and they are now all in Baton Rouge, where, from all accounts, they are likely to remain. I do not know how Banks can get around making an attack on us, and then again, I cannot see how he can do it because his men will not fight.

Sunday, March 22: Heavy firing below between midnight and day this morning, but I cannot learn the cause of it. From 2 p. m. until 4 p. m. yesterday the enemy kept up a steady shelling at the steamboats that were unloading at the landing. They shoot with marvelous accuracy, and they have one gun of most extraordinary range. It must be at the very least calculation 5 miles and I think that it is fully 6 from where they fire to where the shell falls. The old citizens who are about here say that it is eight miles, but I know that there never was a gun nor ever will be one that will shoot 8 miles. I will cut the distance down one half and say 4 miles, and still it is extraordinary shooting, though I am ignorant as regards heavy ordnance and it may be a common thing to shoot 5 or 6 miles. All the shells fall about 100 yards from my quarters and occasionally one comes into the yard.

I think after a while they will get guns of range sufficient to shell Port Hudson from the Gulf of Mexico. The gun they fire at us must certainly be some new patent.[23]

Our boats took with a leaving pretty quick, some of them to Bayou Sara and some of them up Thompson's creek, where they will remain awaiting orders.

Saturday, March 28: I have not written in my journal for some time, the particular reason being that I have been too lazy to write.

There is nothing of importance going on. Raphael has been made Major of Buford's brigade and he turns everything over to Captain McGuire, who is the Post Quarter Master now. I am to go with Raphael. All the men who were under Raphael have made him a present of two stars to go on his coat. Four of us are having two stars made for him out of two $5.00 gold pieces, which will be completed in a few days. No news from the Yankees.

---

[23] These shells were fired from an 8-inch Parrott gun mounted aboard the Union gunboat *Genesee*. The Confederates referred to these missiles, which were about two feet long and two hundred pounds in weight, as "Limping Toms." The shells were plainly visible in the air and would sometimes skip over the ground at short intervals before finally exploding. One observer has written that the shell looked "something like a beerkeg." John S. Kendall, ed., "Recollections of a Confederate Officer," *Louisiana Historical Quarterly*, XXIX (October, 1946), 1122.

"*Tired, hungry, and worn out*"

CHAPTER IV. JUNE, 1863–OCTOBER, 1863

Clinton, Tuesday, June 1, 1863: It has been a long time since I have written in my journal—two long months and since that time a great many important things have transpired, but I shall confine myself to my own peregrinations during this time without attempting to give anything like a correct account of what has been done by the armies on both sides since the first of April last.

I am now writing at home upstairs with no one to bother me except a little negro boy who is beginning to talk quite distinctly now.

I shall now proceed to give a very short account of—

1. My personal adventures, trials, troubles and tribulations.
2. As well as I can remember, the leading points in the conducting of the war up to this time.
3. The present aspect of things.
4. My thoughts as to the future.

Gen. Buford made Raphael his Qr. Mr. and this gave him the rank of Major. Raphael insisted upon my going with him, and as I had promised him some time before that when he went away from Pt. Hudson that I would go with him, I could not well get out of it now, though if I had consulted my own feelings in regard to the matter, I would have remained at Port Hudson. As matters afterwards turned out, my leaving with Raphael, was the best thing I could have done, because it saved me from the horrors of a siege.[1]

About the first of the month of April, having transferred everything over to Captain McGuire that we had on hand in the Quarter Master's Department, Captain (now Major) Raphael packed up our effects to start with General Buford to join General Johnston's army in Tennessee. He rode up to Harrisburg in company with General Buford and Staff while I took passage on the cars to Clinton. I did not reach home until about one o'clock next morning on account of the cars running off the track several times. Colonel Pond and I rode on the engine in front of the smoke-stack and had a very tedious and unpleasant time of it and it was made still worse by the conductor's placing two trunks on the platform where we were sitting very cozily up to that time. However, we managed to get through pretty well although we were very glad to reach the end of our journey safely. We had a crowd of soldiers on board too.

Buford and Staff did not arrive until the next day about 10 or 11 o'clock. We remained two or three days—that is Raphael and I, but the others went on to Osyka [Miss.] the day previous to our departure. The day after they left, Raphael, Colonel Jackson, commandant of an Alabama regiment, and myself, and a driver whose name was Battson, started in an ambulance for Osyka. We campt that night within 12 miles of Osyka and the next day about 10 o'clock arrived at Osyka.

Where we campt that night was a house in which dwelled an old lady with several children, two of whom were girls nearly grown and the eldest, who, by-the-way, was very pretty, looked like she was [pregnant] although she was not married, or at least if she was not in the family way, Colonel Jackson and I were deceived.

We halted the remainder of that day and night at Osyka. Having a little more bedding with me than I thought absolutely

[1] Buford's Brigade was ordered to Jackson, Mississippi, with instructions to join the forces of General Joseph E. Johnston and co-operate in the defense of Vicksburg. Patrick was thus spared the long siege of Port Hudson which, although on a smaller scale, was just as severe as the siege of Vicksburg. Port Hudson surrendered to Union troops on July 9, 1863. *Battles and Leaders*, III, 586–98.

necessary, I sent two pair of blankets home by Bloom and Adler who were on their way from Jackson, Mississippi to Clinton.

The next day we left for Jackson and arrived there about 5 o'clock and after having all the baggage taken from the cars, we obtained a room at the Confederate House near the railroad. We had all our books, papers, etc., put away in the cellar of the house to remain until we wanted them.

I remained there several days until Raphael procured a leave of absence to visit his family at Mobile, and he obtained an order for me to return home and remain there until I received further instructions. Going from Jackson to Osyka I fell in with Felix Delee. I telegraphed home for a conveyance, but after remaining there two days, and no conveyance for us making its appearance, Felix and I hired a vehicle belonging to Dick Rigby to take us. We had not gone more than three miles from Osyka before one of the fore wheels of the concern came all to pieces and there we were. Felix took one of the horses and went forward to see if he couldn't hire another vehicle, and while he was gone, Frank drove up with mother in the carriage, and Hardesty's old Henry was driving the two mules with the wagon.

Felix had returned by this time with a buggy wheel that he had borrowed from someone. This was put on to Rigby's buggy, and Felix and I got in the wagon and we all started back home.

It was long after dark when we crossed the Amite River. When we got opposite Rogers' place the mules took fright at something and ran away with the wagon. I managed to get out behind, when I saw that old Henry was already out and the reins dragging the ground, but Felix was lying in the bottom of the wagon asleep. Everything transpired so suddenly that I hadn't time to give Felix any warning, and away the mules went with the wagon. Clatter, clatter, clatter it went as it bounded over gullies, roots and stumps. The sound grew fainter and fainter, until finally it ceased altogether. Henry had by this time got up complaining that he was hurt, but I knew that this was all put on to cover his cowardly abandonment of the reins. We walked on up the road for about half a mile, until we came to a portion of the wagon, hind wheels, and a little farther on we saw the wagon body. I called Felix. He answered from under the wagon body, which, in falling off, had turned bottom side up, with Felix on the under side. We raised it up and enquired if he was hurt. He got out and shook himself, and after a thorough examination he said that he was all right. This was a fortunate escape. Farther on we found the fore wheels, and still farther on we found the mules fastened to a tree. Someone had tied them there.

We managed to get home in the other two vehicles and the next morning I sent Frank out after the mules and wagon.

I remained at home until the 6th June [1863] awaiting orders from Raphael, but I could hear nothing more from him. The Yankees had already made one raid upon the town, and I had been informed by the Comdt. of the Post, that the evacuation of the place had been decided upon, and it was to be accomplished on the night of the 6th June.

I accordingly decided upon leaving that day and as I could hear nothing from Raphael I determined to rejoin my Regiment as a high old private once more. I was to take Frank and the wagon and go to Brookhaven [Miss.], thence on to the regiment wherever it was.[2] Clay Davis was going with me as far as Magnolia, Miss. He was telegraph operator at that place and had been over home on a leave of absence, and was now returning to his post again. Not wishing to make the trip from Brookhaven to Johnston's army alone, if there was any company to be had, I went round to see Moses, who was at home on furlough and asked him if he wouldn't go. He said he was not ready.

As I was standing in the front door, ruminating on things generally, I saw Clarence Bell and W. D. Lea pass by in a buggy. As Clarence was a member of the 4th the thought struck me that he would probably like to go.

I went down to his house forthwith, and met him at the gate* as he got out of the buggy. I made the proposition to him, representing that if he felt desirous of returning to the Regiment this

---

[2] On May 1, 1863, the Fourth Louisiana was sent out from Port Hudson to intercept Grierson's raiders (see D. Alexander Brown, *Grierson's Raid*, Urbana, 1954) but, failing to do so, it was ordered to hurry northward and join Johnston's army at Jackson, Mississippi, and co-operate in the efforts to relieve Vicksburg.

would be the best opportunity that he would have, as he would have company and save the expense of this journey to Brookhaven, which at this time was quite an item, for he could not hire a team to go there for less than $75.00 or $100. He said he would go and the arrangement was made that I should drive out to Isaac Jackson's and wait for him and Lea there, and that we would go from Jackson's to Lea's and remain all night and make an early start next morning. We went over to Lea's and remained all night.

I had known Lea's wife during her school-girl days, and seeing her again reminded me of the many happy hours I have passed away with her and the other girls that went to school to old Mr. Taylor in Clinton, among whom were several very pretty girls, who were then my sweethearts, for I was a fast young man in those days, and could always boast of 5 or 6 true loves at the same time.

I could relate a great many things in regard to my young lady friends and sweethearts, but, although those days have long past, I do not think it proper to mention all those little affairs that occurred under the intoxicating influence of love and passion.

I have always been very fond of ladies' society, but as for the "frail fair ones" the "nymphs de pare" I have no use. But I must return.

Lea treated us very hospitably, and he lived well. The next morning when we were ready to go, he made us a present of a fine ham and other edibles to take along with us, and accompanied us several miles on our way, to point out the right road, for all of which we thanked him, "and shoved our boat from shore."

[A portion of this page was cut from the original diary. It seems, however, that Patrick and his companion traveled for some distance before they approached a native and requested water.]

We didn't ask nor desire anything more of him than a little water. He came out to where we were making our arrangements to camp, for the purpose, I suppose of seeing who we were, and what we were doing in such close proximity to his possessions, and this was all right enough.

I asked him if he would give us some water. " Yes! Yes! Certainly you can have some water. I have a well in my yard, but that is for the use of my family, but if you will drive your wagon round below the horse lot you will find an old well there, and I think you can manage to obtain some water out of it, as much at least as you will require." We drove around as directed, he following, and continuing to talk incessantly all the time.

" Mind now " said he " don't drive against that little tree " pointing at the same time to a little scrubby black-jack that was standing by the road-side " that is a fine little tree. Don't drive over those rails " he continued, as we approached a pile of pine saplings that were lying in a pile before us. " I intend to make a fence of them; now here's a nice little grassy place that will just suit you, drive this way and stop your wagon right here."

I began to think he was exceedingly kind, and I thought we had fallen into good hands for once, but still I didn't like his not giving us some of the good water out of the well in the yard and he seemed to be devilish particular about a little worthless rubbish.

" Now gentlemen " said he " you are perfectly welcome to anything I have, and I will do anything I can to accomodate you and make you comfortable."

" Where are you going? "

I told him we were going to rejoin the army. " What Brigade do you belong to? " I told him. " Just help yourselves gentlemen to anything that will be of any use to you. I would rather you wouldn't turn your mules in the lot. Can't you tie them just as well out here? "

I told him I could. That I didn't wish to put them in the lot, but preferred having them outside near where we would sleep.

" I am sorry that I have no corn to give you, as mine is about out, but if I had any you should have it, but unfortunately I have not purchased any lately."

I replied that we had an abundant supply of forage and would not require any of his. " I would invite you in to supper but the table has been cleared off, and there is nothing left." I thanked him, telling him that we were very well supplied with rations.

When we produced our store of provisions, he didn't see any bread, although we had plenty. He didn't wait for us to ask for it. No indeed! He was too polite for that.

" I wish I had some meal to give you to make bread of, but we are nearly out, and what little we have is musty, and not fit to eat, and we have a long ways to bring it from the mill," which last I afterwards found to be a lie, as the mill was not more than a mile and a half from his house for we past it on our way to Magnolia.

By this time Frank had produced the bread from our " Commissary."

" Ah! I see you have some bread. That's lucky. I intended if you didn't have any to send for my cook and have some made for you. So it will save me the trouble."

" Where did you say you were from? " I told him. " Clinton! Oh! Yes—Clinton! Aha! A right pretty little place I suppose. I have never been there but I have heard it spoken of very often. What did you say your name was? "

By this time I had begun to tire of his talk, and disgusted with his *bogus* kindness for I now saw his whole drift, which was in the first place to ascertain who we were and all about us, and in the next place, to have us where he could keep an eye on our movements, and I felt a perfect contempt for him, because he reminded me by his voice and manner of speaking and actions generally of Parson Poole, one of the most contemptible individuals of the human species.

I answered him rather abruptly that I had never told him my name.

" Ah! Oh! Yes! I beg pardon, I declare I do. Excuse me " he continued in a whining sort of tone " I suppose you would not mind telling me what it is; I really beg pardon though, I thought I had asked you before, He! He! He! " and wound up with a sickly sort of laugh.

I had a great notion to get out of the wagon and kick his stern all over his own premises—but " *in the first place, firstly* " I doubted my ability to do that, because he was a larger man than I, and in the next place, I concluded he wasn't worth kicking even if I could administer the dose without resistance. I therefore concluded that the better way would be to make a clean breast of it, and get the load off my stomach, and put it on to his if he wanted it, so I told him my name; I told him all our names; I told him how old I was, where I was born, where I had lived up to the breaking out of the war, when and where I had joined the army, how long I expected the war to last, and went on to say that if I knew myself, that I would tell him where I would go to when I died. He stood looking at me with his hands in his pockets, until I got through.

" Can I do anything more towards making you comfortable? " said he.

" I don't think you can " I replied " as you have already done a great deal, and we could not reasonably ask you to do anything more."

He went away under the impression that we felt ourselves under eternal obligations to him. He was a *full blooded Yankee* and no mistake.

Clarence Bell got very tired, and was constantly wishing that he had never left home, and would propose to me to turn back and as he said, let old Johnston and his army go to hell. He cursed the pine roots and stumps, and the hot weather and the dust, to his entire satisfaction.

We met a negro riding a mule. " How far is it to hell old man " said Clarence.

" I dunno marster, but I speck if you should happen to drap off, you'd soon find out," said the darkie showing a row of ivory. Clarence *dried up*.

I never knew before that Clarence was so much addicted to drinking. If he had been as fond of his mother's milk, as he is of whiskey he would have been awful hard to wean.

Clarence saw some chickens on the road side that morning and tried to catch some of them but failed.

At noon on the second day we stopped at a spring of clear, cold water, where we bivouacked for a couple of hours and then went on.

The second night we camped on a creek near the site of an old

115

mill that had been destroyed by the Yankees on one of their raids, within a mile and a half of Brookhaven. We arrived at this camp sometime after night. There was an impassable bridge over the stream near the mill which we thought was all right, but when we drove on it the mules refused to go. It was very dark and on getting out to examine the premises we found a number of planks gone. As it was impossible to turn round we unharnessed the mules and shoved the wagon back by hand.

From this camp we heard heavy firing all night at Vicksburg. Early next morning we entered Brookhaven. I saw more signs of the Yankees, in the way of blackened ruins of buildings and camps near the town. After we reached the village I dismissed Frank with his wagon and sent him back home. We took the train from Brookhaven for Jackson about 9 a. m. We arrived at the getting off place, about three miles South of Jackson at 11 a. m. The rail-road for three miles below Jackson had been destroyed by the Yankees.

As my carpet bag was very heavy and the weather excessively warm, we hired a negro with a two mule wagon to take us up to Jackson. It seemed to me that this was the hardest riding wagon that ever I got into. One of the mules had what the negro called a fistula on his shoulder, and he bled so profusely at every step that I thought he would not be able to go. Every time we stopped there was a pool of blood at his feet.

We stopped at the house of a citizen and asked for a canteen of water. The lady said that she could not afford to fill our canteens as water was too scarce but that we could have a drink. Clarence emphatically pronounced it a hell of a country, said that it was bad enough to go without whiskey, but when the water rations were cut off too, he intended to resign (Clarence was a *high private*).

This scarcity of water prevails all through this section.

We saw Colonel Allen, our old commander, at Jackson. He was just returning from Richmond. I enquired of him the whereabouts of our Regiment and he informed us that it was on the Big Black River 10 miles west of Canton, and that the best way to reach them was to take the train to Canton and then get on from there the best way that I could.

About this time we began to feel a little hungry and our *grub* had *gin out*. We bought a bologna sausage and a pound of crackers. I think I shall remember that sausage, for it *didn't agree with my feelings*, and I felt like I had been metamorphosed in a *caison* for a six pounder, and Clarence hinted at having found something similar to a dog collar in the middle of the sausage, but I didn't believe him.

We took the train at 2 p. m. for Canton and arrived there at 5 p. m. same day. On getting out of the cars at Canton, I saw an officer standing in the door of a house near the depôt, and I enquired of him the wherabouts of the troops. He answered me very abruptly and very ungentlemanly, that it needn't concern me where the troops were, but to go immediately and report myself to the Provost Marshal. I repeated to Clarence—who was hard of hearing what the fellow said—and it seemed to render him very uneasy and he enquired of me what we should do. I told him that we would go and obtain accomodation at a hotel in the town until we could ascertain where our Regiment was. We went to a hotel, the only one in the place, and asked for lodgings but were informed that the house was full. We got our meals at the hotel, but had to sleep on the gallery on our blankets.

I saw Raphael at Canton and told him that I intended to rejoin my regiment.

The next day we found a wagon going empty to Big Black, and we obtained permission to go on it. We reached the river about sundown and remained there with a Kentucky Regiment until our Regiment came along next morning.

At Canton I exchanged my carpet bag for a knapsack. When the Regiment came up I saw Kilbourne and he told me to put my baggage in his ambulance.

We encamped on a stream of stagnant water called Bear Creek 1½ miles east of Big Black and eight miles west of Canton.

We marched from our camp on Bear Creek to a camp on Big Black, thus bearing towards Vicksburg again on the Canton and Vicksburg road. This was a splendid camping place, being a

117

lovely and retired grassy plot, covered with luxuriant grass, perfectly level, and having on three sides large and noble forest trees, and there was a splendid spring of water, that afforded a good supply.

This was near Beattie's Bluff, in the vicinity of which is laid the scene of [William Gilmore] Sims' story of the "Border Beagles."

We remained at this camp about a week, when we moved on to our next camp, about nine miles farther on the road towards Vicksburg just beyond a little town called Livingston where we were fortunate enough to find another spring of good water. Livingston is a poor looking village with perhaps 150 or 200 inhabitants. The next morning we marched about eight miles farther on towards Vicksburg.

(Here my journal commences again regularly. The reason why I didn't keep it in this manner all the time was because I didn't have paper and pencil convenient, but I shall endeavor to keep a daily record from this time.)

Wednesday, June 24, 1863: Last night it rained very hard. There are only two tents in the Brigade. Gen. Maxey [3] has one and Col. Hunter has an older one, that leaks very badly. Capt. Kilbourne, Col. Hunter, Parson Godfrey, Jim Doyle, Jim Blow and I are messing together.

Between Canton and Jackson on the railroad I noticed large fields of corn thrown away on account of the negroes all running away to the Yankees.

I have heard very rapid firing during the last two hours in the direction of Vicksburg. An assault on the works I presume.

Thursday, June 25: Weather very cool and bracing for the season. Our camp is very pleasantly located, being in the thick woods with plenty of shade and first-rate water.

The whole of this portion of the country is very poorly watered, and there are no running streams between Big Black and Canton and very few springs. The planters use cistern water, altogether. To use the water of the Big Black will not do, for there is so

---

[3] Brigadier General Samuel Bell Maxey.

much decayed vegetable matter in it, that it is certain to bring on sickness. The majority of the planters own large plantations and own a great number of slaves. The soil is alluvial and is very rich, producing splendid crops of corn and cotton. A planter whose place is only a few miles away, says he will make this year 100,000 barrels corn, and perhaps more. The citizens are said to be aristocratic and purseproud.

Our rations are meal, beef and salt, and hardly enough of that.

Wednesday, July 1: We are ordered to move this morning. Moved on towards Vicksburg 5 miles and camped near a hollow filled with muddy stagnant water. We suffer for water.

Thursday, July 2: 10 a. m. We have just passed the village of Brownsville. The citizens were standing at their gates with buckets and pitchers of water, handing it to every man that passed. This was the most acceptable thing that could have been offered us.

We met a carriage this morning containing some handsome young ladies, and one in particular looked very pleasing with her sparkling eyes and rosy cheeks. I have thought of her twenty times today as I was marching along through the heat and dust and almost dying with thirst.

The weather is very warm, and the heat of the sun is over-powering. Two of our regiment fell from sunstroke today. We are now only three miles from the enemy's pickets.

Sunday, July 5: The weather is very dry and the roads a foot deep in dust. It is rumored that we are to leave today. 6 p. m. We have received orders to move at half past one tonight.

Monday, July 6: Instead of getting off at 1 o'clock as ordered, we did not move until after daylight. The astounding intelligence has reached us that Vicksburg has fallen. Pemberton has surrendered.[4] We are in full retreat towards Jackson, Miss.[5] We

[4] July, 1863, was a tragic month for the Confederacy. Grant surrounded Vicksburg and undertook a memorable siege of that city. Vastly outnumbered and with his troops suffering from hunger and lack of supplies, Pemberton surrendered his army on July 4—the day after Lee's defeat at Gettysburg. A few days later Port Hudson fell and Federal forces controlled the Mississippi from its source to the Gulf.

[5] The command had expected every day to receive orders to break through the Big Black swamp and attack Grant's rear. But the chance never came and at dawn on

have had a terrible march to-day. *No water*—dust, dust, dust. My God it is awful. The citizens all along the route take the buckets off the well ropes to prevent our getting water—and we are suffering for the want of it.

Clarence Bell, and Jim Nash went into a planter's house and asked for water. He told them he had none. They then offered $2 for three canteens full. He accepted the money and gave them the water.

I didn't get any sleep last night, nor have I had anything to eat for twenty-four hours and I feel pretty well worn out. The heat is intolerable and the dust awful. I never want to be on another retreat.

Tuesday, July 7: Off again this morning towards Jackson. Reached Jackson about 12 M.

Friday, July 17: There has been more or less fighting during the last ten days and the enemy have thrown a great many shells into the town.[6] We received orders a little after dark last night, and we moved on towards Brandon. Reached Brandon just as day was breaking. Very tired and sleepy. Kilbourne's two servants Bill and Henry ran away last night.

Saturday, July 18: Took up the line of march at daylight— made 13 miles and camped at a mill pond.

The men are very low spirited and have been ever since they heard of the fall of Vicksburg. I never saw such depression. Desertions are frequent.

Monday, July 20: Moved at one p. m. Another terrible days march. The men and horses fall by the wayside every few hundred yards. I never saw anything like it. The cry is water, water, water. Got into camp about 10 at night—tired, hungry and worn out.

July 6 the men were instructed to effect an immediate retreat without stopping until they reached Jackson. Kendall, "Recollections of a Confederate Officer," *loc. cit.*, 1145.

[6] Patrick is referring to the "siege" of Jackson. As soon as Johnston received the bad news of the Confederate surrender at Vicksburg he fell back to Jackson. On July 9, Gen. Sherman, commanding three corps of the Federal army, appeared on the scene but instead of attacking he laid siege to the city. On the sixteenth, after a week of scattered skirmishing, Johnston evacuated Jackson and retreated eastward. Sherman did not pursue him but burned the city and retired to Vicksburg on July 23. Stanley F. Horn, *The Army of Tennessee* (New York, 1941), 220.

Our men are deserting us by the hundred.

Thursday, July 23: There is nothing new. Our army is rapidly diminishing. Hundreds are deserting every night. I stopped at the house of a small farmer today to see if I could have some washing done. While there I had a conversation with the lady of the house. She said that fifteen or twenty of the soldiers called at her house and represented that they were sick and asked for food and lodging. She says she put herself to a great deal of trouble and inconvenience, and deprived herself of nearly everything she had, for they are poor, to accomodate them. She gave them both food and lodging. They left before day the next morning. On looking about next morning she discovered that her dairy had been entered during the night and all her dishes taken away and everything in the dairy either missing or destroyed. On going into the garden she found that all her vegetables were gone. They had also left the fence down so that the stock got into the field and were destroying the whole crop. The family is left in an almost destitute condition. This is only one instance out of a thousand, nay, one out of ten thousand.

Friday, July 24: We moved our camp some 4 miles today and it is thought that we will remain here some time. We are near a creek of clear running water being the first we have seen in a long time.

Saturday, July 25: I am anxious to hear from home. The last time I heard from there the Yankees were approaching the place, and no intelligence has reached me since that time. Kilbourne and I went out in search of forage to-day, but we could not find any for sale. This section is very poor; there's nothing in it. There is one redeeming feature amid all the desolation, and that is the remarkably fine well water. The creek water is better than any we have found yet, though it is not as good as that we have about home.

We stopped at a house on our way back to purchase some honey and while there I fell in love with one of the feminine gender.

She was like Juliana in the song " tall and slender, and slender round the waist." When she straightened up good and unwound herself, she appeared to be fifteen feet long and when she rose from her chair she reminded me of the unfolding of the huge serpents we sometimes see in shows. Her face was thin and sharp and her nose keen enough to split a hair; she was slab-sided and had very large hands. She had very long legs being split up almost to the chin. Her legs looked like straws and were bowed like a pair of hams. Her dress came down a little below her knees and she wore very heavy shoes, about a number 7 I should judge, and no stockings. When she once got in motion " take keer." She went plum across the house at a stride.

Tuesday, July 28:   Kilbourne has gone to Morton [7] today and I am paying off the officers. Desertions still continue.

Wednesday, July 29:   I am getting along very well and about as well satisfied as a man could be under such circumstances. If there is no room for self reproach and an absence of physical pain I think any man ought to be able to make himself contented. Contentment is the one great thing. It is the summit of human happiness. But no man should be contented to remain idle and inert and of no use to himself or others. We should all live to some purpose.

Friday, August 7:   I have been very busy for the last five days extending pay-rolls and paying off the troops.

We have received orders to move in the morning. We are bound for Enterprise, Miss. [8] Our horses do not fare very well now. Three green cornstalks per day for each horse. The desertions are more frequent than ever, and they leave by whole companies, officers and all. The Mississippians and Tennesseeans are nearly all deserting. I have heard of no Louisianians going yet.

Saturday, August 8:   I was awakened a long time before day by sharp talking, the rattle of chains and harness, the tramp of men and mules, besides various other sounds equally disagreeable. First Charlie Scharch a teamster was cursing another teamster named Easly, both loud and deep. It seemed that Easly had deserted the night before, and had carried off all Charlie's cooked rations. At length he subsided, and I had hardly fallen into a

[7] Morton Station in Scott County, Mississippi.
[8] The regiment was ordered to Enterprise to prevent an advance of Federal cavalry which threatened in that direction.

comfortable dose again before Pete Green the wagon master opened in full cry, about the loss of a Gov't horse, supposed to have been carried off by Easly. This however proved not to be the case. Pete finally hushed up and I again closed my eyes, hoping to get a good nap before day. Vain hope. Jim Doyle had got into the tent and opened his battery of words upon us. He was abusing Craig and Daniels for appropriating some provisions he had purchased. He poured his hot shot and shells on their devoted heads, until the " first sweet dawn of light " began to appear through the trees in the orient and I got up feeling drowsy and nervous—and ready for the day's march.

2 p. m. We are now at a railroad station called " Forest." Jim Blow and I rode about 3 miles in search of water. We at length found some muddy stagnant stuff, but we were very glad to get it. We raked off the black scum and pitched into it. As we were returning I saw Jonathan Embree in an ambulance. I didn't recognise him at first. He once boarded at our house. He was a clerk for a short time for Levi Bloom & Co," [9] but he drank so much that they would not keep him. He looked pale and emaciated. He said he was captured at Baker's Creek by the Yankees and had been sick for a long time.

The troops go through by rail and the wagon train goes across the country. I shall go with the latter.

These open pine woods are very hot—the tall pines afford no protection from the sun.

Sunday, August 9: Off for Enterprise this morning.

Monday, August 10: Made 25 miles today. Country very poor.

Tuesday, August 11: Up by the time it was light, but didn't get off until after sunrise. Reached Enterprise about 11 a. m. where we found the Regiment.

The country all around here is as poor as it can be.

Wednesday, August 12: Drew clothing for the Regiment today. Bought me some cloth to make shirts. Also 2 pair silver sleeve buttons.

[9] A dry goods and grocery establishment in Clinton.

I called at the house of a citizen to see if I could get my shirts made. I found a homely girl and her mother at the house. In answer to my enquiry as to whether they could make my shirts, the old lady said I could get them in a few days, if I would leave the cloth, and give her the measure of the shirts. This I did.

While here I saw a fair instance of how the Tennessee boys work their way with the citizens. It has always been a mystery to our regiment how the Tennesseeans managed to procure such a quantity of fresh vegetables, milk, butter, and everything else, while we were starving for them, and offering any price. When our boys went about the citizens they seemed surly and unaccomodating and showed no disposition to grant us any favors, for which I could not blame them because the soldiers I know to be a great nuisance.

When I went in, I found a gaunt, sallow faced Tennesseean sitting in the little parlor. He looked like he had been reared from infancy on goobers, green apples, persimmons and dirt. His eyes looked like two bullets set in a pile of clay. He was occupying a chair near the centre of the room, with his hands stuffed into his pockets, and his feet crowded into a pair of number eleven government brogans.

After I had been there a short time I ascertained that the object of his visit was to purchase a chicken. The lady said that she had a few—but that she wished to keep them for her own use, as it was an impossibility to purchase them 'through the country, and besides that some of her children were sick and she needed what few she had and could not think of selling them. This would have been enough for me, but it wasn't half enough for my Tennessee friend.

" Well " said Tennessee who spoke in a drawling tone " we uns (Tennesseeans nearly all say we uns and you uns) we uns hain't got nothin' to eat hardly, and the feller what stays with me is sorter sick, and I want to buy a chicken for him."

" I would like very much to accomodate you " replies the lady " but as I informed you just now I haven't one to spare."

" Well but you know how it is with us poor soldiers in camp, we can't git nuthin " whined Tennessee.

The lady repeated what she had already said, but Tennessee begged until she was almost forced to let him have it, and finding that it was impossible to get rid of him, she had one caught, though I know at the same time she wished him at the devil.

He took the chicken and commenced again. " Hain't you got some buttermilk? "

" Yes " she replied with an air of resignation " I have some but I expect to reserve it for dinner."

" Well " drawled Tennessee once more lengthening his counten-ance, which had almost resumed its natural appearance after receiving the chicken " I hain't been very well, and I have the heartburn mighty bad, and everybody says buttermilk is a mighty good thing for the heartburn and I think you ought to let me have some. Now can't you let me have a little? "

Tennessee went out to get his milk and I left, thoroughly dis-gusted with his pertinacity, with him, and with his whole tribe in general.

This is the way that the citizens are annoyed by the soldiers, and for this reason I dislike to enter the house of a citizen for any purpose whatever. The Tennesseeans are very annoying in this way; more so I think, than the troops from any other state. They are great peddlers and speculators on a small scale. They will sell anything in the world they possess and they think every one else will do the same thing.

They will come around our mess fire and want to trade for the dinner that's cooking.

The other day as I was riding from town with a small bundle on my arm, I met a great many Tennesseeans and everyone would ask me what I had to sell. I met one fellow by himself, pulling along in the hot sun, with the sand about shoe mouth deep and the perspiration pouring from his face.

" What you got to sell Mister? " said he stopping and wiping the streams of sweat from his face.

" Nothing " I answered.

" Well, did you see anything up that way that looked like it was fit to eat? "

" Yes."

" What was it? " said he apparently much interested.

" I saw a pair of old pants hanging on a fence that I think would make good soup."

" Kiss my —— and go to hell —— damn you " said Tennessee very much incensed. I rode on.

The water is better than any we have had.

Friday, August 14: Issuing clothing to the Regiment.

Sunday, August 16: I understand we are to go to Mobile. I was made Q. M. Sgt. on 1st Aug.

Saturday August 22: I have been sick for several days—and I feel quite unwell today.

Sunday, August 30: Left for Mobile.

Monday, August 31: Arrived in Mobile.

Thursday, September 10: Hall's Mills, Ala. near Mobile. Kilbourne and Hunter left for home at 3 p. m. They took a four mule wagon with them for the purpose of bringing back such things as may be sent to the men in the field by their friends. I have sent for a number of necessary articles.

There are no mills here and the only thing that could have given it the name of Hall's Mills, is the site of an old mill, apparently not used for years and partially demolished. There is a narrow, deep, swift, clear running stream, that turned the old mill in its palmy days. There is a clear running spring here, but the water is mineral of some kind and affects the health too much to use constantly, and we therefore use water from the creek alluded to above.

This has been a camping ground for troops ever since the war began. It was primarily a camp of instruction for all the Alabama State troops. A great many of Bragg's troops were stationed here during the time he had command of Pensacola. There are about 150 houses standing. They are placed in rows, regularly, and this regularity and the size of the buildings gives it the appearance of a small village. Some of the buildings are quite spacious and two stories high. Others again are mere log huts. The timber for a mile all around has been cleared away, forming a large and splendid drill ground, the terror of the soldiers.

The place has an exceedingly lonely appearance, and to look around it gives one the blues.

Saturday, September 12: We were ordered to Mobile this morning. I let Jim Doyle have my horse and I went in the buggy with Mr. Godfrey.

We arrived at Mobile about 10 a. m. and went into camp on Government Street near battery No. 9. We are to have lumber furnished us to build winter quarters here, but building barracks is no sign that we will remain any length of time. I hope we will not be ordered away before next spring because it is really awful to move about in cold weather and I always dread it. We have no tents and we are compelled to take the weather as it comes.

Col. Allen has been made a Brigadier and the day before we left Hall's Mills, he made us a speech, and shook hands and bade farewell to his old Regiment. It was quite affecting and there was scarcely a dry eye in the Regiment. He was loved by the men, for he was always their friend, and a braver man never lived, than that same Col. Allen. May success attend him through life is my wish, and I believe when I say this that I speak the sentiments of the whole Regiment. He leaves for the Trans-Mississippi Dep't tomorrow to join his command.

My health is improving.

Sunday, September 13: The weather is pleasant enough now, and the nights are getting cool enough to sleep with some degree of comfort.

Last night in company with some of my comrades, I attended a concert of negro minstrels at Odd Fellow's Hall. The music was poor, the songs and jokes were stale, and altogether it was a miserable affair. After the performance we had an oyster supper and then paid a visit to St. Michael Street.

Saturday, September 26: I took a long ride this afternoon. Went out 2 or 3 miles on the Shell Road, down on the Bay and thence nearly all over the city.

Monday, September 28: I saw Billy Lane at the Battle House to-day! he informed me that the business houses (or nearly all of them) in Clinton had been destroyed by fire. He is just from home and on his way to Bragg's Army.

I am reading " Vanity Fair " by Thackery and I think it is a first rate thing.

Thursday, October 1: It rained pitchforks last night and when I awoke this morning I found myself surrounded by water a foot deep.

My old horse has got to be a bigger fool than " Watch." I have heard that " Thompson's Colt " was noted for being extraordinarily foolish, but in my humble opinion, I do not think he could " lay over " my horse. He has always been very docile until last night. Just before dark I went to give him a bundle of fodder and when I got in about ten steps of him, he got scared at me, or the fodder, or maybe both. I had him tied with a very heavy grass rope and it was impossible for him to break it. He pulled and pulled, until I thought his head would be separated from his body. He got the rope drawn down over his ears, and there he stood, as stubborn as he could be, with his ears pulled down over his eyes, and sticking straight out before him, and every time I would come any ways near him, he would almost break his neck pulling at the rope. I finally went up anyhow, and gave him the fodder and feed of corn, but he wouldn't touch it.

This morning when I got up I went out to see how the old fellow was getting along, and there he stood with the rope still pulled down over his head and his ears pointing towards the tree to which he was tied. He looked the very picture of stubbornness, and I couldn't help laughing at his woe-begone appearance. I tried to get up to him. But, no sir! I couldn't come that, without insisting upon his pulling his head off. I went away and allowed him to remain in that condition nearly all day, until he finally took a notion to eat " suthin " as old man Elder says. After this I found him as gentle as ever, and I could tie him with a thread ever after and he wouldn't attempt to break it. That grass rope gave him a lesson worth remembering.

Sunday, October 4: I have not been to church since we have been here. I would have gone to-day, but I have a boil on my nose which causes it to look too much like a brandy blossom for me to make my appearance in church. I have not made the acquaintance of any ladies since I have been here and as I am in the same dilemma that Flora McFlimsey was, viz. " nothing to wear," I think it very probable that I shall not endeavor to squeese myself in.

Thursday, October 8:   Kilbourne and Hunter returned from home to-day, both looking well.

"Up to Dalton and back to Mobile"

Mobile, Alabama, Saturday, March 26, 1864: Here is a long gap; nearly six months.

While riding out one day not long since I lost my notebook containing all my phonographic notes, since the 8th October last, but I will endeavor to fill up this from memory as well as I can.

One evening about the first of November '63 I was sitting by the fire in front of my quarters where we were encamped on Government Street. It was a dismal evening. A slow rain was falling, and the wind swept by, cold and chilly. Wallace Matthews came up to where I was sitting, thus solemnly ruminating on better days gone by, and remarked that it was a very unpleasant night. He said he had but one blanket and to sleep out on the open common, such a night as that promised to be was more than he could endure. He told me that he intended to go round among the citizens and see if he couldn't find one humane enough to give him a shelter for the night, even if it were nothing better than a dog kennel. As I was quite unwell, I observed to him that I wished him to see what he could do for me also. After a little while he returned saying that he could obtain a room for himself and one for me—that is a room for the two together —provided he would bring a note of recommendation from his Captain. This he obtained from Captain Fiester, and over we went. The house was nearly opposite our camp and just outside the breast-works.

On knocking at the house we were met at the door by the lady of the house, and he introduced me to her, as Mrs. Golthwaite. She told us we could occupy the room already pointed out by her to Mr. Matthews, and told us to make ourselves as comfortable as possible. Matthews forthwith led the way to a room in the basement, which was very comfortable, with a good bedstead, mattrass and fireplace, and we soon made ourselves perfectly comfortable, by building a fire and spreading our blankets on the mattrass, besides divers and sundry other little arrangements. We had tables and chairs and were fixed up about as well as we could desire. It beat out-doors " all hollow." I slept well that night; much better than I had for a long time previous. There is a great difference between a plank and a mattrass.

I took a survey of the premises next morning. The building was a very nice one and quite commodious. The grounds were handsomely laid off, and planted all over with a variety of trees and shrubs, which were very well arranged. The whole place had a cheerful, pleasant look, and I liked the idea of having my quarters there.

I liked the kitchen arrangements very much. The kitchen was built over the cistern and a pump was fixed in the middle of the room near the stove. The cook had no trouble in getting an abundant supply of good, clear water at a moment's warning. Mrs. Golthwaite treated us very kindly indeed during the time we remained there, and frequently sent us little delicacies, which were thankfully received and duly appreciated by us.

On the 19th November '63 I received a furlough to go home. Mrs. Golthwaite very kindly filled my haversack with every thing that was nice, and at 5 p. m. on Friday the 20th Jake Burns assisted me to carry my knapsack down to the depôt. Jake and I took a farewell drink together, and away I went for Meridian.

It rained all night long. I arrived at Meridian a little before day. It had ceased raining and had turned cold. It was very dark and as I was not acquainted with the village, it was with difficulty that I found a hotel. I did at length succeed after sloshing about through the mud and water and stumbling over the cross-ties and parts of old machinery for nearly half an hour.

I got into the hotel and deposited my luggage in one corner. There was a stove in the room, but there was such a crowd around that I couldn't get near it. After standing around for a long time, some one vacated a chair and I got an opportunity to warm myself.

About 7 a.m. I took the train for Brandon, where I arrived a little before sundown.

I obtained passage from Brandon to Crystal Springs a distance of 35 miles, in a buggy with a Capt Chadwick.

From Crystal Springs to Liberty, I went in a two horse or rather two mule conveyance with a man named Jim May, who kept a hotel at Crystal Springs. He charged me $75.

I found Clinton very much changed in appearance. The long row of stores on the east side of the square known as " Brick Row " had been destroyed by fire, as also had all the buildings on each side of " St. Helena Street."

I also found a great change in the ideas and sentiments of the people. They were trading liberally with the Yankees, and hauling cotton to them all the time. This illicit trade was carried on to an astonishing extent. The cotton was never carried to Baton Rouge by the men—the women always took charge of it, and rode down on the cotton. The guards would allow the women to pass.

I heard a great deal of complaint against our cavalry serving in this vicinity. All the way down from Crystal Springs to Clinton, I heard the citizens denouncing the cavalry and many of them told me that they would prefer seeing the Yankees to seeing our cavalry. I thought this was a very bad reputation. Widows and those families whose heads were in the army complained more than the others. The cavalry who were guarding the roads near the enemy's lines would allow the cotton to pass on the payment to them by the owner of $10 or $20 per bale, and when those persons would return with their wagons laden with the articles they had purchased with the cotton, they would again levy a tax on them by taking such things as they desired. Others carried the matter farther still and would demand the money of persons they met on the roads. These men were called " *cotton tollers* " and "*Jay hawkers*" but they were nothing more nor less than regular highwaymen. They would steal cotton from the gin-houses of the planters and send it to Baton Rouge. Some of them accumulated large amounts of money. I was astonished at all this. Nearly everybody seemed to have lost all sense of right and wrong and *Honesty* the jewel was decidedly at a discount.

I remained at home a little over three weeks, but everything looked so gloomy that there was little or no pleasure in remaining, outside of the gratification of being with my family.

Having procured a conveyance to the Rail Road, I left home to rejoin my command about the 18th December 1863. During my short stay at home, I had made a little money speculating, and before leaving Mr. Jackson's I loaned him $200, and made Uncle Giles McKie a present of $50. I also gave Aunt Epsy [1] $75 before leaving Clinton.

I went to Brookhaven in the conveyance I had. The weather was very cold and the ground was frozen during the whole trip. My vehicle broke down once, which detained me one whole afternoon, but as good luck would have it, I was not more than half a mile from a blacksmith shop where I had the machine repaired. I didn't mind the delay much, as there were two good looking girls at the house, and as they had plenty to eat I remained all night. I took the train at Brookhaven to Crystal Springs. From Crystal Springs to Brandon I went in buggy. At Brandon I took the train again for Mobile.

While walking about the city I met Tom Fiester, who, as he had left home the day after I arrived there, I thought was with the Regiment, which was then at Dalton, Ga. [2] I wished to go on to Dalton next morning but he insisted upon my remaining until next day and we would go together. So I postponed my departure until the next day, but as he was not ready, we were to go the day following. As he was never ready we postponed the matter

---

[1] Aunt Epsy Draughon Davis, Robert's mother's sister.

[2] The 4th La. Regiment had been transferred from Mobile to Dalton, Ga., where they joined the Army of Tennessee under General Joe Johnston. After the disastrous Chattanooga campaign, Bragg had been relieved of his command. Johnston had assumed command of the army on December 27, 1863, at Dalton and was attempting to instill new life into the dejected Confederates. Horn, *Army of Tennessee*, 305–315.

from day to day until we had been in Mobile ten days. We did however finally get away.

Tom Fiester had a lot of stores consisting of several very large heavy boxes, filled with clothing for our Regiment, which he was to deliver to the men on his arrival. Tom ascertained that his brother Henry was lying at the point of death at the village of Tuskegee, Ala. and he got off the train between Montgomery and West Point, leaving Jim Doyle and myself in charge of the stores, with instructions to await him at West Point. We went on to West Point, and got our stores off the train, but we could not find any place to store them, so we had to put them under the car-shed, and guard them all night. It was quite cold too. We expected Fiester according to promise but he didn't come, so Doyle and I determined to take the train on to Atlanta that night.

At 9 p. m. Fiester still not making his appearance, we got everything on the train and started for Atlanta. It was a terrible night. It commenced raining a short time after we started and rained all night. On arriving at Atlanta which we did several hours before day, I told Jim that we would endeavor to find some place to put the stores and find a bed; that if we failed in finding any place to store them that we would seek some rest and protection from the storm ourselves, and let the stores go to the devil. Fortunately we found a man, a member of the 30th Regt. (La.) who said he had some stores to guard and would also take charge of ours, and we went off in search of a hotel.

After cruising around in the Egyptian darkness and wading through mud and water ankle deep, we at length found a hotel. We enquired if we could be accomodated with a bed. The man in the office informed us that the house was crowded. We then asked for a clean place on the floor—that we were amply supplied with bedding. He said that if we had blankets, that he could supply us with a room, and a bedstead with a mattrass on it. This we gladly accepted, and slept very well until next morning. This refreshed us considerably because we both needed rest very much. We got a first-rate breakfast, for the moderate sum of $2 each and our beds he didn't charge us anything for, which I considered exceedingly liberal for a hotel keeper in these days of extortion.

" Would you like to look over this morning's paper, Miss? "

At 6 a.m. we took the train for Dalton. We were unable to obtain transportation for our boxes, and we left them in charge of the man in the 30th to bring on next day when he brought his own. It continued to rain incessantly all day and the earth was completely flooded with water.

On the train I was sitting immediately fronting a very pretty young lady. She had dark hair, dark eyes, fair complexion, and regular, handsome features. I admired her. She kept her eyes almost continually on me—and I never looked towards her but what she was gazing at me. I finally came to the conclusion that I would rake up an acquaintance some way. With this very laudable end in view, I drew from my pocket, a morning paper.

" Would you like to look over this morning's paper Miss? " I enquired, in the politest manner I knew how.

" How do you sell 'em? " she asked.

I explained to her that I was not a newsboy nor a " *dealer in trifles.*" That I was a glorious son of Mars—a " bold soger boy " a fighting chicken, a regular game cock and one that would undoubtedly do to tie to, and added that I offered her the paper, thinking she would like to read the news. She said she didn't care about reading it. As the ice was now broken we continued the conversation for some time, and I soon discovered that she was very illiterate, though possessed of good common sense.

I noticed that she was constantly spitting some dark colored fluid from her mouth. I thought she had the toothache, and had perhaps something in her mouth to cure it. I looked on the floor and there was a great puddle at her feet. It resembled tobacco juice very much, and by George it was tobacco juice, for I saw her spit out the old chew and put in a fresh one. I " wilted."

A soldier sitting near me remarked, " she is mighty good looking but she is awful on tobacco."

About 5 p.m. on the 31st day of December 1863, I landed at the village of Dalton, Geo.

It had ceased raining but the ground was one grand loblolly from the tramp of thousands of men and animals, and the running to and fro of supply and baggage wagons. The clouds still looked lowering and the weather was growing colder rapidly.

There was nothing to be seen in the vicinity of the depôt, except a few houses which looked as though they were deserted, all the fencing and everything about the premises having been torn away by the soldiers I presume. In the distance on all sides, the prospect was anything but cheerful. All looked "naked, brown and sear" and the back-ground of this uninviting picture, was formed by a chain of dark and gloomy looking hills, which seemed with their frowning rugged sides to preside over this apparently God-forsaken district. Jim Doyle and I left the heaviest of our baggage at the depôt in charge of the guard who happened to be from our Regiment, and went in search of the camping ground of the old 4th which, after a toilsome walk of over a mile, through mud and water, we at length reached, almost worn out, for we both had a considerable amount of baggage to carry. On reaching the camp we found that the Regiment was tolerably well fixed up, all having very comfortable log houses.[3]

I took up my quarters with Bill Montan and Moreau Purdy. That night (Dec. 31/63) the ground froze very hard, and during the remainder of our stay there which was twenty one days I think, the ground didn't thaw. It was impossible to do any writing on account of the ink's freezing. I would place the inkstand in the warm ashes, but when I dipped my pen in it, it would freeze before I could transfer it to the paper.

I never experienced such cold weather, or I never spent such a disagreeable time, as I did during my stay at Dalton. I was very well provided with thick clothing or I really believe that I would have "gone up the spout."

Ten years ago while on my way to school in Tennessee, I was delayed at this place for several days, but I didn't think then that I would revisit, as a half-starved, half-frozen Confederate soldier. Then everything before me seemed bright and joyous, for it was summer and all nature seemed gay and happy, and it corresponded with my feelings, for I had no cares upon my mind, nor anything whatever to trouble me. But now it was different. I felt dejected and heartsick as I wandered over those cold, bar-

---

[3] The 4th Regt. arrived too late to be of any service and the Louisiana soldiers followed the retiring Confederate army into Dalton.

ren, cheerless hills. The wind sighed along in mournful cadences, through the dismantled forest trees and over the rugged hilltops, and I could not help thinking of the comforts of home and all its pleasures when I contemplated this desolate scene.

Tom Fiester didn't arrive for nearly a week after I got there. He informed me that his brother Henry was dead. He died at Tuskegee, Alabama of consumption, the disease having been brought on by exposure during the siege of Vicksburg. Poor fellow! He escaped all the shells and balls to linger a few months and die in an obscure village. I think I would have preferred sudden death from a cannon shot, to a lingering illness, which would inevitably result in a dissolution of body and soul.

The rations while we were at Dalton were worse than any we had had yet. It was thrown down in the butcher pen and was covered with mud and dung and a decent dog would have turned up his nose at it, but a hungry man will eat almost anything.

One morning the glad tidings came that we were ordered back to Mobile. The men were wild with delight and congratulated each other upon the happy prospect of leaving this dismal place. A declaration of peace would scarcely have been hailed with greater delight than was this order.[4]

We were ordered to be ready to move to the Rail Road at daylight, but so anxious were the men to get away, that they were all ready with their baggage long before the day broke though we didn't get away until after dark that night. The trip down was a very unpleasant one to all hands, and particularly so to me.

It rained a little shortly after we left Dalton and when we reached Atlanta, it was very cold and the rain had turned to sleet.

John Bradford was quite sick and so was I. We were both threatened with pneumonia. We were compelled to remain all night in Atlanta, and I knew that it would not do for John or me to endeavor to sleep out in the open air in our present con-

[4] In early February, 1864, word came to Johnston from General Polk in Mississippi that Sherman was advancing eastward from Vicksburg with an army of 35,000 men. Polk reported that the Federals had crossed the river at Jackson and were presumably headed for Meridian and then Mobile. On orders from President Davis, Johnston sent several regiments back to Alabama to assist in the defense of Mobile. Horn, *Army of Tennessee*, 315–16.

dition. I therefore went out although I was scarcely able to walk and searched around until I found a room for John and myself. If it hadn't been for obtaining this room I don't know what we would have done, and I know that we would have fared very badly, and would in all probability have been down with pneumonia which, by the way I have had three times already.

The next day we left Atlanta for West Point, and the weather still cold. On arriving at West Point I hurried immediately to the only hotel there was and secured a room for myself and Jno. Bradford. We were both still unwell and had grown worse instead of better.

From West Point to Montgomery I had a very good time. I was in a cabcar which had a stove in it. In this car were Kilbourne, Hunter, Dr. Hereford, Dr. Craig [5] and one or two others. They played poker all the way. Kilbourne was the only one excepting myself, that was not in the game.

After reaching Montgomery which we did in the night, I found myself much worse, though I managed to keep on my feet. I saw Jno. Bradford and he said he thought he couldn't go any farther. I told him that it was impossible for me to render him any assistance because I was utterly exhausted, and could scarcely drag one foot after the other.

The next morning we left Montgomery for Mobile, where we arrived about ten or eleven o'clock that night. I found Hunter after searching about some time in the dark and obtained his permission to go to a hotel, as I was entirely too unwell to do anything more than go to bed.

I procured one of the many cabs standing near the steamboat landing and I repaired immediately to the City Hotel on Royal Street. I preferred stopping at this place, for many reasons—the principal one being because I was acquainted with an Irish chambermaid there who I knew would wait upon me.

[5] J. M. Craig, surgeon. Dr. Craig kept a diary during the march of the 4th Regiment through Georgia, Alabama, and Mississippi, in the closing months of 1864 and the spring of 1865. This short diary is of particular interest because Dr. Craig kept a memorandum of the casualties in the command. See John S. Kendall, ed., "The Diary of Surgeon Craig, Fourth Louisiana Regiment," *Louisiana Historical Quarterly*, VIII (January, 1925), 53–70.

I was sick at this hotel for about two weeks and during this time Margaret (I didn't know her other name) waited on me and treated me very kindly. After I had been at the hotel about two days, who should step in but John Bradford. He looked the worse for wear, and if his looks were any indications of his feelings, he must have felt perfectly wretched. He said he was no better than when I parted from him at Montgomery—that he started on to Mobile the day after we did, and that he was now completely used up, though he thought he would call and see how I was getting along, having learned that I was at the hotel. I was glad to see him and I tried to persuade him to take a room next to mine, but he would not consent to this, saying that he thought it would be better for him and me too to go to a hospital.

I told him that I didn't like the idea of a hospital and that I would remain where I was unless I got much worse. He told me that he was going to the Louisiana Hospital, which was kept exclusively for the benefit of Louisianians, and that he wished me to call on him in case I should recover before he did. This I promised to do and exacted the same promise of him. He went on to the Hospital while I remained at the hotel.

After a day or two Kilbourne and Dr. Hereford called upon me, and insisted so strongly upon my going to the Hospital, that I finally consented. The La. Hospital, to which I went was in the charge of the Sisters of Charity and I found them exceedingly kind. I was put in the same ward with Jno. Bradford, who was quite sick by this time. My name and Regiment and date of entrance into the Hospital was tacked to the bed-post at the foot of my bed, and I was considered " one of 'em." This was the first time that I ever entered a Hospital as a patient and it was also the last time. I remained there two nights and days, and that was enough. I was still able to walk, and I resolved to leave. I reported the fact to the physician in charge, but he insisted upon my remaining because I was not well by any means. I insisted upon going however and he finally consented to give me a discharge.

I would have remained there, but there was no fresh air allowed to come in the room, and the smell from old sores and wounds, mingled with the scent of " *drugs, chemicals and dyestuffs* " was more than I could endure, when it could be avoided.

I hired a cab which I found upon the street and returned to my old quarters at the City Hotel, where I remained until I recovered. John Bradford was sick for a long time after I got well and according to promise I went up to visit him frequently, which seemed to relieve the tedium of his illness and apparently afforded him much pleasure. John got straight and " *at himself*," in the course of time however.

About this time Kilbourne and Hunter both received furloughs to go home. As my health was so bad, it was apparent to both of them that I was not very well qualified physically for field service, and they wished before they went home to obtain for me some easy situation and with this end in view they introduced me and recommended me highly to a Major Woolfolk, Qr. Mr. of Gen. [James] Cantey's Brigade.

Woolfolk said that he required a man of some experience and capacity in his office, and would be very glad to have me with him, but according to the laws of Congress it would be necessary for me to go before a Medical Examining Board and if after examining me they pronounced me unfit for field service, then I could ask for and receive a detail where I wished. Dr. Hereford was extremely anxious to have me go with him to East Louisiana. He was going there as Medical Director of the district and his headquarters would be in Clinton and by going with him I would be at home all the time. But I declined his offer, because I didn't like to remain at home and be pointed at as a home soldier, and another reason was that I didn't wish to be connected in any way with the cavalry, because it had such an unenviable reputation, both at home and abroad.

I went before the Medical Examining Board and stood the examination and they pronounced me totally unfit for field service, and at my request recommended a detail with Major Woolfolk, Qr. Mr. of Cantey's Brigade. I went on duty in this Brigade because the general supposition was that it would remain in Mobile all the time, as it had already been there two years,

141

and there were no indications whatever of its being ordered away. So I went into Maj. Woolfolk's office as his clerk.

This brings me to the 24th March 1864. I have written this up as well as I could from memory and all the main points are inserted though as a matter of course there are a thousand and one little incidents unmentioned, which were in my daily journal.

Thursday, March 24: This morning I awoke about 1 o'clock, and as I felt not the slightest inclination to sleep and was tired of lying in bed, I got up. After I got up I was in nearly as bad a fix as before, for I had no candle and I was too poor to buy one. I dressed myself and blacked my boots by the light of the moon, which shone most gloriously through my window. I went down to the market, but it was so early that there was no one there except a few fish dealers.

I took a long walk up the street until I saw the eastern horizon across the bay tinged with light and then I turned my steps towards Woolfolk's office, of which I had the key. I built up a fire, for it was rather chilly, and drawing out my Shakespeare, I read " As You Like It " until breakfast time, after which I came down and proceeded with my day's work as usual. To-day I wrote a long letter to mother, which as there is no mail communication now, I expect to send by some of the boys in the Regiment who have received furloughs and will leave in a day or two.

From what I have seen of Woolfolk I like him very well, and I think that he and I can get along without any difficulty.

Cantey's Brigade is now at a station called Pollard on the Montgomery and Mobile Rail Road, some 60 or 70 miles from Mobile and about 3 or 4 hours run from the city.

There is another clerk in the office with me by the name of Hart Collins, from Clayton, Alabama. He seems to be a very clever sort of man, though he is rather dictatorial in his manner. He dictates to Woolfolk what he should do and what he should not do. He is conceited too, and thinks he knows it all.

Yesterday I made the following resolutions—

    I. That I will drink no more liquor for the space of 12 months unless prescribed by a physician in case of absolute sickness.

II.   That I will attend strictly to business and always be at my post.

III. That I will shun bad company.

IV.   That I will not swear.

V.   That I will read at least one Chapter in the Bible daily, if practicable.

VI.   That I will not contract useless debts.

To-day, I have adhered strictly to all the above articles.

Very rainy, bad weather and extremely unpleasant out doors.

I stopped drinking on Sunday, 20th of March, 1864.

Friday, March 25:   Came down to the office at the usual hour. I am boarding with an old French lady on St. Francis Street, by the name of Moore but I certainly cannot continue there much longer for I have to pay One Hundred and twenty five dollars per month board while I receive only Ninety dollars per month, and the old lady said this morning that she intended to raise the price of board. I receive three dollars per day in lieu of everything else. Out of this I must board and clothe myself with board at $125 per month. Now this is utterly impossible and I must make some arrangement by which I can sustain myself. It seems to me that the Confederacy is about played out of provisions.

The troops only receive ten pounds of meat per month with corn meal and salt.

This is a beautiful day after a very rainy afternoon and night. My money is all gone and I am once more without a cent.

There are more rumors of recognition afloat but I do not place any reliance in them.

I saw Major Raphael, my old Pt. Hudson *boss*, the other day on the street. He informed me that he was in the cavalry service now, and that he was going down to Clinton with Gen. [Thomas H.] Taylor, who is placed in command of the cavalry down there.

I wrote a long letter to Jim Mansker to-day and as I had not sent off the one that I had written to mother, I left the office and walked up town to see if I could not find some one to send them out to the Regiment by, so that they could be forwarded home. On reaching Royal Street I saw Ben Johnson sitting on

143

the steps of the Customhouse and I handed them to him. Ben observed to me that he intended to go to Clinton in a few days and asked me to go with him. If there was any way to go I think that I would apply for one, but I do not think that there is very good policy in walking 220 miles through a barren country.

I have complied with all my resolutions except #5.

Saturday, March 26: I arose this morning about daylight and blacked my boots, shaved and dressed. Read two or three chapters in the Bible and a part of Hamlet, had my breakfast and came down to the office.

I am dead broke again without a cent in the world, not even enough to buy a box of matches of which I stand very much in need, nor a candle to go to bed by, but it makes little difference as I am getting so that I can adapt myself pretty well to circumstances. A week or so ago I was so low down that I was forced to sell my pocket knife, for which I received $20.00, which was a very small price for it. I wanted tobacco and so I sold the most useful article I had and I sorely felt the use of it afterwards.

A Frenchman, who boards here, was kind enough to repair the lock of my valise which had been broken on the way from Dalton to Mobile, and I think this is about the first thing that I have ever had done for nothing since I have been in the army.

I have adhered to all my resolutions except No. 6.

Sunday, March 27: I arose right early this morning and read a few chapters in the Bible. I am writing in my room at old Mrs. Moore's before breakfast. I think spring has come at last. I hear the swallow twittering in the air and this, I think, is a very good sign.

I will give a description of my boarding house. It is an old rackety concern that looks as though it had been built before " Noah was a sailor " and is in very bad repair. My room measures about 10 by 12 feet, containing a single bedstead with a feather bed on it. The walls are plastered but as the room leaks very badly, the ceiling is falling off in places. There is a dilapidated old wash-stand in one corner on which is a broken basin and a pitcher with the spout broken off. There is a row of pegs suspended from which are a pair of my old pants and a vest, an old mirror that seems to have been a very good one in its palmy days but which looks now as though it had performed a journey from the 4th story window to the pavements and had been in the retreat with Johnston's army from Big Black with the Yankees at their heels. Yet there is enough of it left in the corners for me to see how to shave and comb my hair. The frame is very old fashioned, and I presume was very fashionable a hundred years ago. When I look at it I sometimes wish it could give me a history and a likeness of the many persons who have stood before it. I have no doubt many a dandy swell has shaved his countenance, pomatumed and combed his head, and given his fancy cravat the last fashionable touch before that glass, previous to making his appearance in church, the ball-room or the theatre.

How many a fair maid has viewed herself in that old mirror, lacing her corsets, arranging her curls, and painting her cheeks. Perhaps it was some old maid on the wrong side of forty, trying to make herself appear but " sweet six-teen," or maybe some old lantern-jawed preacher or deacon of the church, strapping his razor and shaving away on a face as large and rough as a rawhide.

I have no doubt old glass you could tell some funny incidents if you could but speak. What a pity it is you can't and had you kept a diary, wouldn't it be a rich affair.

There is one window which has so many broken panes that I am well supplied with fresh air whether I wish it or not. A very good fire-place (though I never have any wood to make a fire, and it had as well not be there), a door with a lock to it, an old chair, table with leaves to it on which lie my shaving apparatus, my Bible (given me by Mrs. Moore) my Shakespeare and sundry old books and magazines, my old cob pipe.

Mrs. Moore is old, ugly, ill natured, fond of scandle and deceitful, and she is in a terrible way this morning and is pitching into all of us generally, which makes it extremely disagreeable. I hope that we may be able to get off to-morrow anyhow. The old woman says that she intends to charge us $40.00 a week now and I cannot stand it so I am making some other arrangements as soon as possible.

This is a lovely pleasant day and if this weather continues long, we will soon hear of something doing among the Yankees.

I have no hope now of the war's stopping before Lincoln's term expires, which will be the 4th of March, next, and I hope to see the day when peace will be restored to our unhappy and distracted country. Oh! what rejoicing there will be when that blessed day arrives. I am thankful I have survived as long as I have. I ought not to grumble at what I have to do for I am much better off than most of the boys who started out with me, for they have a much harder time than I do. They have short rations while I have a plenty; they are compelled to stand guard and have to go under strict military discipline, while I have nothing to do at night and can go to bed when I please; they are compelled to sleep in all kinds of places, while I have a good bed and room. I have cause to be grateful. This all comes of having business habits and having good friends and being able to write a good hand.

I intend to leave Mrs. Moore's to-day and board with Collins until we leave for Pollard, which will be in the course of three or four days at the fartherest. All that delays us now is that the boxes in which to put our books and papers is not yet finished. As soon as that is done, we will leave, although Mobile has got to be a second home to me, I believe I will get along better over there than I will here. I will be out of the way of temptation which will enable me to combat more successfully my appetite for strong drink, which has got almost too firm a hold on me.

I read General Johnston's official report of the military operations in Mississippi last night, and he throws all the blame of the fall of Vicksburg on General Pemberton. He says that Pemberton disobeyed orders in every instance, which I have known was the occasion of the fall of Vicksburg.[6]

Monday, March 28: Yesterday, I left old Mrs. Moore's boarding house and I am now boarding with Collins and sleeping at his room. His room is No. 111, Dauphin Street and he hires a

[6] Most Civil War students believe that the fall of Vicksburg was inevitable but that Pemberton might have saved his army had he heeded the orders of Johnston. For example see Horn, *The Army of Tennessee*, 215.

mulatto woman way down on Conception Street to cook for him. We have first-rate fare. We will leave here in a day or two longer, certain.

The weather is bad again with a slow rain falling and a cold wind blowing. Hunter is expected back in the course of a few days.

When we get over to Pollard, I intend to write home in diary form and I think that I shall make me a book in which I will keep a copy of all my letters as I frequently like to read them over. I am getting so now that I can write Phonography very well and if I have leisure, I shall endeavor to abbreviate a little more than I have done.

I find that I am $290.00 in debt, but this I hope to be able to liquidate before a great while. The new currency bill just passed by Congress has put the people in the Confederacy in quite a commotion.[7] The price of everything has gone up at least 50 per cent during the last two days. This bill is nothing more nor less than a repudiation of a part of the Confederate debt. Bad policy is my opinion. When any State or Government begins to repudiate it is getting in a mighty bad way.

I have complied with all the " laws " to-day.

Tuesday, March 29:   I retired very early last night and I arose this morning before day and blacked my boots and came down to the office by the time it was getting light.

I think we will be able to get off to-morrow. I learned yesterday that there were two letters in camp for me which I would like very much to get before leaving town. I was told that they came by mail. If this is the case, I do not know who they can be from as there is no mail communication with Clinton that I am aware of, though they may have been dropped in the office by some one who brought them by hand to this place.

I shall read a few acts in " Hamlet " this morning. Dear old Shakespeare. He is the only companion I have now and I never get tired of reading him.

I received two letters to-day—one from mother dated February

---

[7] Patrick is probably referring to the Act of February 17, 1864. This was a highly complicated law which provided a last desperate measure to reduce the Confederate currency and increase its value. Coulter, *Confederate States of America*, 160–63.

1, and one from Mrs. Montan dated December 16, 1863. I learned from mother's letter that she had sold two hogsheads of sugar to Woulkway at $1.25 per pound, which was entirely too cheap. I hoped that she would keep it until she could do better than that with it, and since the passage of the new currency bill the money is almost worthless.

Woolfolk leaves to-day for Pollard with positive instructions to us to go to-morrow, so we must go *nolens volens.* Well! I care not. It matters little where I go, so it is all one to me. I had as well be at Pollard as Mobile and perhaps better, for it may be more pleasant there than here.

Pollard, Thursday, March 31: At 2 o'clock, I got aboard the steamer " Senator " and left for Pollard. There was nothing of interest which occurred on the route. We arrived at Pollard about 9 o'clock last night. We had all our books and papers along and a considerable amount of Quarter-master's stores. The stores we were compelled to leave at the terminus of the railroad under a guard of which Dave Thompson is the sergeant. I am stopping at the hotel, or rather what purports to be a hotel, kept by a man named Welsh. It is certainly the poorest affair that I ever saw in the way of a tavern. My bed is a poor concern, but of this I do not complain for I am used to sleeping in all sorts of places and I am also accustomed to the hardest kind of fare, but this beats anything I have found yet. On the table we have nothing but bread and meat (fresh pork) both miserably cooked, and the pork without enough salt on it, this with corn-meal coffee without milk or sugar comprises the bill of fare at Mr. Welsh's hotel, for all of which he charges the very moderate sum of twenty dollars per day.

I expected Collins to sleep with me last night, but he did not do so. After I had been asleep a short time last night, some one came in my room and woke me, saying that Mr. Collins intended to sleep with Hamilton and that he (Collins) had sent him to sleep with me. I told him all right, to roll in, which he did. He had not been in bed long before I found out that he had the itch, but as he was already in the bed and had been sent by Collins, I did not say anything, but I did not like the idea of sleeping

with a man who had this lothesome disease. However, there was
no help for it, so I just kept my side of the bed and insisted on
his keeping his side, which he did. I hope that I will not contract
the disease. This morning as soon as I saw Collins, I asked him
why he sent a man to sleep with me who had the itch, and he
replied that the fellow was a liar, that he did not send him there,
that Hamilton had refused to allow him to sleep with him on that
account.

Pollard is a railroad station on the Mobile and Montgomery
Rail Road and is 52 miles from Tensas River which is the
terminus. From Tensas to Mobile, it is 22 miles which is traveled
by steamboat, making the whole distance from Pollard to Mobile
74 miles. This place is high and dry in a pine woods with excellent water. It is rather lonely here, but it will suit me very well
for I do not care much for company and I am well enough satisfied if I can only get enough to eat and a pretty good place to
sleep. I have no mess arrangements made yet and I am stopping
at this miserable hotel on expenses which Woolfolk must pay as I
have no money.

This is a regular March day. The wind has been very high
ever since early morning, though it is not at all cold.

My library now consists of a Bible and Shakespeare and " The
Manual of Phonography " which latter I have not studied any
in the last six months, but which I intend to thoroughly master
this summer if I have time.

I see no indications of a move towards Dalton yet.

Saturday, April 2:   Nothing new going on to-day. I have been
pretty hard at work getting up receipts and making out invoices.

We have some trouble about our cooking arrangements. We
cannot get any one to cook for us. We have a negro woman
cooking for us now, but she says that she cannot cook any longer
than Monday, and I do not know what we are to do as we have no
cooking utensils and even if we had, we have no time to cook.

Yesterday being the first day of April, the place was filled with
women. They are very poor people and the wives and daughters
of soldiers in the army and they came to draw their rations which

149

are issued to them regularly by the Government every 10 days
beginning with the first of each month.

They are about the ugliest set I ever saw, and they are decidedly hard cases. I have been from Dan to Beersheba, but as
little Bloom the dutchman used to say " nevare before did I see
such a ting by Got." The old ones are long, lean, lank, spindle
legged and wiry looking and are so thin that a strong breeze would
apparently blow them over the tops of the tall pines among which
they were born and reared. They have sharp noses and thin lips.
The younger ones are nearly all short, thick set, chubby girls.
Some have sallow, sickly complexions, and look as though they
had lived on craw-fish, terrapins and dirt all their lives. Others
are dark and about the color of a new saddle, with coarse, black,
straight hair which gives them a very ordinary and *niggerly* look.
Their dress is very common indeed, though some of them sported
their Sunday finery. They appeared to be in the depths of ignorance and if " Ignorance is Bliss," then are they truly happy.

I saw nearly 100 of them, but there was not one good-looking
one in the crowd, nor one that was even passable. I saw some
young men, acquaintances, and I suppose, beaus of theirs, walking
about with them and they appeared to be as green as the girls
and matched them first-rate. They walked along with their hands
in their pockets, their old wool hats set jauntily on one side of
their heads and their soiled, dirty pants rolled above their boot
tops, with a bold, defiant sort of a swagger as much as to say
" Now, look at us. Ain't we just the thing? " The girls talked
very loudly and vulgerly to which their companions generally
replied with a horse-laugh. This is a true picture of the citizens
of the backwoods of Alabama.

Wednesday, April 6: The weather is extremely cool for the
season and last night was almost cold enough for frost. I have
12 blankets to sleep upon and I am comfortable enough and I
also have plenty to eat. Louis Allen of our regiment, is in the
brigade Commissary of Cantey's old brigade and as I draw rations
from him, he always gives me as much as I want.

To-day, we commenced on our quarterly returns which I hope
to be able to finish this week.

Friday, April 8: The weather is very unsettled. It rained nearly all day yesterday and last night it poured down in torrents with a great deal of lightning and thunder and a heavy wind. This morning is dark and cloudy and although it is 8 a. m., I can scarcely see to write. There is every prospect of another stormy day and what makes it more disagreeable still, is that it is so cold. We have no chimney to the house that we occupy. Collins curses the weather for five minutes at a time, and hardly takes breath. He says it is time for warm weather, that he has made up his mind to it and by God it ought to turn warm. This way of having wintry weather in the spring doesn't suit him. We are getting clear of our stores very rapidly, which I am very glad of for they are a great trouble.

There is one thing that Woolfolk does which I do not like, and that is, he sells shoes and blankets to the officers' negroes, while the poor private who is fighting for the country goes barefooted and without sufficient covering. I think this is a great wrong and Woolfolk ought to be reported for it. A soldier comes in with his toes sticking out of a pair of bottomless shoes, with a thin threadbare tattered blanket across his shoulders, and says " Major can't I get a pair of shoes and a blanket? " " No sir " is the abrupt and uncivil reply. The soldier says no more but leaves the house. A staff officer comes in.

" Good morning Major Woolfolk, how do you do sir? "

" Good morning Captain. I am very well thank you. Come in."

The Captain comes in, takes a seat and directly he draws out a bottle of whiskey.

" Major, suppose we try a little of this. I brought this with me from Mobile and I think it is much better than the rot-gut they have about here."

Woolfolk, who was never known to refuse a drink helps himself. They talk a while longer and the Captain proposes another drink, and down goes another sockdologer of the " rifle brand." In the meantime a colored gentleman of African *descent*, makes his appearance, and loiters around the door. Finally, Woolfolk, who is pretty " high up " by this time, sees the darkey, and enquires his business. The Captain doesn't give the negro time to reply, but says,

"Oh! that's my boy, Major, and I came round to get a pair of blankets and a pair of those English army shoes for him. Can I get them?"

"Certainly, certainly, Captain. Mr. Patrick give this negro man a pair of blankets and one pair of those best English shoes, and make a memorandum of it against the Captain."

I do so, but at the same time I wish in my soul that I had the physical strength and some one would give me the authority to kick the whole trio out of doors. I would go without my "*grub*" three days, just to kick their posteriors good all around Pollard. Of course the negro is not to blame. It is not his fault, but then like poor Tray he is in damned bad company and ought like him to take the consequences.

I don't like to speak disrespectfully of my *boss* but just at this "petickler moment" I shall spend my opinion, it will not take long nor occupy much space. *He is a damned fool.*

Woolfolk is the poorest business man that I ever had connections with. His returns for the quarter ending 31st of December, are still on hand although I made them out the first thing after I got into the office. I have spoken to him at least a dozen times about it, but he always puts me off by saying that he will attend to it. If he does not send them off during this month, he is liable to be dropped from the rolls, as he only is allowed 4 months in which to make his returns and it is expected that he will send them on within 20 days after the expiration of the quarter. It is now the 4th month and still he shows no signs of doing anything. Well! It is not my fault. I have done my part and if he does not see proper to do so, I cannot help it. His cash is also in a bad condition. He has received large amounts from the Chief Quarter Master which have never been entered upon his books and it is impossible for me to make a balance unless the account had been properly kept. He came down to the office the other morning in a great flurry, saying he wished me to make up the cash as the inspector would be along directly to inspect his books. I told him it was impossible for me to make it up the way it was down on his books.

" Well," said he, " I must make up a statement of some kind."

I told him that I could force a balance of some kind that would probably do to get clear of the inspector for the present, but it would not do to send the returns on in such a manner. He told me to make up anything that would do to get rid of the inspector, so accordingly, I forced a balance on the books and made a false entry, which, if it was known, is enough to cashier him. I handed him over the statement, but as the inspector was taken sick his books have not been examined yet. He hates to talk about business and it is almost impossible to keep him to the point for 5 minutes at a time. He does not come about the office for days and days and knows nothing about what is going on in the department. Everything is perfect straight, though, except that cash arrangement.

I have been patiently, or rather impatiently awaiting Hunter's return, but he has not come yet that I am aware of. I expect some letters and a few articles of clothing by him when he comes.

Tuesday, April 12: Weather again cloudy, with strong indications of another disagreeable wet spell. [William E.] Baldwin's Brigade is leaving for Selma, Ala. A portion of them left yesterday and there is still a large number awaiting transportation. I suppose they will get off some time today. There is a great deficiency of rolling stock upon this road and transporting troops is a very slow business, and from the number of accidents that occur it seems to be a very dangerous one. Their rolling stock is so limited, and the demand for them so great that they are compelled to keep the same cars running all the time, and when they get out of order they do not take time to repair them, but continue running them until something gives way and then a number of lives are lost.

There was a grand review of the troops this morning by Major Gen. [Dabney H.] Maury, which betokens a move, but this is the only indication I have seen as yet. If we are ordered away I would prefer going to Virginia to any other place. Anything is better than the Army of Tennessee. I am disgusted with that.

Collins and I have changed our "boarding house" again. We are messing with Allain of my Regiment and a young man named Worthy, both very clever fellows and both in the Commissary Dept. We have employed a white woman, who lives with her husband in a little shanty hard by, to cook for us. This we find much nicer and better than the negro cook. And besides this the white woman takes care of our rations, while the negro stole them all.

When I went to breakfast yesterday morning I heard one crying as though in mortal agony, and on looking out I saw a negro woman, near the door of a little cabin not far away, and she seemed to be in great distress. I asked my landlady what the matter was. She said the woman had lost her baby only a few minutes before. She fell upon her face upon the earth and bewailed her lot most frankly. I never saw anything like it. Collins remarked that if she belonged to him, that he would punish her for making such demonstrations of grief. I observed that the love of offspring was apparent in both man and brute; that it was implanted there by the Almighty and the poor negro felt her loss as severly as would the Queen of England had she lost one of her children.

Wednesday, April 13: All of Baldwin's Brigade got off this morning. There is nothing new that I can hear of. Gold is quoted at 171 in New York. This gold question will whip the Yankees yet, according to my way of thinking.

We are very busy making up the quarterly returns now and we hope to be through this week.

There is the most glorious news from Tennessee. Forrest has taken Memphis with about $2,000,000.00 worth of stores and two thousand prisoners and has telegraphed to Mobile for room for his prisoners. This has not been confirmed yet and it may be all a hoax.[8]

Thursday, April 14: Nothing but rain, rain, rain to-day and a

---

[8] Once again Patrick's information was in error. A part of Forrest's command had captured Fort Pillow, on the Mississippi River, forty miles above Memphis, and not Memphis itself.

very cold rain it is. The weather is more like December than April.

I put myself to some trouble last night to purchase a paper in order to see what the news from Memphis was, but to my disappointment, there was nothing in the paper in regard to it and so I have come to the conclusion that it is all a humbug.

Friday, April 15: Gold in New York is 173½. This gold question will certainly prove the down-fall of the Yankees.[9]

Colonel Hunter has returned and I have received letters from mother and Sis with dates of the 6th inst. Sis advises me not to join the cavalry. Mother sent me one pair of pants, three colored shirts and one white one, one silk handkerchief and three or four white ones, three pair of cotton socks.

I received a letter from Bill Knox this morning saying that my clothing would not be along until Jim Marchant arrived, which would probably be some time yet, as Hunter has extended his furlough 15 days on condition that he would bring everything along that was to come to the regiment. So it will probably be some time before I receive them. Bill states in his letter that Judge Smith has fined William Gurney $10,000.00 and three months imprisonment and Dominique Zimmerman $5,000.00 and three months imprisonment for making whiskey.

Mother sent me by Hunter, $20.00 in Georgia bank money. This I have not received yet and it is still in Hunter's possession. Yesterday, I wrote to Tom Fiester to get it from Hunter, sell it on the best terms possible and hand the proceeds over to John Bradford to be credited on a due-bill that he holds of mine for $280.00. I do not know how I am to pay John this amount, but I think that I can extinguish it before a great while in some way.

Sunday, April 17: After I had been in bed a while last night some one came to the window of my room and rattled the glass. I asked who was there. "Old Simon Buckhart," was the reply. It was Wallace Matthews who had come over from Mobile as a guard over some ordinance stores. I opened the door and let him in. He brought a newspaper which contained the news of

---

[9] The gold fluctuations produced a complex of problems for the North. This point is discussed in Randall, *The Civil War and Reconstruction*, 452–55.

the capture of Fort Pillow by General [James R.] Chalmers, etc. I desired him to remain until the next trip of the cars, but he said he could not do it, that he was bound to return that night.

He told me that Colonel [William F.] Pennington kicked up the devil in Mobile while on a spree. He started out to camp in the Dauphin Street car and acted so badly that the conductor tried to put him out, but did not succeed. This made Pennington very angry and when he arrived at camp, he had a guard detailed under a sergeant with orders to go down and arrest every conductor they could find and bring them before him immediately. The guard went down and found that the conductors had got wind of it and had sent some boys in their places, so the guard returned and reported accordingly. This is a pretty way for a man in command to act.[10]

I wrote a long letter to Hunter to-day. I hear it rumored that the 29th Alabama has been ordered to Mobile. The 21st went yesterday. I would like to know what in the devil they mean by sending the troops back and forth in that way.

Gold is 175¾ in New York. It continues to rise and I hope it will keep on. That is the thing to whip them. I prophesy peace in less than 12 months.

Wednesday, April 20: Our brigade has to move away in a day or two. From what I can learn it is to Dalton they are ordered.

8 p. m. The 29th and 17th Alabama Regiments are in front of the office, near the railroad, awaiting transportation by the road.

I have been hard at work all day long, trying to make up the quarterly returns. We have prevailed upon Woolfolk to consent that we should send off the returns for the 4th quarter of '63 and we will mail them to-morrow. He stuck his name to them, but he hasn't the most distant idea what their contents are. A nice man truly to fill so important a position as Brigade or Division Quartermaster.

Thursday, April 21: I have been lucky enough to borrow a copy of Byron from a young man in the provost marshal's office.

---

[10] This was only one of many such episodes involving Pennington. Only a few months earlier he had survived a duel fought with the terrible navy 6's at ten paces. Kendall, "Recollections of a Confederate Officer," *loc. cit.,* 1148–49.

It has been so long since I have read Byron that it is almost new again. I have read nearly the whole of Shakespeare again. I never get tired of glorious old Shakespeare. I wish that I had a copy of Moore. I had one but I loaned it to a young lady who was kind enough never to return it to me. I told Matthews to try to get it, which he said he would do. I think it is a mean thing to borrow a book and not return it, although I obtained my Shakespeare that way, though I did not intend to commit a theft. At Enterprise, Mississippi, the book was boxed up and sent away with the regimental baggage before I knew anything about it. I was absent from camp and Jim Blow had the book boxed up along with our mess arrangements, and stowed away on the train where it was impossible for me to get at it. It was in this manner that I stole the book and I still have possession of it. I know it is of more use to me than it is to the owner because he can procure another, and has other books to read besides, while I have not these advantages and this single volume is a whole library to me.

The left wing of the 29th Alabama is still here and is to leave to-night or in the morning. Cantey's Brigade is to go to Atlanta and there await orders, so it is not absolutely certain that they will go to Dalton.

Friday, April 22:   When we went to breakfast this morning, there were two girls at old Mrs. Sowell's (our boarding house) and after conversing with them a while Collins and I got to kissing them, which seemed to correspond with their feelings, and we were getting along finely when suddenly a voice cried out " God damn you, stop that. Are you going to make a whore house of my place? " On looking round who should it be but old Sowell, who had thus suddenly put a stop to our amusement.

I intended to pay no attention to what he said, but to go on about my business, and started away. Collins got very angry however and went to where the old man was, and cursed and abused him considerably. As might have been expected this made the old stud very wrathy. The upshot of this business was that before dinner time that day the old lady, Mrs. Sowell, sent a messenger requesting me to inform Mr. Collins that he couldn't come into the house any more, but that it was all right with the balance of us. The messenger said that she would cook for me as long [as] I wished her to, that I was worth all the others put together. I went up and had a talk with Sowell about the matter, and endeavored to talk him into a good humor, but the old sinner wouldn't hear to peace on any terms, so far as Collins was concerned. I then spoke to the old lady about it. She said she didn't care anything about the matter, only the old man said that if Collins came to the house any more he (Sowell) would drive her away. She remarked that he was an old fool and a brute in the bargain. She consented that we should bring Collins' meals to him, and thus the matter stands now.

Later. The old heathen swears that his wife shall not cook for any of us, and this has busted up our cooking arrangements once more. Damn the luck I say. I haven't time to cook or I would do it myself. However we will be off in a short time and we can get along some way until we leave.

"*Johnston is in full retreat*"

CHAPTER VI. APRIL, 1864–JULY, 1864

Pollard, Alabama, Saturday, April 23, 1864: We leave for Dalton, Geo. in the morning, so that Sowell and Co. may go to the devil.[1] All the troops have gone except Gen. Cantey and staff and as I am an attache of the staff I am still behind.

Sunday, April 24: Left Pollard this morning about ten o'clock. We had a very pleasant trip from Pollard to Montgomery, and arrived here about 5 p. m. Allain and Worthy told me before we left Pollard that it would be unnecessary for me to carry any cooked rations along because they had plenty to do us all. Acting upon this advice I came away without any, and I find now that they have nothing at all to eat. Worthy and I went around to hire some one to cook our rations for us, but we failed in this. We managed to borrow a pot at last and we cooked some meat.

Monday, April 25: I went up town this morning and bought some bread, for which I paid the sum of two dollars per loaf and they were very small loaves at that.

It costs a sight of Confederate money to live these days, and I do not see how poor people subsist.

Tuesday, April 26: All day I have been annoyed endeavoring to store some Quartermasters stores, that we wish to deposite here until we can send for them, because we have not sufficient transportation to take them along with us. Woolfolk knows nothing about business and he is in my way. If I were rid of him

---

[1] Patrick's command had been ordered back to Dalton to reinforce Johnston and the Army of Tennessee.

and clothed with the proper authority I could get along much better. To make the matter worse, he is stupidly drunk all the time, and even if he had the capacity his unsteady habits would render him entirely unfit for business. Unsteady habits, I say? Well, I will take that back. He is the most regular man in his habits that I ever saw. *He gets drunk every day regularly.* Nothing could be more systematic than his drunkeness.

Arrived at West Point at 7 a. m. having left Montgomery about 10 p. m. I was in company with the Brigade Commissary and we carried our stores along in the same car. He had about twenty barrels of flour along and a large quantity of sugar, besides meat and other things. During the night we were awakened by the brakeman, who said that we must get up and remove the freight from the centre of the car where we had stowed it, to the ends. He said that the weight must all be over the wheels, otherwise the car was liable to break in two, or be thrown from the track. When I got up I noticed that the car was swinging terribly, from side to side, caused by our rapid motion. We were going at great speed because we were behind time. We moved the freight as directed, and soon settled down to sleep again, and reached West Point without an accident.

Wednesday, April 27: Left West Point at 6:30 a. m. this morning and arrived at Atlanta at 5 p. m. with everything safe. We had a very pleasant trip to-day. Remained all night at Atlanta.

Thursday, April 28: Left Atlanta at 2 p. m. Have our baggage car attached on to the engine of the passenger train and arrived at Kingston a little before dark. We left Kingston at 9 p. m. and arrived at Rome about 11:30 p. m. I slept in the cars all night. I have slept in the cars every night since I have left Pollard and on the whole of this trip, I have felt very well, much better, in fact, than I have on any other similar trips.

Rome, Georgia, Friday, April 29: Woolfolk had everything moved over to camp today and had the tents pitched. Although he can procure a good house that is vacant and stands within a hundred yards of us, yet he will not do so, but prefers sleeping in the dirt like a hog. I suggested to him the propriety of taking the house but he would not hear to it. He says he is soldiering now and he must sleep on the ground. He is a bigger fool than Thompson's colt, and it is said that he swam the river to get a drink of water, and afterwards ran himself to death attempting to leave his shadow behind him.

Thursday, May 5: On the 3rd, we had a heavy frost, though the weather is quite pleasant to-day.

Woolfolk was so beastly drunk the other day and yesterday, he could hardly walk. He is very cross and peevish and makes himself very disagreeable.

We have orders to march and I suppose that we will be off in the course of a few hours.

Between Rome and Calhoun in General Cantey's buggy. Left Rome at about 1 o'clock and made only about 5 or 6 miles on account of the wagon broke down and stalling.

Woolfolk was very drunk to-day and was very insulting in his language to me. I expect to leave him the first opportunity.

We went into camp about 5 miles from Rome. I am writing in General Cantey's buggy and Allain has been with me nearly all the way assisting me to unharness and feed the horses. Our camp was near a church and reminded me very much of Hepsibah Church at home.

Friday, May 6: Between Calhoun and Resaca. I arose this morning about daylight and fed the horses. We reached Calhoun about 12 Noon and halted to rest and feed the teams about a mile beyond the town of Calhoun. There are any amount of springs all along this road. Arrived at Resaca about 3 p. m.

Resaca, Saturday, May 7: Last night I slept on top of a hill in an open field, and this morning I found myself quite wet with the cold dew. When I am exposed to the dew it generally makes me feel very unwell and causes me to look very pale. As long as I can get a tree or bush to sleep under I do very well, but somehow I cannot stand the dew. Woolfolk is sober today for a wonder, I suppose he cannot get any liquor.

Resaca is only about fifteen miles south of Dalton, and is a Rail Road Station. I heard heavy firing towards Dalton today and a fight is momentarily expected.[2] We have orders to move again and our baggage has been reduced to feather-weight.

I visited a spring a little while ago, near the banks of the Oostanaula River which runs close to the town. This spring is in a cave of solid rock, some twenty feet deep, and the water is very cool indeed.

I dreamt last night that I was married to a young lady that I never saw before and although the ceremony had been performed yet I was totally ignorant of her name. As she was in the company of several of her relatives and friends, I did not wish it be known that I had married a young lady whose name I was ignorant of. I would not ask what it was in the presence of others and the consequence was that I never did find out because I awoke before I had an opportunity of asking her privately what it was.

Sunday, May 8: We are kept in readiness to march, though we are still in the same place. Woolfolk has a clerk, or a nominal clerk whose name is Daniels—J. B. Daniels. He is from Columbus, Ga. where he was a merchant of some repute, in the clothing business. He is a middle aged man, tall, fine looking, and wears flowing side whiskers after the English fashion. He does no work for he doesn't know how, and is always in my way. He is very fond of whiskey and when he gets a few drinks of whiskey in him, he calls himself the " great one price emporium," which was the advertising heading of his mercantile establishment. As for the good he does Woolfolk or anyone else he had as well be at home. He is fractious and contentious to the last degree, and take him altogether he is a great annoyance, for he not only will not do anything himself but he is always calling upon some one else to wait upon him. He called upon me, not seeing any one else to call, to bring along his heavy valise. I told him just to allow it to remain where it was until I brought it, and off I went. He was very indignant, but I cared nothing for his indignation.

Monday, May 9: Last night as I was sitting by the camp fire

---

[2] On May 5, 1864, General Sherman moved out from his fortified position near Rocky Face Ridge, Ga., as the opening maneuver of the Atlanta campaign. His mission was to attack and destroy Joe Johnston's Army of Tennessee and to capture Atlanta, the great nerve center of Southern communications. Horn, *Army of Tennessee*, 322 ff.; *Battles and Leaders*, IV, 247-344.

before my tent, a scout rode up and getting off his horse, stood by the fire. He said the enemy were only about five miles distant, in large force coming through Snake Creek gap, and that he had come in to report the fact to Gen. Cantey the commanding officer. Cantey in my opinion is a poor dependence for a commander. This morning a brigade of cavalry came into the town. The General enquired who was in command here. The answer was, Gen. Cantey. " Well " said he " he is a damned poor General. I have come in with my whole force, and neither he nor any of his troops were aware of it until I was in their midst." This was so—they had come right in upon us, and they had never been challenged because old Cantey had not thrown out a single picket. I would have known better than that myself. Here the enemy are, liable to come in upon us at any moment, and no watch kept to give us warning.

About breakfast time, firing began to be heard about three miles west of the town. This afternoon the enemy's advance troops came up close to the town, having driven in our pickets, and engaged our troops pretty smartly. Later in the day they came in much closer, but were driven back by our forces. Our artillery opened upon them pretty brisk. They charged our lines twice, but failed to make any impression. Loss slight.

Tuesday, May 10: No firing up to 12 M. to-day. Loring's [William W.] Division will be here from Rome to-day, and we have received some troops from Dalton, which will make our force about eight thousand men. Enough I suppose to check the enemy for the present. There are two gaps near this place, one of which only was guarded, and the enemy made their approach through the unguarded one. It certainly was a great oversight in not placing a strong guard at both those points. They are now very near the Railroad and have already cut the telegraph lines between this place and Dalton. Their force is estimated at 10,000, but if they are not right sharp we will capture the whole of them.

The news from Virginia is that we have captured two Major Generals and other commands.[3] We have whipped them terribly

[3] Battle of the Wilderness fought in northern Virginia, May 5–7, 1864. The victory spoken of by Patrick was of little significance. Gen. John B. Gordon attacked the

in eastern Louisiana and captured a great number of prisoners.[4]

Wednesday, May 11: The sky is overcast and very threatening. I transferred a lot of clothing to Reynold's [Daniel H.] Brig. today.

Everything is stripped for the fight and the hills and knobs overlooking the town, on which we have batteries of heavy ordnance, are covered with troops. The infantry is in line of battle, the artillery horses are harnessed to the guns and caisons and some of the men are lounging about, others are leaning against the pieces and sitting upon the caisons. The artillery drivers are standing listlessly beside their trusty horses with one arm slung over the saddle, ready to mount at the word. Everything is as still as a churchyard, but all hands are wide awake and ready to open the ball.

Generals Cantey, Vaughan, Martin, Grigsby, Hood and Polk [5] are together upon their horses, upon a rising ground, evidently very calmly surveying the scene of the expected conflict. Couriers are galloping from point to point along the line, bearing dispatches. Upon an eminence to the right, the men are working hard, throwing up an embankment, behind which to plant a battery I suppose, as the horses are being unharnessed from the pieces. There is evidently a heavy thing on hand, for the troops are pouring in from Dalton. The enemy's force is estimated at 150,000 with a large amount of artillery.

An old lady came in yesterday reporting that the enemy were at her house, some three miles distant, with five hundred thousand men and seven hundred pieces of artillery down in her orchard. Bully for the old lady. I would like to know her estimate of our forces. Last night as I walked up to my campfire, a green fellow, who had never heard the roar of a gun, until now, enquired of me the news. I repeated the old woman's story as being the latest

---

Union right flank late in the day on May 6. The movement was of little consequence but two Federal brigadiers—Truman Seymour and Alexander Shaler—were captured.

  [4] Although the action took place in western Louisiana, Patrick was obviously referring to the defeat of Bank's Red River expedition at Mansfield and Pleasant Hill.

  [5] Brigadier General James Cantey, Brigadier General Alfred J. Vaughan, Jr., Major General William H. Martin, Brigadier General J. Warren Grigsby, Lieutenant General John B. Hood, Lieutenant General Leonidas Polk.

intelligence from the enemy's lines. His eyes grew as large as saucers.

" The geewhillikens " said he " we can't fight all 'o them; why Mister hain't the whole face 'o the yeath, kivered with 'em? I *allus* said old Cantey would git us into jist such a scrape as this, the durned old fool. But then he ain't a keerin,' *he's* all right, he'll keep oute'n the way, I'll bet on that and I fur one says, git up and git, while times is good."

Last night was a terrible night indeed. The wind blew almost a hurricane and the rain poured down in torrents and I thought that the covering of the wagon in which I was would certainly be blown off. This afternoon was very cold and it feels like it would frost before morning.

Thursday, May 12: We were ordered farther down the road yesterday. The fighting along the front is going on pretty brisk to-day. I consider Gen. Johnston the best General in the Confederacy, not even excepting Robt. E. Lee, but this is one time that old Sherman came near over-reaching him. I will always consider it a mere chance if he gets well away from Resaca.

I broke through my resolutions yesterday and got drunk, but I shall not do so again soon.

The whole of Johnston's army is here and so is the Yankee's forces. I said more than a week ago that the fight would be transferred to this place instead of Dalton.

Saturday, May 14: The fighting has been raging all day long and has been the fiercest of any day yet. Nothing particularly gained by either side.[6]

We are encamped about 2 miles from Resaca with our train.

Adairsville,[7] *Sunday, May 15, 10 a. m.:* Left our camp near

---

[6] The battle of Resaca was fought May 13–15, 1864. Initial Union attacks on Confederate entrenchments were repulsed. On the 15th, however, word reached Johnston that other Union troops were crossing the Oostanaula on pontoon bridges below Resaca. Endangered by this flanking movement, Johnston's forces fell back across the Oostanaula, destroyed their bridges and retreated back toward Calhoun. *Battles and Leaders,* IV, 263-66.

[7] After leaving Resaca, Johnston had hoped to find a favorable position near Calhoun, but there was none available. After resting for a few hours, the command moved on eight miles to Adairsville early in the morning of the 17th. Patrick, traveling with the supply train, had already arrived in Adairsville two days earlier. On the 17th a

165

Resaca about 2 o'clock this morning and Captain Gardner, who was slightly wounded in the leg, came over in the buggy with me to this place and has taken the cars for some place below.

Heavy firing and fighting is going on at Resaca. I left the train and drove on ahead to this place. It begins to look a little like a retreat, though nothing but the wagon train have left yet. I waited at this place until nearly sundown for the wagon train before it came along.

Kingston,[8] *Tuesday, May 17:* Yesterday evening, we camped about 2 miles this side of Adairsville. The reason why the train did not come on as it should, was because Woolfolk was lying in the house drunk and asleep and would not get up although two couriers had arrived with orders for him to move. I am getting more and more dissatisfied with him every day. He has not any any sense worth talking about when he is sober and when he is drunk, this little amount leaves him. He is the poorest apology for a quarter-master, or as I may say, for a man that I ever saw.

The prospects are very gloomy for us at present. Our forces have fallen back across the Oostanaula River and a great many of the men had to jump in and swim the river to prevent being captured. The enemy has taken our batteries on the hills with the guns there-on and have doubtless captured a large number of small arms and a considerable quantity of stores. This looks very bad for our side, but as there are so many rumors, I cannot place much confidence in what I hear, though I have not the slightest doubt that Johnston is retreating.

The troops have certainly seen a very hard time of it, lying in the entrenchments for nearly a week without rest. If ever a people ought to be independent, I think that we ought.

I think that I shall go to the creek and take a wash. I have not put on any clean clothing for about 3 weeks and I think it is time that I was doing so.

The wagon train has been passing ever since 12 noon and it is

---

sharp skirmish was fought which checked the pursuit for a short time. *Ibid.,* 266-68; Horn, *Army of Tennessee,* 326-27.

[8] Johnston's troops moved down the Western and Atlantic R. R. and passed through Kingston. A line of battle was formed near Cassville with their backs to the Etowah River. *Ibid.,* 327-28.

now 5 p. m. and still they come. Johnston is in full retreat and there is no doubt that we have received a good thrashing from the Yankees. I suppose that our train will be ordered away to-morrow morning or maybe before. I am under the impression that we will not stop short of Atlanta, if we are lucky enough to get there.

I took a good bath in a stream close by and put on some clean clothes which has made me feel a great deal better. There is one of the boldest springs here that I ever saw. It gushes out of the solid rock as thick as my body. I would like very much to send 'a little home but it is impossible just now.

Wednesday, May 18: We were ordered up early this morning to be ready to march. This was not unexpected to me for in fact I expected to hear this during the night. We left Kingston about 9 o'clock this morning with an immense wagon train ahead of us.

I have marched about 24 miles to-day. From Kingston we went to Cartersville and then to this place. I stood the march pretty well and I could have gone 5 or 6 miles farther if it had been necessary. The only inconvenience I found was that my feet became a little sore. If I can only keep my health.

Johnston is in full retreat and this is the second retreat I have been on with him. The thing is not through with yet and they had better mind how they fool with him for they are getting a long ways from their boats with a good army and a cautious man in front of them.

Thursday, May 19: We have not moved camp, though wagons have been passing all day.

I wrote a short letter home to Sis to-day. I made my first attempt at washing a shirt to-day. I washed two but as they are not dry yet, I do not know how they will look.

Camped at the Allatoona hills.[9]

---

[9] Johnston had planned to make a stand near Cassville but with two of his commanders urging abandonment of the position he decided to continue the retreat. On May 20, the Confederate troops passed the Etowah River, abandoning strong fortifications protecting the bridges across the river. Johnston then moved his forces into the broken Allatoona heights to the south of that stream. On the 23rd Sherman's army crossed the Etowah at Stilesboro, below and to the west of Johnston's position. The Confederate Corps moved in front of the Union forces and on May 25, 26, 27, a

Big Shanty, Saturday, May 21: We arrived at this place about 1 p. m. to-day. I have walked about 8 miles to-day. Yesterday we encamped at Allatoona which is about 8 miles above this.

Weather warm and roads dusty though good water is plentiful.

Two of Cantey's staff now ride in his buggy and I am knocked out of the ring entirely. It beats anything I ever heard of, that aides-de-camp should be in the rear of the army. These have been with the wagon train all the time, endeavoring to protect their precious carcasses from the deadly missels of the enemy.

They talk about the ravages of the enemy in their marches through the country, but I do not think that the Yankees are any 'worse than our own army. This morning when the train was passing the house of a farmer a lady gave to the men all the milk, butter and butter-milk she had. They were not satisfied with this. They took all the chickens she had, robbed all the nests they could find, went to the stables and took all the fodder and not content with this, pulled down the fences and turned their horses in upon the fields of wheat. I am sorry to say this has been the case all along the road by our army. I saw some beautiful fields all wantonly destroyed. The husband of the lady above mentioned is in the army and as a matter of course, was away from home. War is a terrible thing. Our whole force is south of the Etowah River and we have destroyed the railroad bridges and the enemy are still in pursuit. Nothing new from the front to-day.

Sunday, May 22: All quiet in camp. Lying on our oars. This country affords fine water in abundance. The whole country is covered with pennyroyal. On the hills and in the valleys, in the fields and in the woods, in the shade and in the sunshine, the ubiquitous pennyroyal may be seen. The ground all in and about our camp is strewn with isinglass.

I have always understood isinglass to be a glutinous substance prepared from the intestines of certain fish. Nevertheless they term this isinglass. But I am no mineralogist nor geologist, there-

---

battle was fought northeast of Dallas at New Hope Church. Both sides lost heavily. Sherman, having left the railroad well to his left, moved back in that direction on June 4. Union troops reached the railroad between Acworth and Allatoona on the 5th. Johnston also moved his forces eastward to get in front of the Union troops and cover the roads leading to Atlanta. *Battles and Leaders,* IV, 269-70.

fore I do not pretend to argue the point. Of one thing I feel satisfied however, and that is, that all this region is rich in mineral productions, and iron ore is abundant everywhere. Sometimes in lifting up a loose stone, I am somewhat astonished to find it nearly as heavy as a cannon ball. I believe that at one time it was believed that gold abounded among these hills, and I have dim recollections of seeing accounts in the newspapers of gold having been discovered in Georgia.

Monday, May 23: We received orders about 11 o'clock to-day to move beyond Chattahoochee River, which is only about 7 miles north of Atlanta. I started off on foot and walked about 11 miles as hard as I could, but when I got 2 miles below Marietta I was forced to take a wagon. It was not the distance that hurt me so much as the pace at which I travelled.

We arrived at the river a little before sun-down and then went on about 4 miles farther before we reached our camping grounds. I did not get in until 10 o'clock. The teams were very much jaded for they had been driven steadily along all day and the weather was warm and they had no food nor water during the whole time. We marched to-day about 26 miles.

Marietta is the prettiest place that I have seen anywhere in my travels and it is a pity that it should fall into the hands of the Yankees. I saw a beautiful lady as I passed along the streets. The whole town was in an uproar and confusion. The bedsteads and mattrasses were placed in the yards of the hospitals ready for shipment. The nurses, among whom I noticed the big white bonnets of the far-famed Sisters of Charity, were fleeing and were packing up the bedding and other paraphernalia of the hospital. Citizens of all ages and sexes were hurrying to and fro; negroes were staggering along under a weight of heavy trunks and boxes; wagons were standing at the doors of the private dwellings, being hastily filled with the personal belongings of the owner; the galleries and doors were filled with a little of everything in the way of house-hold furniture; citizens were standing about in little groups as if undecided what to do; the female portion of the community were at their gates looking anxiously up and down the streets; the railroad was filled with cars and the locomotives

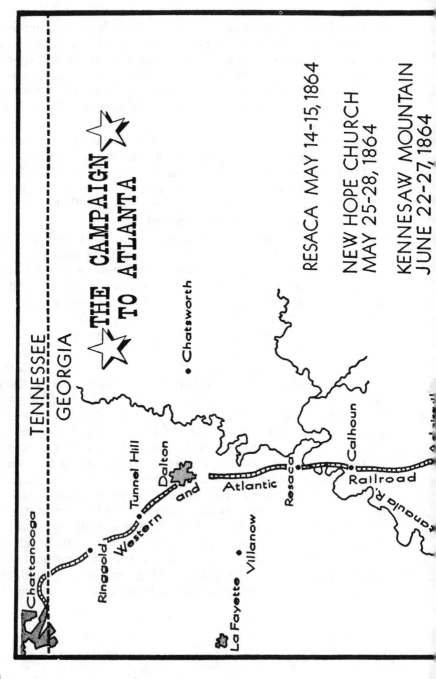

THE CAMPAIGN
TO ATLANTA

RESACA MAY 14-15, 1864

NEW HOPE CHURCH
MAY 25-28, 1864

KENNESAW MOUNTAIN
JUNE 22-27, 1864

TENNESSEE

GEORGIA

Chatsworth

Chattanooga

Ringgold

Tunnel Hill

Dalton

Western and

Atlantic

Resaca

Calhoun

Railroad

La Fayette

Villanow

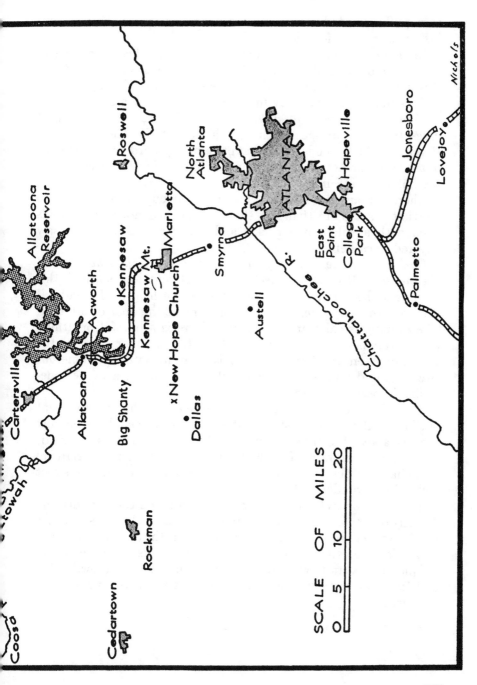

SCALE OF MILES

0   5   10   20

were puffing and shrieking up and down the track. All was confusion, worse, confounded.

Johnston will fall back below the Chattahoochee River where he will doubtless make a stand, because if he ever intends to fight, this is the place for him to do it, or else he must give up Atlanta and its important railroads to the enemy without a struggle.

Camp Wilderness, Tuesday, May 24: We are in camp about 4 miles from the bridge on the south side of the Chattahoochee River in a thick woods. I am having a pretty hard time of it now, but I hope for better times soon. Collins is sick and went off to the hospital on Sunday last.

There are any amounts of ticks and red bugs and it seems to me that I get more than my share of them. I notice the woods filled with a wild honey-suckle and they are red. I never saw any red ones before.

Camped in the woods South of the Chattahoochee River. Wednesday, May 25: I feel rather sad and low spirited this evening and I get so very often and I cannot help it. I wonder if it is so with every one. I am sitting alone at the door of my tent. The evening is calm and beautiful. There is a blissful breathing in the summer air; a placid depth in the summer heaven; the trees are green and lovely; the air is fragrant with the numerous sweet-scented wild flowers; a beauty, a grandeur, a peace indescribable pervades everything.

The wild bee hums by in the gathering twilight and the faint outline of the moon with her attendant stars can be seen just peering above the tree-tops and in the distance across the fields of a neighboring farm, I hear the sharp crow of some patriarchal shanghai; the plaintive lowing of the cattle mixed with the sweet bells of the wandering herd.

There is a brass band along with our train and they are playing " Shells of Ocean " and as the familiar notes of this sweet air are gently wafted in delightful cadences over the woody hills and dewy fields of the quiet forest, numberless visions of home in happier hours and sweet reminiscences of the past crowd thick and fast upon my soul and bring to view a green spot on memory's wide waste.

There is nothing in the world that reminds me more of home than those old familiar airs that I heard when life had brighter appearances than it does at present, and causes me to feel more keenly my present position and to long the more earnestly for peace. But alas! There is no peace for the end is not yet.

> How many moons will rise and wane
> How many months languish
> Ere peace, the white-winged Angel comes
> To sooth the nation's anguish?

But I am getting off on a sentimental strain and I shall dry up.

Thursday, May 26: I received a letter from Sis last night with one from mother also enclosed. From this I learned the following —Benny Wall was killed in the battle on Red River and Wesley Wall, is a prisoner. All of Henry Skipwith's negroes have gone to the Yankees. Boatner Chapman has gone to Virginia to join the Washington Artillery.

We are encamped way off here in the woods where we cannot hear any news. Sis says that it is rumored at home that our regiment is to be sent down there to operate in conjunction with the cavalry.

Saturday, May 28: We are still in the same old camp. There has been a good deal of fighting during the last few days and we have repulsed the enemy.[10] I do not know whether the 4th Regiment is at Mobile yet or not.[11]

Wednesday, June 1: The other day " The Great One Price Emporium " (Daniels) went to Atlanta and brought out a jug of whiskey, and we had a jollification. " The One Price " is very heavy on the drink, and when about half seas over becomes theatrical. I have laughed at him sometimes until my sides ached, although I heartily despise him. He uses, every few minutes,

[10] Patrick is probably referring to the fighting around Dallas at New Hope Church, May 25–28. Although Union troops suffered heavy losses, it could hardly be called a Confederate victory and actually did little to slow down Sherman's advance on Atlanta.

[11] In late May, 1864, the Fourth Louisiana was ordered from Mobile to Marietta, Ga. Arriving on May 25 the men were immediately detrained in order to re-enforce Confederate forces at New Hope Church, where a bitter fight was in progress.

when he is drinking, the latin phrases, " *E Pluribus Unum* " and " *Ad Quantum Sat.* " He sees some one passing by, and calls out " I say stranger, do you belong to the ' E Pluribus Unum ' or the ' Ad Quantum Sat? ' " " If you belong to ' E Pluribus Unum ' come in and take a drink, but if you belong to the ' Ad Quantum Sat,' you don't drink my whiskey."

As a matter of course, if the fellow wants a drink, which is generally the case, he is on the " E Pluribus Unum " side, and accordingly steps in. The " Great One Price Emporium," takes up the jug with the following toast.

" The humble representative of the great ' One Price Emporium,' now offers his congratulations and best wishes, with the kindest regards of the ' E Pluribus Unum ' and the ' Ad Quantum Sat.' " [12]

He passes the jug over and proceeds to quote, with an extremely tragic air, and in a theatrical attitude the following:

" My name is Norval, and on the Grampian hills, my old dad used to feed his sheep, swine and poultry."

He next favors us with a patriotic song in the most discordant, dismal tone imaginable.

> " Hurrah! Hurrah! For Southern rights hurrah.
> We'll hoist on high the bonnie blue flag.
> That bears a single ' E Pluribus Unum! ' By God."

Day before yesterday I mounted a mule and went out in search of something to eat, but I did not meet with much success. I took dinner at the house of a man who bore the extraordinary name of Smith. His wife appeared to be a very nice woman and he was a member of the Presbyterian Church. They gave me for dinner biscuits, fresh butter, butter-milk, syrup made of Georgia cane, which was very good and tasted like our reboiled Louisiana molasses. I had a man along with me and he only charged us both $5.00 for our dinner.

[12] Patrick probably means that if the stranger is an ordinary drinker or desires just one drink, he is of the " E Pluribus Unum " school and is welcome. If, on the other hand, the stranger is the insatiable sort—" Ad Quantum Sat "—and requires a large amount of whiskey to quench his thirst, then he is not welcome since the supply is limited.

174

On my return to camp, I stopped at a house and inquired for almost anything to eat in the way of vegetables, chickens, eggs, etc. The house was full of children of all ages and sizes, but all girls. There were several apparently from 18 to 22, one 14 and another 16 years old. I succeeded in purchasing a dozen eggs for which I paid $5.00.

I saw several young babies and I inquired of the old lady if any of her daughters were married, but she said they were not. " Whose little baby is that? " I asked as one of the younger girls came near me with a child in her arms. " That is my daughter's."

" Why I thought you said just now that your daughters were none of them married."

" They are not married. I have three grandchildren but none of my daughters are married. Can't you see how it is? " she said rather sharply. The light broke in upon me and I became aware that I had unwittingly been treading upon very delicate ground. I told her certainly that I comprehended her, but that she must excuse me for my dullness.

She went on to remark that the country was being ruined, that the war was ruining every one and that her girls were not the only that acted so and that all the girls she knew in this settlement had done just as bad as they. One of the girls aged 14 and the best looking one in the party, I had a notion of paying some little attention to, but before I left I ascertained that every one of them had the itch, and it was not the camp itch which I have seen the soldiers have, but it was the 7-year sort. I concluded that it would be better to forego any pleasure of this kind than it would be to contract this disease.

Last night a little after dark, one of the men came down to my tent saying that there was some one just from the front who wished to see me. I went out immediately to see him and who should it be.but Captain Kilbourne with his negroe Bill. As may be imagined, I was very much surprised to see him for I thought that the regiment was still at Mobile. From him I learned that the whole brigade was at the front, that they had been in a pretty heavy engagement. He showed me a list of the casualties. I do not remember the whole of them for there were some killed and wounded that I was not personally acquainted with. Among the killed was Carl Attler my old mess-mate. Kilbourne is in very bad health and has gone to-day to find some place where he can stay a short time until he recovers.

Last night I was very unwell and my bowels were much deranged though I feel much better to-day.

Thursday, June 2: I am staying in my tent writing and the rain is pouring down. We need rain very much, but I cannot help thinking of our troops that are lying in the trenches without any covering whatever, with only a single blanket to protect them from the damp ground and kept for days without being relieved. Oh, what a life the soldier has. I believe that I am not sufficiently thankful for being kept out of the ranks.

Now, compare my position with a colonel's. I am sitting in my tent protected from the rain. I can lie down and sleep when I feel like it and walk about if I desire it, with little or nothing to do, while he fares no better than the commonest soldier in the ranks. His food is the same; he has no more blankets nor has he any more comforts in any way than the private. It is very true that he holds a more honorable position and receives better pay, but then it requires all that he can make to buy his rations and there is nothing left to purchase his clothing with and he is expected to dress well and to make a decent appearance in society. I know it is a hard struggle with the best of them, and even the Brigade General finds it no easy matter to make both ends meet.

General [William A.] Quarles is delighted with the manner in which our regiment conducts itself in battle and says it is the best regiment in the service. This is high praise, but I think they are worthy of it.

While I have nothing else to-day to do, I think that I shall endeavor to improve myself in Phonography. I can write now much better than I did last year this time—that is, I do not write much better, but I write faster than I did. I would write more after the reporting style, but I am afraid I cannot read it afterwards, and I think it is better to be a little longer at it now, than it is to be bothering my brains to read it in the future.

I sit down sometimes and picture to myself the joys of home

with all its blessings, when I passed my time honorably and profitably. There is one thing I miss more than anything else and that is my music. I had become so attached to my old violin that it had become, as I might say, a part and parcel of myself. I have a fine collection of music at home, if I ever get back home to practice it again.

Sunday, June 5: I have been studying Phonography all day. I have studied more in the last two days than I have yet, and I intend to apply myself to the study of this as long as we remain in this camp, for I have nothing else to do and it may be of some advantage to me here-after. I shall endeavor to write a little more after the reporting style if I never am able to read it.

I would speak more of military affairs, but all that can be read by me afterwards in the papers and books.[13]

Our fare is devilish hard—nothing but corn-meal and the toughest kind of bacon and I am sick and tired of grease, grease, grease. It keeps my thoughts by day and my dreams by night. I have tried half a dozen times to show the negro that is cook for me how to fry some mush, but he is so dull of comprehension that I cannot beat it into his thick head.

I can hear nothing from the front. There has been nothing in the way of a decisive character done yet, though it is to be presumed that something will be done before many more suns rise and set.

Monday, June 6: This day one year ago Clarence Bell and I left home for Johnston's Army, which at that time was on the Big Black, threatening or rather pretending to threaten the rear of Grant's army. I shall ever remember that disastrous campaign and its hardships. The heat and dust were awful. I thought then that twelve months more would bring matters to a close, but there doesn't seem to be much prospect of the war's ending soon. I remember how dispirited the troops were, especially the Tennesseeans. They would not allow the " Bonnie Blue Flag " to be sung

[13] During the greater part of June, Sherman was probing the Confederate lines before Atlanta. The Union forces were established on the railroad at Acworth and Johnston was entrenched just to the south, holding the slopes in front of Kennesaw Mountain. Henry, *Story of the Confederacy*, 384-85.

in their hearing. Curses both loud and deep were hurled against Jeff Davis and the Confederate Gov't.

I see that Ohio has gone for FREMONT as president of Yankeedom.[14] Now I will make a prophesy and time will tell whether or not it will be correct.

I think that there will be no more fighting after June 1 [1865]; that the tale will be told one way or another. In the event that the fighting does not cease by that time, that we will be recognized by France which will be virtually the end of the war and it is a mark of indifference to the Confederacy whether Lincoln is elected or not.

I do not get half enough to eat. I am hungry nearly all the time. Dry corn-bread is bad enough, but I believe it is worse when it is made with grease. As the negro who cooks for us said the other day, " All three of you don't eat as much as a 10 year old boy." No wonder when our stomachs are particularly nauseated.

Wednesday, June 8: The time wears wearily away and the days drag very slowly. I look at it in this way—at the close of every day, I think, well there is so much time gone. I have strong hopes of something turning up in our favor during the preceeding months this fall in the United States during the Presidential canvass. We are just here in camp. I can hear nothing from the front nor anywhere else. But I do not complain and I am particularly satisfied to remain where I am until the whole affair is over which I know cannot be postponed for a great while longer. The only information that I can get is that the Yankees are massing on our right.

I fear the enemy out-number us so far that it will be a difficult matter to whip them, though if we can only force Sherman to fall back, it is equal to a victory for us.

Gulliver's Bill has just returned from the front and informs me that Royal Collins was killed. Poor Royal; he was a good boy and very young to die. He was always kind and obliging and did his

---

[14] On May 31 a group of radicals, who vigorously opposed Lincoln, met in Cleveland and nominated John C. Frémont for the presidency. See Allan Nevins, *Frémont, the West's Greatest Adventurer* (New York, 1928), II, 659 ff.

duty well as a soldier. He was very delicate and was not fit for a soldier and if he had had any business qualifications, he could easily have obtained a detail on a surgeon's certificate, but I do not think that he ever tried to procure a detail. He had no confidence in himself to attempt it.

The enemy is moving to the right of our line and I suppose it will not be long before we hear of a battle. Bill says that the officers at the front told him that the number of the enemy was estimated at 200,000, but I very much doubt this, though there is no doubt that the heavy odds are against us.[15]

Friday, June 10:   This day, one year ago, Clarence Bell and I set out in a wagon from Canton, Mississippi, to join the regiment which was at that time on Big Black River in the rear of Vicksburg. I remember the day very well. It was quite warm and had been raining and the sun coming out afterwards, the steam rose from the earth. We remained all night with some of the 3d Kentucky Regiments which were in camp on the banks of the Big Black, and we rejoined our regiment the next day. There have been many changes since then. Port Hudson has fallen, Vicksburg has fallen and we have lost many prisoners at both places. The enemy has full sway of the Mississippi and nearly all its tributaries, but the Confederacy still holds up its head and presents a bold front. Our memorable order from Big Black to Jackson and thence to Enterprise will long be remembered by me and by all of us that were in it.

I do not feel at all well this morning and in fact, I have been quite unwell for 8 or 10 days. The water affects my health very much and I must find some way to rectify it if possible.

I cannot hear any news from the front other than that the enemy is massing on our right. There was pretty heavy firing yesterday, but what the result was I have not learned.

Kilbourne is trying to obtain a furlough from the Medical Board and he seems very confident of success. I hope he may, for he is not fit for service in the field. He says that he intends

[15] Sherman's army was much closer to 100,000 than 200,000 men. The Union troops outnumbered the Confederates about two to one. *Battles and Leaders,* IV, 281-89.

to obtain a place some-where about home and remain there for the balance of the war.

Yesterday I wrote the following letter to Mr. Lewis though I have not yet sent it off.

In Camp near Atlanta, Georgia
June 9, 1864

Dear Friend,

I have frequently heard it said that there is a wide and beaten road leading to an inhospitable region, where fuel is furnished gratis and a man to stir up the chunks in the bargain, that is paved with the best quality of an article denominated " Good Intentions." My intentions to write have been good, but you know that if I do not turn into a road that is macadamized that I will never reach the place that we all desire to find, therefore, the highway of good intentions is here-by ignored and I leave this beaten track for one covered with rocks of " Practice " and " Execution."

I am now and have been ever since last winter, a clerk in the office of Major Woolfolk, Quartermaster in Cantey's Division. I have got along very well with him, though he is very inattentive to business and drinks to excess. This negligence of his and his dissipated habits will, unless he changes his mode of life, certainly lead to ruin.

I think I hear you exclaim—" He sees the beam in the eye of another, but he does not discern the mote in his own! " But here you are wrong, for I see both, and of the two, the mote is the larger and is to me the most troublesome, and in the future, if I live, I shall use the utmost exertion to eradicate it, and if God is willing with due diligence and watch-fullness, I will prevent its ever obstructing my morals ever again.

I have troubles and petty annoyances too numerous to mention with drunken, uncivil, ungentlemanly officers and ignorant, ill-bred and contentious men, who criticize and pass judgment upon matters of which they are totally ignorant and have not the capacity ever to learn. These are small matters, but you know it is the little things which constitute the sum of a man's exactness.

A soldier's life is that of a slave's, or worse, for he must act as the slave does while at the same time he is possessed of greater sensibility than the slave and his toils and sufferings are not confined to the physical man alone.

I hope this war will close soon, and I have made up my mind that this is the last year of the " Reign of Terror." So fully am I convinced of this, that I am even now making my arrangements for the future, as though it were a foregone conclusion. If I am right, it places me in a better position, and if I am wrong, there is no harm done. You will probably wish to know my reasons for being so sanguine.

Well, I do not know that I can give any really good reason for my opinion. Instead of drawing my conclusions as most persons do, by the slow process of deduction, I have discovered a shorter and easier method, to wit:

I jump at it. Taking for my stepping-stones, the precarious and critical condition of the financial affairs of the North, which, as sure as fate, will come down with a grand crash, and the aspect of political affairs which are very unsettled and are now being stirred up, as the Dutchman says, " mit a stick." I make a jump into the future, land in the middle of the month of January, 1865, and if at that time I do not have in my pocket a document showing that I have been mustered out of the Confederate Service, or that I shortly will be, then am I no prophet nor a son of a prophet.

I have been no nearer Dalton than Resaca, which is 16 miles south of that point. When the enemy first made his appearance at Resaca, there was only one brigade of Cantey's Division, consisting of three regiments and one battery there, though there were some guns placed in batteries on the heights overlooking the town. This force succeeded in checking the Yankees until reinforcements arrived, which by-the-way, did not come a moment too soon, for I verily believe that Johnston barely missed being caught in a bad box, and whatever may be said to the contrary, I shall always think that it was nothing more than sheer good luck and the lack of enterprise on the part of the Yankees that his communication was not cut off. I know that the wires were cut between Dalton and Resaca and all dispatches were sent by couriers.

On Saturday afternoon and Sunday, the hardest fighting occurred, after which we evacuated the place, burning the bridges after us. We lost some guns and a considerable quantity of stores, and some of the men were forced to swim the river (Oostanaula) to escape capture. The order was well made without a doubt, though I am no military man and not capable of criticizing military movements. I have ventured to give you my ideas of what occurred there.

The order has been well conducted through-out and I do not believe that any General except Johnston could have effected it without serious loss. Sherman's plan seems to be to flank us all the time; although Johnston has offered him battle time and again, he invariably declines it, and sets to work at his wire-pulling gun. The two armies are now confronting each other, each maneuvering for a pass. Sherman is massing

181

his men on our right and has planted his troops on the Altoona Mountains. I presume his intention is to form a new base of operation at the Etowah River.

The citizens all along the line of our march had pulled up root and branch, and removed with all their personnel. Folks farther south say that there is not much falling into the hands of the enemy.

The armies are doing nothing now. I say doing nothing for unless there is a heavy fight, we always say there is nothing going on, but there are many killed and wounded every hour, for even if there is no heavy engagement the skirmish is kept up night and day, and the work of death goes on the while like the current of the flowing river, slow and even sometimes, and at others, as rapid as a catarack. There is not a day passes now that many victims are not offered up at the sacred shrine of Southern Liberty and every breeze brings the roar of the artillery.

The morale of the army was never better than it is now and the men are sanguine of success and their confidence in Johnston is undiminished. I will venture to say that if Bragg had conducted this order, that he would now have had a discontented and demoralized army. It has been remarked by everybody that there is less straggling than ever was known before, and every man is at the post assigned him.

I see that General Pemberton has been promoted down hill. He is now in the regiment, a Lieutenant Colonel of Artillery. If they would give the man that never won a battle (Bragg) the same rank and get him out of the way of better men, I think it very probable that our forces would be more prosperous. I did not know until the other day that the 4th Regiment was up here, my impression being that they were still at Mobile. They have been in a pretty heavy engagement and lost between 20 and 30 men.

General Quarles speaks in very high terms of the regiment and says it is the best in the service.

Give my compliments to Mrs. Lewis. When you write, address your letter to the care of Major Woolfolk, Quarter-Master Cantey Brigade, Polks Corps, Atlanta, Georgia.

Your friend,
s/Rob. D. P.

Sunday, June 26: This is Sunday and a gloomy looking day it is too. I am sitting in my tent ruminating over times, matters, and things generally. The day is a rainy one and there seems to be very little prospect of its clearing away before night, so I must make myself contented and while away the slow and cheerless hours as best I can by alternately reading " The Percy Anecdotes," of which I accidently obtained a copy, and writing and thinking, but particularly by vacantly looking out across the dense woods as far as my vision will go by the thick undergrowth.

I have one great annoyance and if I were only rid of that, I think that I could get along first-rate, and that annoyance is one of our clerks named Daniels. He is the most disagreeable man that I ever met in many a long day and I hope that I never will meet just such another. He grumbles and growls all day and night like a bear with a sore head at every one that comes about him, and he considers it the duty of every one around him to discommode himself for his special benefit, and grumbles if it is not done. He expects every one to wait on him and act as a servant to do his bidding at a moment's warning, but I imagine that just about this time of day, he will not order me around for I have given him to understand that I am as good as he, and that I am not one of the kind he has been in the habit of ordering around. He insists upon having the best of everything.

The poor negro Prince, that we have cooking for us, has an awful time, and whenever Prince makes his appearance, it is the signal for a long string of vituperation and abuse. I have heard so much of it that I am particularly disgusted and the negro does not see a moment of peace. He is too mean to talk about. He is forever speaking about " The time he was hurt " (I believe the horse ran away with him and threw him out of the buggy) and wishes to convey the idea that he has been a wonderful man, but that his injuries have affected his intellect, and as he says about 20 times a day, " He is not near the man he was before he was injured." When stumped about anything that gets him in a corner where he cannot well get out, he replies " Well, I knew all these things before I was injured so badly," and if you do not get away, he begins to tell you what an awful time he had while he was sick. He is the most contentious man I ever met and he will take the opposite side of every-thing you say whether you address yourself to him or not. He will always put in his mouth and in order to get rid of his tiresome harang, you must get out of ear-shot. So much for Daniels, the damned old reprobate.

My feelings are very much affected by the weather, and a dark, cloudy, rainy day like the present, generally gives me the blues and brings sad thoughts, and the only way to work it off is to keep my mind employed at something.

I am sitting alone gazing listlessly out upon the dreary prospect, the falling rain-drops, the dripping leaves, and the flying clouds rapidly chasing each other across the darkened heavens. I look back to the events of the past three years. How many changes have come about, how many unhappy days I have spent. I will remember the Presidential election; how eager I was to obtain intelligence as to the probability of Lincoln's being elected, and after it was known that he was elected, how I scanned over the paper to see what would be the probable result upon the southern states; how my worst fears were fully realized. How sad the parting when we left for the army, perhaps never to return. I look back and I can trace my course all the way through in a moment. The noisy, hilarious trip from Port Hudson to New Orleans; the frolics in the city; the smokey, dirty camp at the Military Race Course in New Orleans; the trip from New Orleans to Camp Moore; the work, which was the first I ever did, we had in clearing up the ground for a camp; the weary days passed there in the hot sun, with no protection save our tents; our removal to Biloxi and the time we had there; the time spent at Berwicks Bay; the trip to Jackson, Tennessee and thence to Corinth, the battle of Shiloh; the days spent at Vicksburg, Baton Rouge and Port Hudson, and so on down to the present time.

All this flushes across my memory and I have often wondered how it is that I have come through safely. It is to a Kind Providence that I have indeed and I have cause to be thankful. What will I do after the war? I have asked myself that question a thousand times within the last six months, and I think that it is time to be asking for the war is nearly over now and cannot last longer than this year, and it behooves me to begin to think of what I am to do when peace is declared and I am safe back home. Well, I hardly know what I will do, as everything will have a very different aspect from what it did before and I must adapt myself to circumstances. The great trouble is that I cannot now tell what these circumstances may be.

If I can raise any money, I must go into business of some kind. I have often thought of the grocery trade. I believe that I could make as much at that as I could at anything else by conducting it on a cash practice entirely. I know that no other way will do because I have seen too many men utterly ruined by the credit system. I think that in the course of two years, I could build up a business that would pay me very handsomely and supply me with enough money to supply all my wants, provided everything remains quiet, but this I fear will never be the case. I am fully convinced that no Republic will stand long without internal convulsions that will shake the Government to its very foundation and eventually result in its disintegration and finally its down-fall.

Sometimes I think that Texas would be a good field for operations, but then after our nationality is recognized, that will be the very first place that trouble will spring up again for in my opinion she will sooner or later sever her connections with the Confederacy and set up a concern on her own hook. Though that will be many years hence, but that it will come sooner or later, I am fully convinced. Another argument against removing to Texas is that it will cost so much to sell out everything and start anew, for I cannot get the family as comfortably settled as they are now in Texas without a considerable loss, for as old Ben Franklin use to say, 3 removes are equal to a fire. John Bradford says that he has $5,000.00 deposited in a safe place at home, and when the war is over he proposes to go into business with me. This sum is all in gold and there is no discount on it.

I have resolved never to marry. I intend to live a batchlor all my days and it shall be my special study to render to myself. Sometimes I think perhaps it would be more pleasant to have a good sensible, pretty wife, a rosy cheeked child to greet me when I come home, etc. Then on the other hand there is the responsibility of a family and if anything should go wrong so that I should be pressed for money, it would make me unhappy to think that there were others dependent on me, their wants I probably could not relieve, whereas, if I am alone and anything goes wrong, I may starve or go to the devil and there is no one to suffer but myself. Besides, if a fellow should happen to meet an old friend and get drunk, there would be hell kicked up in the wigwam.

No, I will be a batchlor—that is decided. I will be a grand giantimushia, the great polywampus of my own estate, the " Lord of all I survey " in that concern any-how.

So much I think for my future prospects and matrimonial ideas this rainy Sunday.

Rain, rain, rain. There is plenty of it, but it will make the crops grow. I know that the troops in front are suffering sadly from this weather, though I hope they will not have to endure it much longer.

The infernal Yankees have plenty to eat and that of the best quality, and heavy blankets, and good oil clothes to protect them from the weather. Not so with our men. If they have one blanket they are lucky and oil clothing is rarely ever seen except in the possession of some officer.

Tuesday, June 28: Nothing new. Gen. Cantey and Maj. Wool-folk came into camp to-day. The General seems to be in very bad health.

Wednesday, June 29: Woolfolk and the Gen enquired of me the reason why Daniels and I couldn't get along any better, and I explained to them how Daniels acted. I told them that only a few mornings before, Daniels had thrown all my clothing down upon the wet ground in order to hang his own in place of it, and that I had used some pretty sharp words about it, and that was the reason he had laid in a complaint against me.

" Damn it " said the General " you are as good as he is. If he does such a thing again, throw his clothing out of the tent, and kick him out after them. I'll stand up for you."

When they first mentioned the matter and told me that Daniels had been complaining of me it made me very angry, because he was the transgressor and I was the injured party, and if any complaint were made, I was the proper one to make it. When the General spoke to me about it, I remarked " I'll be damned if I will be any man's servant, and if either of you expect me to knock under to such a man as Daniels, you will be disappointed, for I certainly shall not do it." This remark of mine lead the General to make the one quoted above. I wouldn't have made use of an oath before the General, but my temper got the better of my politeness.

Saturday, July 2:   I am very unwell this morning and scarcely able to get about. The artillery commences at dawn and never ceases until dark. The weather is fair and hot.

"We can't run much further"

Sunday, July 3: We were ordered about 3 p. m. yesterday to fall back south of the Chattahoochee River. Another fall back. I must acknowledge that it begins to look a little squally for our side.[1]

I have had no rations issued to me yesterday or to-day. Charley Redding who is acting Q. M. Segt. went on ahead of the train, on his horse, instead of remaining with it to see how it got along.

We didn't reach the bridge over the Chattahoochee until after dark. This bridge is a very long one. It was impossible to see anything ahead of us, and when we were about half way across we met two other teams on the bridge. As their wagons were empty I insisted upon their unharnessing and backing their wagons off by hand. We had great difficulty in passing them after we got them off, because the road was very narrow and on one side there was a perpendicular wall of rock, and on the other a precipice which overhung the river. We managed finally to pass them, but it was a tight squeese and a very tickelish operation. We went into camp about a mile from the river. I felt very much fatigued pulling at the wagons, endeavoring to get them off the bridge.

---

[1] On June 27 Sherman made a frontal assault on the Confederate position at Kennesaw Mountain only to be repulsed. Not to be stopped, once again the Union troops swung to the right in a flanking movement. With his flank threatened and the bridges across the Chattahoochee protected by slight forces, there was little for Johnston to do but fall back again, cross the Chattahoochee, and move into the hastily built entrenchments around Atlanta. Horn, *Army of Tennessee*, 337-40.

Monday, July 4:   As I had nothing to eat yesterday I feel very hungry today. Jno Richart and I walked down to a farmer's house near by, to see what prospects there were of obtaining a small quantity of that useful and necessary article, poetically denominated " grub." We saw a little girl in the yard and John asked her if we could buy anything to eat. She said we could if we had gold or silver, but her ma wouldn't take paper money. John went into the house and enquired for a little of the article mentioned in the poetical works. The lady of the house piously informed him that this was Sunday; that she had been reading that good book—holding up a bible—and that she couldn't think for a moment of desecrating the holy sabbath, by selling anything whatever, at the same time recommending to get his bible and peruse it attentively.

John whose patience was exhausted—for where is the hungry man whose patience is *not* soon exhausted—answered abruptly.

" Don't talk to me about Sunday and the bible. I'm half starved, and reading the bible will not fill my belly, and even if I should read it, I would not understand anything I read, because I would be thinking about something to eat all the time."

" Well you can't get anything here to-day " replied the old lady " come another day and I will accomodate you," and she closed the door in his face.

I went to a well in the yard to wash my face and hands, and while I was performing my ablutions John went round towards the kitchen on an exploring expedition. He returned after awhile with the intelligence that he had got on the good side of the cook, and that we would have something to eat presently. This was good news. We accordingly waited at the well until the cook informed us that our breakfast was ready, and we went into the kitchen.

Just at this time occurred a piece of the coolest impudence that I ever saw. Just before we sat a large, rough looking, red whiskered man came in, and when we seated ourselves at the table he took a seat also. He pitched into the bread and meat which was all we had, and a very little at that, and after eating the greater part in a very hasty and voracious manner, suddenly rose and left the house. When we came to settle for our breakfast the woman wanted us to pay for this red whiskered fellow, but this we wouldn't begin to do.

I call this full blooded impudence. The whole affair was so sudden that neither I nor John fully understood the thing until the scoundrel was gone, for we were under the impression that he had also spoken for breakfast, and that for the sake of convenience it was placed upon the table at the same time with ours. John and I acknowledged that we were sold and at first we were inclined to follow the fellow up and expose him to the first crowd we could find him in, but we finally came to the conclusion that it wasn't worth the trouble. We afterwards considered it a good joke and had a good hearty laugh when we recalled little by little his curious manoeuvres in endeavoring to make the thing pass off all right while he was at the table, until he could get away.

Firing heavy. Sometimes when I sit down to make an entry in my journal in shorthand, a crowd of greenhorns will crowd around me to have a peep at that " curus riten." It is very annoying to me. A fellow came up just now, a man that I never saw before, shoved himself right in upon me, asking very abruptly " What in the devil is that? " " Phonography " I answered.

" Is it writing? " " Yes."

" Where did you learn it? " " From a book."

" How long will it take you to *learn* me? "

" About twenty five or thirty years."

When I wish to write, I like to be alone and these fellows are impudent and troublesome. I was not aware that there was so much ignorance in the South until I came into the army. Here I am thrown amongst all classes. There is a considerable number around me now, asking questions, and not one of them has even so much as heard of Phonography. They didn't know there was such a thing as short hand writing. There are a great many officers who hold high positions in our army, who are wofully deficient in the commonest English branches, and sometimes their office is one that imperatively demands a common education.

The fortifications we had on the other side of the river are different from any that I have ever seen. Instead of the regular ditch and embankments, they have stuck upright stakes made of trees and saplings into the ground, with sufficient space in the interstices to fire through. One of the engineer corps informed me that this line was built up that way for twenty five or thirty miles. It is a miserable concern in my estimation, and a few well directed shots from the enemy's light artillery would knock those logs northwest and crooked, and kill and wound fully one half the men behind them. Some engineers have remarkably brilliant ideas and this is a specimen. It might stop a charge of cavalry for a while, but that's all it could do.

Tuesday, July 5: The wagon train has been passing all night long and are still going by (10 a. m.). Our whole army is now south of the Chattahoochee River and I presume Johnston will make a decided stand. If he doesn't try it right now, Atlanta goes up beyond a doubt. I think, though, that if Sherman could flank us out of our strong positions north of this, that it will be still easier for him to do it here. We are too weak, and that fact is as palpable as anything can be. But if we do not fight here, where will the struggle take place? Where are we to go to if we give up Atlanta? It has been nothing but a run from Dalton down and there must be a stop somewhere, or we had just as well not have an army in front of Sherman. According to my way of thinking matters look very gloomy, but I'll talk big anyhow. We are very weak, but I suppose we can have the consolation of blustering around amongst ourselves, and shout " big Injun heap." Our army is in good spirits however, and have an abiding faith in Johnston.

Wednesday, July 6: We moved our camp again this morning. Woolfolk is not along as usual, and I am bothered about what course to pursue. I suppose he is off in search of rotgut. He is acting Division Q. M., but I know that Gen [Edward C.] Walthall has no confidence in him, and in my opinion he will not occupy the position long because he is too great an ignoramus.

It's a devilish gloomy looking time for us certain, and I feel despondent. One more retreat and the fate of Atlanta is irrevocably pronounced. It is " now or never."

We did not succeed in getting our pontoon bridges out of the river, before the enemy was right down upon us.

Thursday, July 7: Weather fair and very warm. There is very little firing this morning and I cannot surmise what keeps the enemy so quiet. They must be driving at something or they would be pressing our pickets.

Collins got in a working humor late yesterday evening and commenced cutting some poles to make a bedstead, but after working about half an hour, he suddenly stopped and this morning he is entirely recovered from his working fever. This is usual with spasmodic workers.

Very heavy cannonading immediately after dark at the river. I never heard more rapid firing. It was occasioned by an attempt of ours to "bluff" the enemy away from the vicinity of the pontoons so that we could get them out, but we succeeded in getting only a portion of them.

Friday, July 8: Arose before day, and as soon as it was light enough, I made out some reports of field transportation and mounted a horse and went in search of the officer whose place it was to receive them. After riding nearly all day in the hottest kind of sun, I succeeded in finding him.

Sunday, July 10: We have removed our camp inside the breastworks at Atlanta. We pulled up stakes about midnight and reached our present camp about 9 a.m.

The bridges over the river were burned this morning by our troops a little before day. I don't believe Johnston can hold Atlanta. I am sorry to admit that as the Frenchman says, I am losing "the grand confidence."

The enemy I understand are making raids constantly in the neighborhood of Jackson, Miss., consequently I cannot reasonably hope to receive any communications from home soon. I would like very much to hear from there, but there is no use in fretting about the matter and so I shall take things easy.

This is an awful crisis for our young Republic and a short time now will tell the tale, because if Sherman whips Johnston out of Atlanta, we may bid farewell to this part of the country for I have yet to hear of our ever retaking any captured territory.

I saw McQuithy, a druggist who resided for a time in Clinton prior to the war, to-day. He informed me that he was in the medical department and that all the medical stores were being removed as rapidly as possible to Macon. I learned to-day that all our stores of every description were *in transitu* to Macon and Griffin. This looks as though Johnston didn't intend to make a stand. If he gives up the place where in the devil are we going to? We can't run much further, for we will soon be down to the Gulf of Mexico. I can't see into it. " Further, deponent saith not." Go it Mr. Johnsing. Your head has more brains in it than mine.

Atlanta, Tuesday, July 12: Everything is very quiet, and the city is almost deserted.

Woolfolk is such a wretched apology for a business man that I do not think Gen. Walthall will retain him as his Quartermaster for he neglects his duty or, more properly speaking, he doesn't know how to perform it but as is usual in such cases he thinks he knows it all.

Thursday, July 14: I have been worried, annoyed and be-devilled by my *superior* Woolfolk to such a degree that I have felt no inclination to write in my journal for a day or two past. If Walthall retains him as his Q. M. I shall consider the former as great an ass as the latter.

There is an unoccupied house near us, and Woolfolk obtained leave to sleep in it and as it contains 6 or 7 rooms, I remarked that I would be glad to occupy one of the backrooms as I had no tent and the weather was rainy. He became very indignant, and seemed to consider himself grossly insulted because I spoke of sleeping under the same roof with him. He replied rather sharply that he had engaged only one room for himself. I told him that I could not see how my sleeping upon the floor would injure the building and besides said I, you expect me to do all your writing, and I must do it outdoors with your books and papers all exposed. Well then let me have your tent, as you will occupy the house. " No " said he " I want that for my servant Bill to sleep in."

His brother who was present remonstrated with him on the unreasonableness of the thing, but he made no reply.

The next day the owner of the house came to our camp and I

applied to and received a written permit to occupy one of the rooms regardless of what Woolfolk had said. When he saw me *located*, he didn't say much, though I could see that he was angry. He appears to do everything he can to render all about him uncomfortable and I believe that it really affords him pleasure to see us exposed as much as possible. He puts on a great many simple foolish airs that causes all of us to feel a contempt for him. Well Major Woolfolk, you and I will part company before a great while and you may bet your last dollar on that.

Everything is as quiet along our lines, as though there was not a bluecoat in a thousand miles of us. There has been no fighting for the last 5 or 6 days.

That bird of evil omen, Gen. Bragg, has arrived in Atlanta from Richmond.[2] I think we will be defeated if he has anything to do with it. The army hates him, and cannot endure him. I saw a speech that was made the other day in our Congress by [James L.] Orr of S. C. The way he pitches into Bragg is a caution. The speech occupies several columns in the newspaper. Orr says that Bragg never has benefitted the Confederacy, but on the contrary he has been a very serious drawback and a positive injury to the cause; that he remains in Richmond doing nothing, but at the same time he receives better pay than Gen Lee, who is always in the field; that he was put into the position he now occupies because he was a played out General, and none of our armies would receive him; that he is placed in an office where every petition for promotion must pass through his censorship, and that he will not award justice to those who have fallen under the ban of his displeasure; that he has found fault with nearly every officer that ever served under him; that he has had open ruptures with the most of them; that it is very remarkable that Bragg should have all the bad officers, while the other armies had all the good ones; that if he is continued in his present office, a great many deserving officers can never rise. It is a long article,

---

[2] There was considerable official and popular dissatisfaction with Johnston's long retreat. President Davis was urged to remove Johnston from his command. Davis at length sent General Bragg, his adviser, to visit Johnston in the field and report on the situation. Upon Bragg's recommendation, Davis relieved Johnston and appointed General John B. Hood to assume responsibility for the defense of Atlanta. *Ibid.*, 340-50.

but those are some of the main points. He winds up by saying that all that Bragg is fit for or ever was fit for, is to be put in command of a Camp of Instruction, with a superior to prevent his tyrannising over the men. Right straight talk I think.

He has come here to have a finger in the pie and if this proves to be the case, we may expect to hear of something going wrong in a few days. I presume his first act will be to have someone courtmartialed and the next will be to have him shot. He doesn't think of anything except issuing more stringent orders upon the troops, and that accounts for his being no better General. Gen Johnston enforces stricter discipline than Bragg, but somehow it doesn't have that mean kind of a look that Bragg's does, and the troops all love Johnston and hate Bragg. But enough of the old heathen. We'll see what we'll see.

Col Hunter called to see me yesterday and remained two or three hours. He looks remarkably well and says that his health is excellent. Among other things he alluded to the death of Pres Pond, and spoke of his religious views. He says that Pond remarked to him one day in the course of conversation, that when he left college he was a firm unbeliever in the bible, and that he studied the subject well for the purpose of arguing with others, and the result was that before he had completed his researches, that he was a firm *believer* in the faith. Hunter says that during his last moments he became very solicitous in regard to his future state, and had old father Taylor with him until he expired.

Hunter seems to fear that the enemy will make a raid upon Clinton, and destroy the place.

Friday, July 15: Everything is very quiet this morning. The enemy doesn't seem to be making any attempt yet to cross the river. We have a very strong picket line on this side. The troops are in the best of spirits notwithstanding the hard time they are having. Perhaps, for duration, and the fierce, obstinate nature of the conflict, the present campaign in Georgia is unparalleled in history. It is now about 70 days since the opening of the campaign beginning at Dalton. Few of these days but what there has been fighting along our lines. These were followed by weary nights of incessant toil, oftentimes of fighting and building breastworks and entrenchments. Our men have seen a hard time, passing wearied nights of restless anxiety with the cold, damp ground for their beds, sleeping on wet leaves or branches of trees, sometimes on rails to keep them out of the mud, and frequently their rude couches were rendered too hot for them by the pattering bullets which came to disturb their slumbers. There is no child's play in soldiering. "Up to the rack, fodder or no fodder" is the word, to use a vulgar phrase.

Our army is like a lion at bay, now and then turning in desperation on their relentless pursuers. They have literally disputed *every inch* of ground from Dalton, down to our present position. Their unexampled, desperate, fighting qualities have even won the admiration of the Yankees, and as they say, " it begets a sad regret that we are not engaged in a holier cause."

There is a terrible state of things all along the line of the enemy's march from Dalton down. All the fighting men are in our army and the old have fled to the woods. The Yankees have burned the houses of the citizens with all their contents, and driven their wretched inmates, houseless, homeless, starving outcasts to perish of cold and hunger. It is said that numbers of affrighted, starving women and children may be seen huddled together in the woods, where many of them perish of cold and want. Old and young, grey headed matrons and timid girls—clinging together in hopeless misery. It is terrible to think and it must be a thousand times worse to behold. And this is war, great, glorious war. I think I shall make this my motto in the future. Never appeal to arms, if the same end can be arrived at by argument. I have seen enough myself to convince me that there is not the slightest improbability in what I have stated above. If I only had the fanatics of the North and fire eaters of the South, in equal numbers in a pen together, I'd make " dog eat dog." I'd " *make Rome howl* " for once.

I thought I had seen good water in my time, but I must acknowledge that the water we obtain from a well hard by bangs anything I ever met yet. It is the purest, the coldest and the best water that I ever swallowed. I cannot drink more than half a glass at a time because it makes my teeth ache. Any one who should hear me say this would simply come to the conclusion that I was lying. The owner of this well needn't spend any money for ice—it's already mixed for making lemonade and mint-juleps.

Saturday, July 16:   I received a note from Hunter this morning acknowledging the receipt of some sugar that I sent him. He enclosed me a copy of a piece of poetry written by Rev. H. C. Lewis, entitled " Jimmie Muse my Joe Jim."

Our regiment and the 30th Lou. have been transferred from Quarles' Tenn Brigade, to [Randall Lee] Gibson's Louisiana Brigade. It has created great dissatisfaction in the 4th.

Monday, July 18:   I have been quite unwell for several days and to-day I am scarcely able to sit up. I have very severe pains in my back and limbs generally. Quite an unexpected and startling announcement this morning. Gen Johnston has been removed and Gen Hood takes command. I have no doubt old Bragg has had something to do with this. The command was first offered to Gen Hardee, but he declined it, saying that Johnston's views and his corresponded, and that if Johnston couldn't give satisfaction, neither could he. It was next offered to Hood and he accepted it. Hood is a fighting man. When we first fell back below the Chattahoochee Hood insisted upon Johnston fighting the enemy there, and went so far as to say that if he didn't do it, that he (Hood) would give battle with his corps alone. This is all very fine talk, but we are not strong enough to go into a pitched battle. If we had been Johnston would have tried it long before this. From what I can learn the army is dissatisfied with the change.

Tuesday, July 19:   I am very unwell this morning, though I feel a little better than I did yesterday. I am very weak and hardly have strength to walk about, and every one tells me that I look very pale and haggard.

There is not a railroad running out of Atlanta but what is out of fix. All but one have been cut by the enemy, and that one has been torn up by the explosion of a locomotive. Our means of subsistence are extremely precarious, and we are literally " living from hand to mouth." According to my view we are in a very ticklish position.

Just as I thought—Woolfolk is to be relieved from his position as Division Quartermaster. I thought if Walthall was any account he wouldn't endure Woolfolk's style for any great length of time.

It is cloudy this morning and has been raining a little. There is no fighting. Both armies are massing on our right and a few more days will doubtless show something.

Before the band left for Gibson's Brigade yesterday, they played some familiar airs, which reminded me of the times we had along the Gulf coast at the beginning of the war. Speaking of the band reminds me of Davis, the drummer. He is certainly a philosopher. I saw him the other day, and he was bareheaded. " Hello Davis " said I " where's your hat? "

" I haven't any " he answered " someone stole it."

" Well, what are you to do for another? " I asked.

" Do without I suppose " said he.

He didn't seem to be at all annoyed about it and seemed to be perfectly well satisfied without a hat. I wish I had such a disposition. I believe I would get along through the world better. If I had been without a hat I should have been perfectly miserable until I could get another. Davis on the contrary made himself perfectly easy and contented until he could get another hat, because as he said, " Kicking up hell would not bring him a hat any sooner." I think when a man makes up his mind to take everything easy and not to fret about anything, that he gets along through the world much more pleasantly than one who is always grumbling and growling.

Charley Redding who has been acting as Forage Master of the Division has been ordered back to his Regiment by Gen Walthall. His Colonel was the cause of it. From what he says the Colonel of his regiment is a " mean old cuss " and doesn't wish to see any of his men filling easy positions. I never saw a man seem to disrelish anything as much as Charley did this and I cannot blame him, but at the same time when a man knows he *must* do a thing, however unpleasant it may be, he had as well go and do it. I feel sorry for him because he seemed to dread it so much, and if he had received his death warrant he could not have appeared more despondent.

Wednesday, July 20:   Woolfolk is to be relieved today. Sometimes I think the war is nearly closed, and then again it looks like it had but fairly commenced. I begin sometimes to lay out plans for the future, but I generally come to the conclusion that endeavoring to look ahead is useless though I do not see how the war can last longer than this year, because I am fully satisfied that we cannot hold out longer than Jany or Feby next unless something turns up in our favor and that devilish quick.

4 p. m. Fighting like "hell a beating tan burk." It appears to be about our centre. They are at it hot and heavy.[3]

Later—Charley Redding came in just now, minus his left hand. At least it is so badly shattered that I presume it must be amputated. Polks old corps was the only one engaged. Our forces attacked them in their works, and drove them out with a large number killed and wounded on both sides. The general impression seems to be that we have not gained anything by the operation. Hood is determined to fight; there's no doubt about that. I suppose he intends to "make a spoon or spoil a horn" and if he doesn't look sharp, he'll "spoil the horn." Charley Redding slept with me this night and complained very much of his hand. He has been to the hospital, but it is so crowded with the wounded and dying that they say they can do nothing for him until morning.

Thursday, July 21:   There is pretty rapid firing on our left and centre this morning.

3 a. m. There's slow regular artillery firing all the time, but nothing like an engagement, although yesterday about dark all hands were under the impression that "the fur would fly" from one side or the other to-day. I fear we will not be able to hold Atlanta, for the enemy is too heavy for us, and they have taken "old Joe" away from the helm.

Well! my opinion is that if Hood follows up the policy inaugurated yesterday, we will either drive the enemy back or we will go up the spout ourselves. There seems to be general dissatisfaction among the men on account of the headlong way in which they were put in yesterday, and they think that "it costs more

[3] Battle of Peach Tree Creek, near Atlanta.

than it comes to." They say that Hood cares no more for the loss of his men, than Grant does of his in Virginia. From all I can learn I am inclined to believe that the advantages gained yesterday are not at all commensurate with the loss sustained, and from the comparative silence to-day, I hope that Gen Hood may reconsider matters, abandon his aggressive policy and await the enemy inside our lines. His course would do well enough I think, if we had plenty of men, but this is not the case and as a matter of course he knows it. I am forced to the conclusion that we must either give up the place, or they will surround it, and then I know " the dog's dead."

Friday, July 22: At about one o'clock this morning we were ordered to pull up stakes and move. We drove our train down in town, where we remained until after daylight. I saw a sight this morning that I never saw before and never wish to see again. A lot of cavalry, said to be the 7th Alabama Regiment, went all over the business part of the city breaking open the doors as they came to them, and robbing every house of whatever it contained, carrying away with them such things as they desired and throwing such as they did not like into the streets. They had sacks tied to their saddles and seemed to have come prepared for the business, and all through the day cavalrymen could be seen with their horses literally piled up and almost concealed by the plunder they had on them.

They started to enter the establishment of an old lady who kept a shop, but the old lady didn't seem disposed to submit, and she drew a pistol and threatened to shoot the first man who entered. They went in, however, took her out of the house and as her hair had become dishevelled in the affray they caught up her streaming locks and dragged her up and down the streets by the hair of her head. They then entered the house, taking away what they wanted, and making an everlasting smash of things generally.

There was another hard fight about 2 p. m. to-day on our right.

Saturday, July 23: There was some very hard fighting yesterday afternoon. Hardee charged the enemy on our right and drove them back. I can learn nothing reliable, only that we drove them back capturing quite a number of prisoners and some artillery. We lost heavily. There is not much firing this morning.[4]

Sunday, July 24: This is the most extraordinary weather that I ever saw. Every man has on his coat and all hands are huddled around the fires.

I saw a wounded Yankee yesterday that was a perfect sight to behold. I will try to describe him, though any picture that I can draw will fall short of the mark. He is at the hospital. He is a tall, spare made man and his clothing is entirely too large for him. He was dressed in the blue coat and pants of the Federals. His coat fits very loosely and hangs upon him like a shirt upon a bean pole; his pants will wrap easily around his thin, spindling legs twice. His legs, which are not much larger than pipe stems, run down into a pair of huge boot legs, and his feet are extremely large and not at all proportioned to the balance of his body, and it would appear impossible for him to carry such a weight of leather with such a slender pair of legs. He was wounded in the lower jaw and as it is much swollen it protruded nearly an inch beyond the upper one. When I saw him he was sitting on the ground with his head hanging between his knees, which latter stood up some distance above his shoulders, like two sentinels. The color of his clothing could scarcely be distinguished, for the vast number of flies which swarmed in myriads over him. Taken altogether I think he was the most singular looking object that I have seen in many a long day.

This morning I passed the grave of a Yankee who died yesterday, and I just thought to myself, now, old fellow, you have travelled a long ways to secure a very small spot of earth, when you might have purchased ten thousand times as much nearer home and much cheaper than you got this. You were not satisfied to remain at home, and let us alone; you must come to the South to murder our citizens, burn our houses, desolate our homes

---

[4] This was the battle of Atlanta. The action referred to by Patrick could hardly be called a Confederate victory even though General Hardee had dealt the Federals a heavy blow. He had captured some two thousand prisoners and eight guns. The attack was a disappointment to Hood, however. The Confederates had been forced back to their original position with heavy losses—losses which the undermanned Army of Tennessee could ill-afford. Horn, *Army of Tennessee,* 355-59.

and lay waste our country; to make war upon women and children, turning them out to die of cold and want, without the slightest compunctions of conscience. You for one have met your just reward, which is a grant of land from the Confederates of three feet by six, in an obscure spot, where your friends, if you have any, will never be able to find your body for there is nothing to mark the spot except a small hillock of red clay, which a few hard rains will wash away and it will disappear forever. "So mote it be" as the Masons say.

Tuesday, July 26: I received from Hunter the following note.

> DEAR BOB,
>
> Your's of this morning was handed me by Jno Richart. Many thanks for your kindness. I enclose you the $20 Geo. bill. Capt Fiester says he has sent you word a dozen times about it. He tried in Mobile to dispose of it, but without success. I also enclose a very rough copy, made by Jim Doyle of "Jimmie Muse my Joe Jim," what a truly Christian spirit is exhibited between these ministers of the gospel!
>
> The order transferring us to Gibson's is in Walthall's office, but has not yet been enforced. I suppose it soon will be. It is very distasteful to all of us. "May your shadow never grow less."
>
> Your Friend Truly
> S. E. HUNTER

Atlanta, July 28, 1864: Weather very warm today. Another hard fight on the left. Attack made by our side. Hood will have our whole army killed off if he doesn't change his policy. If we had plenty of men this would do. He is entirely too reckless.[5]

Atlanta, July 31: From the fact of my being attached to a different Brigade, different Division, and even a different Corps, I was not aware until yesterday that our Regt. was in the fight of the 28th. Our loss was very heavy.[6] It was a perfect slaughter.

---

[5] The battle of Ezra Church, four miles southeast of Atlanta. There the corps of Confederate General Stephen D. Lee collided with Federal forces. What started out to be a small engagement soon grew to battle proportions. Again and again the Confederates attacked but were unable to dislodge the Federals. By the end of the day the Confederate troops had been repulsed with heavy losses. After the battle of Ezra Church the siege settled down for almost a month. *Ibid.,* 360-64.

[6] Out of 240 men present for duty the Fourth Louisiana suffered 82 casualties.

I managed to get off to the Hospital where the wounded from our Regt. were and I did all I could for them. I gave them all the clothing I had of every description.

I fear Bill Knox will not recover. He requested me to write home to his family, which I will do as soon as possible. With the assistance of some others I carried him into the woods, and procurring some water and a sponge I washed his body all over and put clean clothing upon him. The flies are awful. In spite of all that can be done, they will deposite maggots in the wounds of the men, and there is scarcely a wound that is not full of them.

Monday, August 1: I have just had a conversation with Maj Mulherin, Comy of Walthall's Divis. and he says he needs a clerk very much and desires my services. I told him that I had seen enough of Maj Woolfolk, and that I would accept the place he offered me. He appears to be a very nice man.

"Where's everybody gone to?"

CHAPTER VIII. SEPTEMBER, 1864

South of Atlanta, Friday, September 2, 1864:[1] I have had a terrible time of it since the last entry in my journal. On Thursday afternoon we were ordered to move, but we didn't get away until after dark. The city was being evacuated as rapidly as possible. Some of the boys were acquainted with several young ladies who resided on the street we were then on, and some one proposed that we should call upon them before leaving. To this a general assent was given, and we hurried on at a tremendous pace in order to get ahead of the train and have as long to remain as possible. This very rapid walking or rather run I should call it, caused a sudden soreness in my legs, and before reaching the house I found that I could scarcely walk. We went in and found several young ladies. We had some music on the piano, singing, etc. and remained until we thought our train had overtaken us.

The night was very dark and upon going into the street we found it crowded with men, horses, and a little of everything. We couldn't see much, but we could hear a perfect babel of voices in every direction. In the darkness I became separated from my squad, and I looked around for them in vain. I went over the town in search of them but failed to find them. I then concluded that I had better hurry on after the train and get out of the town

---

[1] After almost a month of siege, during which for some reason Patrick made no entries in his diary, Sherman began on August 25 the last of a long series of movements which finally resulted in the evacuation and capture of Atlanta. Union troops occupied the city on September 2.

before the enemy captured me. As I walked up the street I came upon a lady standing at a gate, and she made some remark to me and I stopped to talk to her. I asked her for some water and she went into the house and brought some out. She appeared to be very much troubled on account of the city falling into the hands of the enemy. She was badly frightened. I gave her the best advice I could. She insisted upon my remaining until morning as a protection to herself and her children, but I told her such a course as that would be the height of folly, because I could be of no assistance to her and my remaining there would certainly insure my capture.

About this time I heard a terrible roar, immediately ahead of me, down the rail-road. At first I could not imagine what it was but after a time I ascertained that it was shells exploding. Gen Hood had ordered a train loaded with ammunition to be destroyed to prevent its falling into the hands of the enemy.[2] I could see how to walk for a long distance by the light of the shells and the burning cars. My road lay paralel with the track and as I approached nearer and nearer the burning train, the sound became perfectly deafening, and the fragments of shells, hurtled through the midnight darkness over my head with an ominous rushing sound. I walked steadily on. I met no one, neither did any one pass me. After walking about two miles, the explosion of the shells suddenly ceased, and I knew by this that the train had been totally destroyed. Hearing such a tremendous continued noise for such a length of time, and ceasing so suddenly, made it appear very lonely. I sat down to rest. It was very dark and I could hear no sound whatsoever. The God of Silence reigned here. I have heard that the Egyptian darkness could be felt. The silence was so profound that it seemed to me I could feel it. It caused a painful, uneasy sensation.

I got up after awhile and walked on. I knew the wagon train

[2] Six railroad trains of ordnance stores and ammunition as well as large supplies of provisions were burned to prevent them from falling into the hands of the enemy. In a dispatch dated September 4 to General Bragg in Richmond, Hood stated that this action was necessary "owing to the wanton neglect of the Chief Quartermaster of the Army [who] I am informed is too much addicted to drink of late to attend to his duties." *Official Records*, Series I, Vol. XXXI, Part V, p. 1018.

was on ahead of me, and I would use every exertion to overtake it. Several times I stopped and listened, thinking I heard the tramp of men and horses, but it was a mistake; the summer night breeze sighing through the dense foliage of the lonely forest trees that threw the still deeper darkness of their shadows across my lonely way. I began to feel pretty well used up, but I travelled on as well as I could. By daylight a whole division of infantry had overtaken and passed me. How far I walked I do not know. Once during the night I mistook the road and travelled it several miles, and on finding out my error I was compelled to retrace my steps. About daylight I was so sore and stiff and I thought I could not walk any farther. As day began to break and I could see about me, a lot of ambulances were passing. I enquired for the chief surgeon in charge. He was pointed out to me. I stepped up to him saying.

" Doctor I am completely worn out, and I wish to ride in one of your ambulances, for a short time at least."

" Our ambulances have too much load on them already and you must walk," was his reply.

" Well " I answered " you see my condition. It is with the greatest difficulty that I can move, and in a few hours more the enemy will be along, picking up such unfortunate stragglers as myself, and I shall soon be in a Yankee prison."

" Can't help that " said he.

" No I suppose you can't help it. Just look at the ambulances you have, and just look what is in them. I see bedsteads, mattrasses, cooking utensils, washtubs, and from one to three great lazy strapping negroes in each one of them, but yet you can't give me any assistance. The government has supplied you with those conveyances for the benefit of the wounded, sick, and disabled, but I do not see a soldier in any of them. Nothing but your damned old camp trumpery and a lot of indolent negroes. All of your sort ought to be in hell right now."

He listened to this and rode on without another word. There were others besides myself that were almost past traveling, but they received no assistance from the ambulance crowd. Well *let them rip*, but there is one thing certain, I have nothing to thank them for nor will I forget them soon.

Directly after daylight, I stopped at the cabin of a negro and got some water and rested awhile. After this I started on again, though I was so much exhausted that I thought I would be forced to give up. It was at this time that I found the will had such a control over the body. I verily believe that it was mental exertion alone that carried me on. I walked so slow that other men over-took me, passed me and were soon out of sight, while I was hobbling almost in the same place.

Saturday, Sept. 3: [3] I continued to walk on though I was com-pelled to stop and rest about every hundred yards. About 8 or 9 o'clock a. m. as I was toiling up a hill I heard a familiar voice exclaim.

' Ello Bob! what the 'ell's the matter? "

I looked around and who should it be but Bill Gurney mounted on a very small mule.

Said I, " Get down off that mule Bill, I'm used up and I want to ride a little."

" Will do it—by God. Hi never see a feller 'ard hup yit, but what hold Bill Gurney was willin' to 'elp 'em. Damned if I did." Saying this Bill dismounted, and handed me the bridle rein.

He looked at me a good while, and finally said he " What'n 'ell *his* the matter anyhow? I never see a feller stove up like that before, damn me if I did." " Well git-up " he continued, seeing that I didn't mount.

I had made several vain attempts to mount, but Bill hadn't noticed it. With very great difficulty by stooping down and taking hold of my ankle with my two hands, I had managed to place my foot in the stirrup, but when I attempted to raise my leg to throw it over the saddle, I failed signally. I told Bill that

---

[3] The repulse of Hardee's corps at Jonesboro on August 31 ended any hope of saving Atlanta. Hood's most immediate problem was to evacuate his positions around Atlanta, escape Sherman's victorious army and re-establish himself somewhere along the Central Railroad below Jonesboro. This withdrawal was successfully made by retreating to Lovejoy's Station, a few miles below Jonesboro. Sherman discontinued the offensive, however, and retired his troops into Atlanta. Horn, *Army of Tennessee,* 367-70.

his mule would be useless to me unless he assisted me to mount, because I was too sore and stiff to get up unaided. Bill assisted me on the mule, and we went on about two miles and stopped at a house to get some water. There were two ladies at the house, and we enquired of them if they knew any house off the road in an out of the way place, where I could remain for a couple of days until I got able to walk. One of them answered that she did. Her sister-in-law, she said, was a widow and would receive me at her house very cheerfully. This she knew because her sister-in-law, Mrs. McWilliams, had told her to direct any disabled soldiers she might see to her house and they would be welcome.

This was good tidings for me in the condition I was in then, and I told her that I should certainly avail myself of the lady's kindness. She endeavored to point out. the way from where we then were, but this proved a rather difficult task, as I was so entirely ignorant of the country. She told me then to go on to the next house on the roadside, and that from that place it would be a very easy matter to direct me to Mrs. McWilliamses.

I rode the mule and Bill walked along by my side, until we reached the house on the roadside. It was not a large house though a very comfortable one, and there seemed to be no one about the place. The gate was open and I rode into the yard, Bill following, and I managed after so long a time to dismount and Bill hitched the mule.

" Damned if I believe there's anybody here " says Bill.

" Well " said I " it doesn't look much like it, but at any rate we will go in and see."

We went in and there we saw an old woman lying in bed. She raised partly up and I observed that she was very much emaciated. Her eyes were sunk deep in their sockets and glittered like diamonds. I involuntarily started back so unnatural and weird like was her appearance.

" Good day madam " said I, but she returned no answer. I turned around and looked at Bill. Judging from Bill's remark, he must have construed this look of mine into a question of what he thought of her case.

" By God, she's going to die " said Bill in his deep gruff tones

" she don't know anything, there's no use talking to her." We entered the next room and there we saw a young woman lying in bed. In the middle of the room stood a cradle in which lay a child apparently sick. Near the bed sat a man with the branch of a peachtree in his hands, keeping the flies away.

" How do you do sir " said I " you seem to have a sick family? "

" Yes, Sir, very sick. My wife's dead, my mother is sick and so is my daughter and that little baby."

I told him I was sorry to intrude under such circumstances, but I was exceedingly anxious to find the way to Mrs. McWilliamse's. He gave me the necessary directions and we walked out.

" I'm tired of walking " says Bill. " I'll get in the saddle and you get hup be'ind."

" All right " said I " unhitch your mule."

Bill mounted and rode near the gallery of the kitchen and in accordance with Bill's instructions, I got " hup be'ind," and away we went.

I know we must have cut a handsome figure for the mule was very small, not much larger than a good sized rabbit, and it seemed to have had entirely too much of nothing to eat for some days past, for it would stagger from side to side under this double weight. Every time it would step into a gutter our feet would touch the ground. It beat walking though, an even two to one.

" 'ood's [Hood's] played 'ell 'asn't 'e? " said Bill by way of getting up a conversation, for we had been riding along silently for some time.

" I should say he had " was my response.

" If they'd let hold Johnston halone, 'e'd a played 'ell with him, wouldn't he? "

" I think he would " said I.

" Well " said Bill turning round rather suddenly to look at me as well as he could " what's 'ood done hany'ow? Where is everything and where's everybody gone to? Where are they going to? I don't know where I'm going to, damme if I do. Haw! Haw! Haw! " laughed Bill " if that haint the best joke I've 'eard yet." Bill for the want of something better to talk about gave me the full and complete history of his wedded life but as it would

" It beat walking though, an even two to one "

require too much space to note it down, besides being a violation of confidence I shall not repeat anything on that head. We finally reached Mrs. McWilliamses and I must acknowledge that it was not quite as commodius and comfortable a place as I expected to find it. It was a log cabin containing only a single room, stuck in the middle of a cornfield without any enclosure whatever around it. A little ways from it stood the kitchen which was a *fac simile* of the dwelling only it was much smaller. It looked like the larger one had been in the familyway, and had been relieved of a young one, and there it stood seeming to say " here I am, just like you."

Bill and I dismounted and went in. We found Mrs. McWilliams in the kitchen. She was a young woman and rather good looking, and a widow, her husband having died in the army. She had some young children. There was a disabled soldier, a young, good looking fellow, already there and had been there as I learned afterwards for some time. He was a Mississippian and lived between Vicksburg and Yazoo City. His name was Porter. He and she seemed to be on the best of terms and appeared to understand each other. She invited us in and gave us a glass of good fresh buttermilk. I explained to her my condition and she willingly assented that I should remain at her house as long as I saw proper to do so.

Bill now said he must go, and I went out with him to where his long eared quadruped was hitched. I used every argument that I could think of to induce him to remain at least until the next day, as I thought a nights rest would enable me to travel without much difficulty. There were two reasons for my wishing Bill to remain with me. First—I was in a strange country and alone and as I didn't know what might befall me I wished to have some one with me in whom I could place confidence, and who would be willing to render me assistance if necessary. Secondly—I wanted to have the benefit of riding Bill's mule occasionally which would be a great help because any one who has walked a great deal knows the immense relief afforded to the wearied limbs by a ride, be it ever so short, on horseback. It is not like sitting down to rest. There seems to be something in the motion of the horse that dispels fatigue quicker than almost anything else.

I knew Bill was hungry and I thought I would bring my arguments to bear on the most vulnerable point, so I drew pictures of fried chickens and chicken pies, fresh butter and milk, besides vegetables of every description, cooked in every imaginable shape. Bill stood for some time in silence and I thought I had come the gentle shepherd over him, but finally he said

" He'd like damned well to 'ave some of that, but then by God what good would it all to hib the enemy gits 'old of me? "

I had done all I could to detain him, but it was useless, and as Bill rode slowly off down the lane I returned to the house.

Mrs. McWilliams pointed out a bed saying that if I felt disposed I could lie down. I knew that if I could only go to sleep it would benefit me more than anything else. So I lay down, but I was sore and in pain, and I was so nervous withal that sleep was out of the question. Sometimes I would fall into a little doze, but my nervous system was so deranged from excitement and fatigue that the slightest noise would awaken me with a start, and I would find myself trembling all over, and the perspiration starting from every pore. I went out to dinner. I felt hungry but when I sat down to the table I could not eat anything. I drank a glass of buttermilk and went back to bed. There was no one in the room except myself and I was lying on the bed. I was sick, sore and weary. I was crabbed, cross and illnatured. I sought repose but I could not find it. Sleep would not come to my relief—rest was not to be had let me turn as I would. I felt embittered against everybody and everything.

A man came to the door and stood there. He was medium size with an old green blanket thrown over his arm. He was pale as a ghost—he was very much emaciated—he was perfectly cadaverous—his clothing hung loosely about him—his general appearance reminded me of starved sickly looking kittens I have seen that had apparently gone all to head—his head seemed to be the biggest part of him—it looked so heavy that it was a wonder his weak neck and spindling body sustained so great a weight.

There he stood in the door with his blanket over his arm. He looked at me and I looked at him. Finally I asked very abruptly.

" Where in the hell did *you* come from? "

He responded in a very weak voice, " I come from the Hospital."

" Well " said I " why didn't you stay there "?

" Because the enemy would have captured me."

" You ought to have stayed there and let them capture you " said I, " because it would have saved our side the trouble of burying you."

" I'm sick " said he " and I want to know if I can remain here for a while."

" How in the hell do I know whether you can stay or not? "

" Well I saw you here, and I thought the house belonged to you. You needn't get mad about it."

" No sir " I answered " the house doesn't belong to me, when I own a house I'll get a better one than this."

About this time Mrs. McWilliams came in. " Mrs. McWilliams " said I " do I look like that man? "

" No " said she " why do you ask? "

" Because " I answered " if I do, I'll go to the nearest tree and hang myself."

The fellow's deep set, hollow eyes began to sparkle. Said he, " I've seen better lookin' men than you are. Youv'e got nuthin' to brag on in the way of looks. I spose you want to make out like you never seen a man that's been sick before."

" Yes, I have seen sick men, but I must acknowledge that I never saw just such a looking object as you are."

During this conversation which was conducted on both sides in the most serious and bitter manner, Mrs. McWilliams was roaring with laughter. As soon as she could speak she said, addressing herself to her new guest " You had better lie down and rest yourself and I will get you something to eat," and turning to me she said " don't say anything more to him. I know he has a funny look, but then you are both sick, and I wouldn't go to quarrelling."

" Well " said my antagonist—if I can be allowed the term— " it wasn't my fault. I came here and he pitched into me. Damned if I aint jest as good as he is, if I *am* sick."

This wound up the skirmish and he laid down to rest, which I have no doubt he needed as much as I did.

About an hour elapsed when Mrs. McW. came in and said she thought the Yankees were coming. I got up and went to the door, and sure enough I heard their drums and bugles. I put on my coat and made preparations to go. My companion of the green blanket enquired what was the matter. I told him that I thought the enemy would soon be down upon us.

"Well! what are you going to do?" said he.

"I intend to leave" said I "as quick as I can, and you had better bundle up and go along too."

"I'm not able to go" said he "and if I was, I'll be damned if I would go along with *you*."

He hadn't forgotten the way I opened upon him when he made his appearance at the door.

I bade Mrs. McWilliams good bye, having first thanked her for the kindness to me and I made my way out to the road, and travelled on towards the army the best I could. This was a slow and exceedingly painful task because every time I stepped I felt as though I was pierced with some sharp cutting instrument. There was such a soreness in my groins that it was with the greatest difficulty that I could drag one foot after the other. My idea was to follow the country road leading from Mrs. McWilliams until I reached the public highway that Bill Gurney and I had left in the morning.

I had just crossed a little creek, where the trees and undergrowth on each side of the road were very thick. I heard a heavy crashing of the vines and dry sticks, and something or somebody was coming at a sharp pace towards the road. Directly a negro made his appearance, with a huge knapsack upon his shoulders, and evidently making very good time. He didn't see me until I spoke.

"Halt there" said I "or I'll kill you."

He looked around and exclaimed.

"Good God, master, don't shoot me. I haint done nuthin."

I questioned him, and found that he was a servant belonging to one of our soldiers in the cavalry service. He was now endeavoring to overtake his master, who had gone on with his command, but the negro being on foot could not keep up. He told me that I had better not go out to the main road as the Yankees were there. He said that he had spoken to and passed a number of them. This road lay to my left and another public road was on my right, and I was fully satisfied that the enemy were coming down both roads, and that my only course was to travel through the woods between the two roads. I thought the negro might be of some service to me and I thought there would be policy in keeping him with me. I told him that he had very little idea of the geography of the country, and that he would rejoin his master sooner by remaining with me than he would to go on by himself. He consented to this arrangement, and we left the road and took a course through the woods as near due South as we could guess.

My progress was very slow because I had to stop every few hundred yards to rest, and as a matter of course the negro had to wait for me. I noticed that he was very impatient at these delays. We had just crossed an open field and I sat down upon a huge rock to rest myself. The negro said he wanted to go to the railroad which lay only a mile or two to the right of us. I tried to persuade him to remain with me, but he said as soon as he had rested and cooled off a little that he would make for the railroad. Suddenly the notes of the clear toned bugles and sonorous drums of the enemy were wafted to our ears upon the quiet summer breeze as we sat upon the rugged rocks.

" What's dat? " enquired the negro.

I explained what it was.

" Well, boss " said he " you walks too slow for me. Ise a gwine," and he began to gather up his budget. I saw there was no use attempting to detain him and I maliciously determined to get a big scare on him if I could before he left me.

Said I " Didn't you tell me you had seen the Yankees on the road? "

" Yas sah, I did. I seed 'em."

" Well, didn't you talk to them? "

" Yes sah: I talked to dem when dey talked to me."

" Well " said I " didn't they ask you where you were going? "

" Yas sah, dey axed me whar I was gwine and I told 'em I was jes gwine down de road a piece and when I got outen sight I tuk to de woods and come across you."

"That's just exactly what I thought" said I. "Now do you know what they think about you?"

"No sah" said the negro, evidently becoming interested, "I don't know what they thinks. I hain't no idy."

"Well" said I, looking as solemn as a graveyard "you're in a damn bad fix. I wouldn't be situated just as you are now for all the money in the Confederacy."

"Why boss, I haint done nuthin' to none of 'em. I didn't even stay whar dey wus. I ges come right off as soon as I could" said he.

"That's it" said I "that's the very thing you oughn't to have done."

"I didn't have nuthin to do wid dem. I never seed dem before" said he.

"That doesn't make any difference" I answered "they consider you a soldier now and you really belong to their army. You told them you were just going down the road a short distance, and now you are away down here. You are a deserter and they know it. You are not only a deserter but you are deserting to the enemy. You are trying now to get with the Confederates aint you?"

"Yes sah, I is."

"They'll kill you certain if they find you again. Did you ever see a mackerel?" I enquired.

"Yes sah, I has."

"Was the mackerel dead?" I enquired.

"Yes sah, all de mackerels I ever seed was dead and full o' salt."

"Well" said I "no mackerel that ever you saw will be as dead as you'll be in fifteen minutes after the Yankees lay eyes upon you."

"Well boss, you walk too slow. Good bye, Ise gwine."

He gathered up his bundle, and the last I saw of him his knapsack was bobbing up and down above the bushes. He had swallowed every word I had said, and I took a malicious satisfaction in knowing that I had frightened him just because he wouldn't stay with me. This is human nature. I felt perfectly miserable and I took a delight in making the negro as uneasy and wretched as possible. It is true that "misery loves company."

The negro was gone and I was alone, sitting upon that old rock in the solemn stillness of the deep woods. I was so sore that I could with difficulty drag one foot after the other, but I must go on. It would not do to remain there. Delays are said to be dangerous, and it was particularly so in this instance. Pictures of Yankee prisons rose before me and the Lord knows how much suffering. With an effort I arose and started on. After walking a while, I struck a settlement road, very plain but apparently very little used. I followed this because it was easier walking than through the woods where the undergrowth was so thick. I had not been on the road long before I heard some one talking. I hid myself behind a tree, thinking it might be some of the Yankee cavalry. I waited for some time but could see no one.

Not deeming it safe to be upon a regular road, I again struck across the pathless woods. I came to a field. It was only a short distance across it, but on account of not being able to raise my feet I could not climb the fence, and had to walk a full mile around it. After going about a mile farther I approached a farm house where I heard voices in conversation. I feared it might be the enemy. After slipping around among the bushes I got a sight of them. They were Confederates, stragglers from the army. I went up and got a drink of water, and enquired of a citizen the nearest route to the public road travelled by the army, and he gave me directions. One of the soldiers said he would go along with me, so we started on in company. We had not gone far before we came to another farm house. A man was standing at the gate as we were passing. He enquired if we wanted something to eat, and we told him yes. We went in. I thought the place belonged to him as there was nothing about him to indicate that he was a soldier, but I ascertained that he was a straggler, having thrown away his gun and equipment.

We went into the house, and he pointed to some flour and bacon in one of the rooms. I told him that I thought he had something cooked and that I had no way to carry the flour and bacon. The owner of the house together with all his family had left the house, and from the appearance of everything they had not been long gone. There sat the water bucket full of water, and the gourd hanging beside it. The beds were tumbled up—men and womens clothing was scattered over the floor—the spinning wheel stood in the middle of the room with the thread hanging from the spindle, and a lot of spun thread lay in a basket near the wheel, besides many other things showing very plainly that the family had evidently left in great haste and trepidation. I went into the orchard and found some very good apples. I went back to the house where I found the others pillaging and appropriating everything they could find. As this was not in my line, I went away and left them to take what they pleased.

They were strong healthy men and should have been with their commands, but instead of that they were roaming in every direction over the country, stealing what they wanted and destroying what they didn't want. Shortly after leaving this place, I again struck the public road along which the army had marched. I stopped at a house to obtain a drink of water, and I enquired of the owner how long since the army had passed. He said the rear guard, consisting of mounted men, had passed early that morning.

Said he "In your condition, I think it will be impossible for you to escape capture, and if I were in your place, I should not attempt to overtake the army because you will be captured before you can do it, and your walk will all go for nothing."

I told him that I should walk on anyhow, and if the enemy did capture me they must take me on the wing, for I should certainly not sit down and wait for them.

I walked on as well as I could, though it was a very slow walk and a very painful one too. I stopped at every spring and well that I saw to obtain water, because I was feverish and it was almost impossible to quench my thirst. Night was approaching and dark clouds began to gather overhead, portending rain. I thought several times of stopping at some house and applying for shelter for the night, but the consciousness of the enemy being behind me spurred me on. Darkness came on at length, and the elements appeared more threatening than ever. It grew darker every moment, and the thunder was rolling in the distance, accompanied by flashes of lightning and the low moaning of the night wind. I had no blanket and I knew that if I should be exposed to the weather and pass a sleepless night, that by morning I should be in a worse condition than ever.

I saw a light shining at a little distance upon the roadside, and I went in towards it. Upon a nearer approach I saw a small cabin, and I determined to apply for a night's lodging at this place. I met a girl apparently about fifteen years old with a bucket on her arm going for water. I enquired of her if I could stay all night. She referred me to her mother who was in the house. I went in and spoke to the old lady, who very politely invited me to take a seat, which I did. I told her the condition I was in; that I had no blanket, and that everything seemed to indicate a night of bad weather.

" Yes Sir " said she " you kin stay, but I hain't got nuthin' fur you to eat."

I told her that made not the slightest difference, that what I desired most was a roof to shelter me from the approaching storm.

I now took a survey of the premises. Here was poverty, squalid poverty! I had never seen a family quite so low down. They seemed to be without the very *commonest necessaries* of life. The house was built of logs with a single room—the logs in places were so wide apart that a man could almost crawl through. A great portion of the roof was gone. In one corner was a kind of bedstead, and on it lay a mass of bedding, or rather what represented bedding, for it was in reality nothing more than a pile of dirty, filthy looking rags. Upon this the whole family, consisting of the old lady and several children, all slept. She told me that her husband had died in the Virginia army and that she had a son sixteen years old in the State militia. She said she had managed to raise some little corn and a few chickens and pigs, but that the cavalry who had been stationed about there had robbed her of everything she had, and had on many occasions, also insulted herself and her daughter very grossly.

About this time the girl returned with a bucket of water and I took a look at her. She was a very pretty girl and if the dirt had been washed off, and nice clothing put upon her, she would have been better than half the young ladies we generally see in our fashionable ballrooms. I lay down upon the floor, but I had scarcely stretched myself out upon the hard planks, when I heard something moving about immediately beneath the floor. I enquired what that was.

" Oh! that is only a pig that I keep under there to prevent the soldiers from stealing it. They tuk all but that, and I put it whar I could watch it."

If I had only waited a moment, I needn't have asked any questions, because the smell that greeted my olfactories would have informed me what it was.

Notwithstanding the noise made by the pig, the offensive smell, and my hard bed, I soon dropped off to sleep and slept soundly until morning.

I awaked a little after daylight and found the old lady already up, sitting by the fire. On looking around I saw the young girl lying on the bed with the greater part of her person exposed. She was a beautifully formed girl, and where there was no dirt her skin was as white as snow.

I looked out doors and perceived that it had rained during the night, but I had slept so soundly that I didn't hear it. I wanted to pay the old lady for her kindness but she wouldn't receive anything, and so thanking her for my lodging and bidding her good morning I started on. I found that although a night's rest had refreshed me very much, I could perceive no diminution in the soreness of my limbs, and that it was about as painful a matter to travel as it was the day before. However, I pitched out and did the best I could. The roads were very muddy and slippery from the recent rain and this made my progress slower and more difficult.

About sunrise I reached a dwelling on the roadside, and I walked up to the gate. I saw a man standing in the door, and near him two young ladies and a large yellow dog lounging about the yard. I enquired if he could give me anything to eat. He answered " No." " Can't you give me a potatoe, I'm easily satisfied and almost anything will do me? " " No sir, I can't " said he. " Well give me a piece of cornbread, you can do that can't you? " said I. " No Sir," was his answer.

" Well go to hell then " said I " I know you can do so if you would, but do not wish to do it."

So I turned away, disgusted with him, his two gals and his yaller *dorg*, and wended my way down the road.

I had not gone more than a mile before I approached another residence. This was a very nice looking place, and I resolved to try my luck again because I was very hungry, and I was compelled to have something to eat because I had eaten nothing except some buttermilk since leaving Atlanta. At this house I found a very kind family. The lady gave me some buttered toast, ham and coffee, all of which was duly appreciated and thankfully received. This breakfast revived me very much and I felt more cheerful. All along the road, I saw scattered and broken wagons and caisons, artillery ammunition of all kinds, and boxes of ammunition for small arms. Some of the wagons had been partially burned. About 11 or 12 a. m. I overtook one of our wagons which had been delayed, and the driver assisted me to get in and I rode the remainder of the day.

I caught up with the rear guard of the army which had stopped to rest. It was Gibson's brigade that brought up the rear and I saw our regiment. I saw Colonel Hunter sitting by the roadside with Craig and he told me that the regiment had been in a very severe engagement at Jonesboro a few days before and that the regiment was terribly cut up. He went into the fight with 110 men and came out with 43. Tom Fiester was wounded and captured. John Bradford was captured, Tom Scott was killed, Jim Doyle wounded, a great many others that he could not think of now. I only talked with him a few minutes and then went on. I had not walked far before I came up with our wagons that had gone after forage.

I never was so glad in my life, as I was to see these wagons. A declaration of peace would not have been hailed with greater joy. I was so stiff and sore that I could hardly get into the wagon, for it was with the greatest difficulty that I could raise my feet. I went on with the wagons, then, to where the brigade was encamped. The wagons were loaded with forage which was issued to the horses in the company and we went into camp near the brigade in camp number 13 near Lovejoy Station. The enemy began to throw shells right among us a little before dark and we were forced to move a little ways and get out of range.

"A weary heart and a worn out body"

Sunday, September 4: About 10 or 11 a. m. we started for Griffin. I saw Major Mulherin to-day, who told me that he wished me to commence work for him as soon as possible. I told him that I would do so as soon as I could obtain my blankets and knapsack which were along with Reid's train.

Monday, September 5: Reached Griffin, Geo. to-day where we came up with the train of Walthall's Division.

This has been an awful retreat, and the army is scattered to the four winds. The country is full of stragglers, and the men are deserting by hundreds. I don't see what delays the enemy. If they would only come on, they can capture the whole concern. I have obtained a transfer to an Arkansas Brigade, and as soon as it is convenient I shall report to Mulherin for duty, which will suit me much better than remaining with the low down vulgar set I am with now. I am still unwell, though I am improving. The whole army seems to be " down in the mouth " on account of our recent defeat.

On arriving I learned from the papers that the Yankees had plundered Clinton and boasted that they had robbed the citizens of $3,000.00 worth of property. I see where old McClellan has been nominated by the Chicago convention which I suppose is all right as he is in favor of the cessation of hostilities.[1]

---

[1] Patrick is referring to General George B. McClellan, who was nominated for the Presidency by the Democrats at their Chicago convention in 1864. Although the

Tuesday, September 6: It rained terribly last night, and I slept in a wagon with a cover on it which kept me dry. I feel very sore indeed and can hardly get about. I went to a little creek this morning and took a bath and shaved and put on some clean clothes which makes me feel much better.

This has been an awful retreat and I saw a great many cannons and wagons broken along the road as I came along, and a large quantity of ammunition thrown away. The whole country is full of stragglers and there are thousands of men deserting and going home. It is a disastrous affair and I think that this army is so weakened and demoralized that it will never be worth a curse again. Hood cannot now prevent the march of Sherman if he feels disposed to come.

To-day I got a transfer from Reid to Mulherin and as soon as I can get a way to go I shall go to the cooking train and go to work for him.

Wednesday, September 7: I feel very stiff and sore yet. The weather's cloudy and I fear we will have another stormy day of it. I feel low spirited, because everything is working very badly for the Confederacy, and I am uneasy about the family at home. I am now waiting for some way to get to Mulherin. His papers I understand are a long ways behind and I will have a great deal of work to do. I feel very thankful indeed to God that I have got along as well as I have, for at one time I thought that it was impossible to reach the train again.

Thursday, September 8: At 10 p. m. yesterday I reported to Major Mulherin, Commissary of Walthall's Division, for duty, and all day to-day I have been busily engaged upon his books and papers. I find that Mulherin has forwarded no returns since the year 1862. I don't know how it is that they have allowed him to go so long without making his returns. I think Mulherin is a very fine man, but as I have been deceived so often, I shall not be hasty in forming a decided opinion. I thought Woolfolk

---

Democratic platform demanded a cessation of hostilities, McClellan insisted upon the preservation of the Union even if hostilities had to be continued. Randall, *The Civil War and Reconstruction*, 619-24.

was a perfect gentleman on our first acquaintance, but I afterwards discovered my error.

My condition is bettered in one respect, and that is I get much
better rations which is a great item. For dinner I had snap beans,
ham, fresh tender beef, biscuits and sweet milk. I had the same
for breakfast minus the beans, with a cup of good genuine coffee
with milk in it and it has made me feel like a new man. This is a
decided improvement on spoiled meal and rotten bacon.

Friday, September 9: We moved our camp a few miles above
Lovejoy's Station. A new man by the name of Doc Cochran, a
member of an Arkansas regiment, is in the office with me. He and
I fixed up the tent which we use for an office and we have gone
to work arranging the papers for this year.

Lovejoy's Station, Saturday, September 10: Sherman has
ordered all the citizens out of Atlanta. He says he will not feed
them. He knows provisions are scarce with us, and throwing the
citizens upon us will have a tendency to make our rations
shorter. Everything is quiet now and the whole army is enjoying
a season of repose which is very much needed.

Our army I think now does not number more than 25 or 30
thousand men and it will be a tight squeeze if we have that many.
There are a great many stragglers all over the country and a great
many deserters also. It is said that the militia have all deserted.
I get no news from home.

Sunday, September 11: I have been hard at work to-day altho
it is Sunday. I do not like to work to-day, but I thought that
Mulherin desired that I should, and so I pitched in. Weather
very fair and pleasant.

Monday, September 12: Making slow progress with my work.
Everything concerned with Mulherin's business is in confusion. It
is a dirty job to right them. Jack Bell came over this morning
and read me a letter from his wife giving a full account of the
Yankee raid at Clinton. She says that the General commanding
made his headquarters at Mr. Hardesty's. She gave us the name
of some of the citizens whose property was all destroyed. She
does not mention my family and I presume from that there
was little or no damage done to them. I hope it is so. She says

that she went to the commanding officer and asked protection for the Bell family and premises, which was granted and a guard placed all around the house and no one was allowed to come in. As the general was so close to our house it is possible Mother asked protection from him. I hope she did. I cannot get a word from there, tho I have noted that letters have been coming in since the raid.

Wednesday, September 14: I received a letter from Bill Knox last night. He is at the hospital at Macon. He seems to be very despondent. He is also in a bad humor for he pitches into some members of the Regiment very severly. I wrote him a long letter to-day.

Still working away at Mulherin's old papers for the year 1863. There is an Armistice between Sherman and Hood for 10 days commencing on Monday last. This is for the purpose of giving time to get the citizens of Atlanta out and all our wagons have been sent to East Point to bring them away. Old Sherman says he is not going to feed them; that they must be supported by the Confederates.

I beat the Major two games of chess yesterday evening and he's considered a very good player. Speaking of chess, I think that when the war is over I shall endeavor to get up a chess club. It would be a very easy matter and would afford an abundance of sport during leisure hours.

Friday, September 16: This morning I got off all the returns for last year commencing with December. I heard General [D. H.] Reynolds make a short speech to his Brigade yesterday evening. He complimented them very highly upon their conduct during the campaign; he said that the Confederacy was going along well; alluded to our victories in the Trans-Mississippi department; that we had done well in keeping the enemy out of Atlanta as long as we did, and that he hoped every man was determined to hold out until we had gained our independence. He said that we had held Atlanta long enough to prevent the enemy from planning another campaign before the winter set in, but in the next breath he says " You have now finished one campaign, and you must prepare for another." If it's too late for the enemy to plan a campaign, I should think that it would be too late for us to plan one.

Collins came over to see me yesterday and while he was here lent me $2.00 which was good as I am entirely without funds and I have nothing to pay my washing bill with.

It is reported that the Yankees are to make another raid on Clinton. I wish our cavalry would go away from there, for they cause the enemy to come out of Baton Rouge and then they can't drive them back and the citizens have to suffer for it.

Saturday, September 17: The morning is quite cool and regular fall weather is here now. I am very anxious to obtain some winter clothing. I will need my over-coat and I need woolen under clothing, for I am entirely out as the clothing I have now is worn out.

The citizens are all being sent away from Atlanta and the Armistice between the two armies will close in a few days, and I have no doubt that we will then move on somewhere else, for I do not see what we can do here. Our army is too weak to oppose Sherman, and from what I can see I should judge that a move in some direction will be made in the course of the next six or eight days.

Sunday, September 18: We are picking up to leave. The day is rainy, wet and disagreeable. I have not heard which way we are to go. I wrote a letter to Mother this morning with the intention of mailing it the very first opportunity.

We have not got off yet, but everything's in readiness to move. I understand that we are to go to Fayetteville. I think it is a move of the whole army. The weather's very dark and cloudy and it has been raining some all morning and if we can judge from appearances I think it will be a very bad day.

At two p. m. we started, but there was so much artillery ahead of us that our progress was very slow. It rained nearly all the afternoon on the road but as I was in the wagon I kept dry. We passed a long line of breast-works on the road, and I saw some graves together with a number of skeletons of horses that had been killed in a skirmish sometime before.

We reached Fayetteville a little before dark and went into camp about ½ a mile from town. As the weather was so unsettled we put up a tent. I did not sleep very well as I felt fatigued and worn down.

Monday, September 19: We were up this morning before day making preparations to move. I have no idea where we are going to. The weather has turned cooler. I have much better rations now than I have had for a long time. I didn't know before that a man's diet could create such a change in his feelings. I feel like a new man since I have got something fit to eat. I have plenty of coffee with milk and sugar and plenty of milk to drink and flour nearly all of the time, and first rate beef and hams.

We were not able to make any progress until after 10 a. m. on account of the artillery being ahead of us. Their horses are in such a wretched condition that they cannot pull the pieces up a hill that is anyways steep without the assistance of about twenty men, and their progress on level ground is very slow and toilsome. The road we are travelling to-day is extremely rough and muddy. The way is filled with large stones and it makes the pulling very heavy. We reached a little place on the Atlanta and West Point road, called Palmetto, about sundown and went into camp.[2]

Tuesday, September 20: I do not like our present camp because the water is not good. I have had good water for so long a time that I am spoiled in this respect. Mulherin received an order this morning to press all the cattle, hogs, wheat and in fact everything that was eatable that he could find among the citizens. This is pretty hard on the natives but this is war and these are unusual times such as we have never seen before in this country.

Wednesday, September 21: I was up this morning at a very early hour and as usual whenever I have time I always read a few chapters in the Bible and make a few notes in my journal. It is dark and misting rain.

[2] About twenty-five miles southwest of Atlanta on the Montgomery and Selma Railroad. Here Hood sought to reorganize and reinspire the army, whose morale had been severely damaged by the loss of Atlanta and steady retreat. Hood's plans were to swing around Atlanta to the west, attack Sherman's communications and attempt to draw him into the mountainous sections of northwest Georgia and there seek a favorable opportunity to attack. *Battles and Leaders*, IV, 425.

The other day on the march I saw Captain Reed a Q. M. in an Alabama Regt. I was in his mess previous to going with Mulherin. I was sitting at the foot of a tree resting. He saw me and supposing I was pretty well worn out and would probably ask some of the drivers—I knew them all and I was very popular amongst them—to allow me to ride, he rode up to a teamster and said, "Don't allow anyone to ride in your wagon. Mind what I say, *no one*, under any circumstances." He then went to each of his drivers delivering the same strict injunctions. After he left he continued to look back to see if I didn't make an application to the teamster to ride.

Yesterday morning he came over to my tent. "How do you do, Bob? I am glad to see you" and was particularly friendly. He soon stated his business which was to obtain a drink of whiskey as he knew that Mulherin always kept it, and he also knew that I had charge of it. I told him that I could not give him any unless he saw Mulherin about it. He is a mean low minded man. He is coarse and vulgar and has very little brains. He insulted young girls all along our route with his dirty proposals, and in more than one instance if there had been any male relatives of the insulted girls present he would have had his head shot off. In one instance a Col. of artillery told him if he caught him at any more such tricks he would take him in hand himself. I despise him. He has a friend, a Capt White, who is a good match for him. They will go their death for whiskey. I never was so glad to get out of a mess in my life as I was to leave that concern.

Thursday, September 22: I think there is a grand move on hand, as every one seems to be getting ready, and I think it very probable that we will cross the Chattahoochee River and go up the country, then there is no telling which way we will go.

I am inclined to write too much and I am anxious to make this book last me the balance of the year if possible but I am becoming very profuse in words and barren in ideas.

I cannot get a word from home. I wrote to sis to send my overcoat and some woolen under clothing if possible, because I consider my obtaining a furlough a very doubtful affair.

Friday, September 23: We had a little fracas to-day in camp.

[Charles A.] Morris Lieut Col. of the 29th Ala Regt., beat Conly [J. F. Connley] the Col. of the same Regiment over the head with a big stick in great fashion. Conly accused Morris of cowardice and this led to the difficulty. Conly was an old reprobate anyhow and I wish Morris had given him more than he did.

Sunday, September 25: President Davis reviewed the troops to-day, and as he rode down the lines there were calls for Gen'l Johnston to be restored to command. The troops do not like Hood.[3]

Wednesday, September 28: This morning when I got up the Major informed me that some one had stolen his valise out of his tent while he was asleep. It contained about $5,000 in money and $40,000 in cash vouchers. He went immediately and obtained a detail of men to search for it. In the course of an hour the valise was found in the woods. It had been cut open and all the money abstracted except $500. which was in one bill and enclosed in an envelope, and had been overlooked by the thief. The vouchers were all recovered. We suspect one of the butchers as there is one of them missing, also a horse from Quarle's Brigade and we think he took the money and made his escape upon the horse.

Friday, September 30: Left our camp at 1 p. m. Crossed the Chattahoochee River on a pontoon bridge a little before dark, having made about eight miles. Slept in an open field upon the rocks. It was a rough bed but I slept very well.

Saturday, October 1: I was annoyed considerably to-day. I took my desk out of the wagon and after considerable trouble I got things comfortably arranged, when it began to rain. In great haste I had to move everything into my tent. I hadn't more than got everything in good order, before it ceased raining and the sun shone out, which rendered it so intolerably hot that I had to move out again. Just as I had got everything to my notion

---

[3] President Davis, accompanied by two of his aides, visited Palmetto to make an on-the-scene investigation to see what could be done to strengthen and invigorate the battered Army of Tennessee. The Confederate President addressed the troops and conducted an informal review in an effort to boost their sagging spirits. It was during this review, made in the company of General Hood, that men in the ranks shouted for the return of Johnston to command. Horn, *Army of Tennessee*, 372-74.

it began to rain again, and I was forced to move into the tent. As I am anxious to get on with my writing this moving backwards and forwards put me very much out of humor.

We have orders to move very early in the morning but there are no bread rations for the troops here yet. They were to have been here early in the afternoon but they have not yet arrived and I do not know how the men can march without something to eat. They have meat rations for tomorrow of bacon. General Hood or somebody else at the head of affairs doesn't seem to understand his business. I wish that I knew where we are to go. I understand that the news has been received officially that the enemy have evacuated Atlanta, but I could not hear in which direction they have gone. We are now on the road to Powder Springs.

Sunday, October 2: Moved today within twelve miles of Marietta. Nothing works right. The trains are all mixed pell-mell. Nobody knows where to find anything or anybody. There are no bread rations. We now miss the master hand of Gen Johnston. Nothing worked wrong while he had command.

Gen Hood has issued a circular in which he says he intends to strike the Rail Road and that the men must be prepared to live upon parched corn and fresh beef without salt for a time, until he can accomplish his purposes.[4] I fear this campaign will prove a failure though I will continue to hope for the best. I have no

---

[4] In early October, 1864, Hood started north to operate against Sherman's communications. By the second of the month, his troops were again on the railroad between Atlanta and the Etowah River. The next day detachments captured Big Shanty and Acworth and on the fifth the fortified post at Allatoona Pass was attacked. Sherman moved a part of his force out of Atlanta and marched northward in time to save the fort at Allatoona. Hood then swung westward, crossed the Coosa River below Rome and again struck the railroad between Resaca and Dalton. On October 13, Dalton was captured but on the next morning the Confederates marched away through Snake Creek Gap to camp grounds near LaFayette. For three days the army remained in camp while Hood meditated drawing Sherman into battle. Advised by his corps commanders that the troops were not in condition to risk battle, Hood turned westward. On the night of October 16, the Confederate commander decided upon his campaign into Tennessee and on the morning of October 17 the army was in motion toward Gadsden, Alabama. Here Hood hoped to accumulate sufficient supplies to launch an invasion into Tennessee. See Thomas R. Hay, *Hood's Tennessee Campaign* (New York, 1929).

confidence in Hood's abilities. He is a good, rough fighter, but when that is said, all is said. He hasn't the knowledge of military affairs that Johnston possesses.

Tuesday, October 4: Loring's division has possession of the road at Big Shanty. If we succeed in holding the road we will in all probability give Sherman trouble yet. There was only a very small force of the enemy there and they were soon dispersed. It is reported that the enemy sent one force of 25,000 to intercept us, but I verily believe that Sherman has been out-witted. It is reported that he has furloughed a whole division and has mustered 15,000 men out of the service as soon as he has been at Atlanta. If he has weakened his force much he will find it a hard matter to drive Hood away.

The rain poured down in torrents to-day, and the walking was terrible through the mud and water. I had an awful time last night trying to patch up an old wet tent. It weighed 500 pounds it seemed to me.

Wednesday, October 5: Moved about five miles to-day and encamped at the foot of Lost Mountain. Our forces have destroyed about twenty miles of the railroad.

After marching all day, I had to walk until near midnight endeavoring to find the Commissaries of the different Brigades, and as the night was very dark and I had no idea of their locality, this was no easy matter.

Thursday, October 6: This has been an awful day's march. It was worse than anything we have had yet. The rain poured down and the roads were flooded. I have been walking knee deep in mud and water all day. We camped near an old camp of the enemy, and I slept upon some Yankee graves all night. We happened to pitch our tents in one of their graveyards. It's the live Yankees I am afraid of, not the dead ones.

We passed through the battle ground of New Hope Church to-day. The line of works was run right through the graveyard and the tomb-stones, the Sheds, the railings around the graves were all torn away.

The woods in all directions were particularly dead. The trees were killed by the bullets and the tops and even huge trees themselves were cut down by the artillery. I never would have thought that bullets would have killed large oaks like these.

I had a troublesome time with my old tent during the night and while Doc and I were sleeping some-one rode over the tent ropes and broke them down and we had to sleep the balance of the night in the open air and this morning we left the old thing lying there.

Friday, October 7: This has been a very beautiful day after a very rainy one yesterday. I have walked nearly twenty miles to-day and I am worn out. We travelled over a mountain ridge road, and it was very toilsome marching.

We are now at a little place called Van Wert, about thirty miles from Rome, Ga. I am fearful that this move of Hood's is not a good one, and will prove a failure.

Saturday, October 8: Marched eighteen miles to-day in the direction of Blue Mountain. I rode all day to-day and I feel better than I did at this time yesterday. I wonder if it will never cease.

Sunday, October 9: We had a heavy frost this morning, the first of the season.

Monday, October 10: The artillery and wagon trains have been ordered to move by one road, and the infantry by another. I am to go with the wagon train in charge of Maj Mulherin's books and papers while the Major accompanies the troops. The Major came to me this morning saying.

"I don't suppose you have much money and as I do not know how long it may be before I see you again, you had better take this," at the same time handing me Fifty Dollars. This was quite acceptable because I hadn't a cent of money. Our route all day has been over the mountains and in some places the scenery was very beautiful. On reaching the top of a mountain I looked back, and saw the little village of Cedartown, eight miles off, which we had left early in the morning. The country for miles around with mountains in every direction lay spread out before me, and the village in the distance reminded me of pictures I have seen. "Distance lends enchantment to the view."

John Niolon, a young man in the Commissary department of an Alabama Brigade, got a little too smart for his own good this morning. John was sitting in the front part of a wagon, riding along very comfortably when Brig Gen [W. H.] Jackson, a cavalry commander, came riding by. John knew the General by sight and for amusement he sung out so that the General could hear him.

" Where was Gen Jackson at the battle of Waterloo? Up to his – – – in blood and hair and – – – – God almighty damn."

This raised a roar amongst those who heard it. Jackson who had just passed the wagon stopped his horse, and waited for the wagon to come up. Said he

" Young man, come down from that wagon." John got down. The general ordered a detail of several men, and when they reported to him, he said " Select the heaviest oak post you can find on that fence, and mind that you get a solid one." " Now young man " turning to John " be kind enough to shoulder that post. You can have the pleasure of carrying it all day over these mountains and if you didn't know where Gen Jackson was at the battle of Waterloo, you will remember where I was on the 10th Oct. 1864. Don't allow him to drop that until you go into camp tonight " he said, addressing the guard. Poor John shouldered his post with the best grace possible.

So much for being too smart.

The road is very rough. Encamped in an old field that was very wet and boggy and went to work and cooked our supper of bacon and bread which we are very lucky to have as all the others have only dry crackers.

Tuesday, October 11: I thought I had seen bad roads but that we passed over today beats anything within my experience. We struck an open pine ridge, which to all appearance had a hard clay foundation, but when the wagons and artillery came to drive on it, the wheels sank up to the axles and the mules were floundering about belly deep in the soft earth.

The woods being very open the wagons and artillery could drive about anywhere, but it was all the same, and as far as I could see, through the woods to the right and to the left, before me and behind me, the wagons and artillery were stuck, and sometimes the whole team would give up and not try to pull.

234

" Don't allow him to drop that until you go into camp tonight "

We eventually got out of this though all the artillery didn't get out until the next night.

We are encamped near the Coosa River.

Wednesday, October 12: We have one day's rest at last, and both man and brute certainly require it. We are delayed here on account of the pontoon not being laid down. It has been put down to-day and we are to leave tomorrow.

I can hear nothing from the army and I do not know where it is but rumor says it is somewhere in the neighborhood of Rome, in fact they were occupying that place yesterday, but I do not see what good it will do us.[5] I am very tired of this thing and I think it is the longest campaign that I ever heard of, at least it is the longest that I have ever been on since I have been in the army.

I hope that this move may benefit us, but my real notion is that it will do nothing more than annoy the enemy, because we are not strong enough to operate with much effect. They out-number us too far.[6]

Thursday, October 13: We are lying here waiting for I don't know what. The reason given for the delay was that the bridge was not laid, but that, I understand, was completed last night, but still we do not move, though there is no longer any pretext on that account. The fact is I don't believe that they know where to go.

Friday, October 14: Last night about 11 o'clock, we were un-expectedly ordered to move with the whole train. Those in com-mand seemed to be badly frightened, and the teams were urged into a gallop most of the time. I rode in a wagon and the road was very rough. Of all the hard riding I ever experienced this was the hardest. It was ram, jam, slam, bang, clatter and jolt, until my body felt as sore as though I had been beaten with a club. My head seemed to be battered into a jelly, it had come

[5] Hood's army flanked Rome and swung around eastward toward the railroad, which it struck at Resaca on October 12.

[6] Sherman was considerably irritated. He wrote one of his corps commanders that Hood's "whole movement is inexplicable to any common-sense theory." *Official Records*, Vol. XXXIX, Part III, p. 177.

so often in collision with the hoops that held up the wagon cover. I shall remember that ride for several days. I would have got out and walked but they were going at such speed that it would have been impossible for me to keep up. This has been the trip of trips. We drove on until sundown, having made thirty three miles without a single halt.[7] We went into camp near the village of Jacksonville, Ala.

Saturday, October 15: I wrote a long letter home to-day to mother. Also a long one to Ann Mark. My letter to Ann contained some little love, but very little, just enough I think to make it interesting if she felt inclined to read a love letter, though there is nothing in it that I would not be willing for the world to see.

I expect an answer to this, and if I don't receive it, this child will never write her another one, that is certain. She used to love me that is beyond doubt, but whether she still feels any affection for me is more than I can say. I do not think that I ought to be writing to her because I do not care anything for her. I believe that there is such a thing as real genuine love and she might really fall in love with me for good although I do not think that she is of that disposition.

I never intend to marry and there is blessed little use in my tampering with the girls, though I suppose there is no harm in writing her a letter.

When I have time I think that I shall open a correspondence with some of the young ladies of my acquaintance just for the amusement of the thing. When the war first began I corresponded with some 12 or 15 young ladies, but this correspondence was too great to keep up and I dropped them off one by one until I finally ceased to write to any of them.

Sunday, October 16: Jacksonville is a very pretty village surrounded on all sides by lofty mountains which have quite an imposing effect. There is a magnificent spring here. I heard the Reverend McFarren of Nashville preach at the Methodist Church

---

[7] The entire train was in danger of capture by Sherman's troops who were moving into the area very rapidly.

to-day. He is quite an eloquent speaker and advances good ideas, but I did not see any pretty girls.

I went to Sunday School at the Episcopal Church this morning where I saw a very pretty girl about 14 years old. She had the largest boobies for a girl of her age that I ever saw I think, and if we were to remain here any length of time I should use every exertion to make her acquaintance certain.

Tuesday, October 18: I went to a hatters' some three miles away, this morning for the purpose of purchasing a hat, but he had none made. On my return I found all hands preparing to move, and in the afternoon we made our camp about a mile south of the town in an old field where wood and water were scarce as usual.

Thursday, October 20: We left our camp near Jacksonville about 12 M and took the road towards Gadsden, Ala. We travelled about ten miles. Weather clear and cold. I have found a plan by which I can sleep very warm the coldest night that comes. As it would be a difficult matter to explain the *modus operandi*, I will simply say that it is made by leaning 5 or 6 rails near the fire at an angle of about 45 degrees, and laying upon these rails a sufficient number of blankets to cover the rails. An old tent cloth that is worthless in its legitimate use serves the purpose admirably. This concern is placed on the side of the fire whence the wind blows, and prevents the wind from carrying away the heat of the fire. Under one of these things a man can sleep quite comfortably on a very cold night.

Friday, October 21: We crossed the Coosa River on a pontoon bridge at a miserable little village called Gadsden. We went into camp about five miles beyond the town where I again got in company with the Major, the whole army being encamped here. I ascertained that we were to leave the troops again and I provided myself with extra rations of meal, flour and bacon.[8]

Saturday, October 22: At 10 o'clock last night the Major ordered me to take a wagon and go back to Gadsden for some soap for the Division. I attempted to cross the creek at the ford, but I

[8] Patrick and the supply train traveled by a route different from that used by the army.

found the ford stopped up, several wagons having mired down in endeavoring to cross. The only alternative was to go back a mile or so and take a road that led to a bridge, a mile or so above the ford. The driver of the wagon was so ignorant of his business that I had to get out and walk on ahead of him nearly all the way because he couldn't keep his team on the road. This creek is the one over which the young lady piloted Gen Forest's command, she mounting behind the General's horse for the purpose. They could not cross at the ford as the stream had suddenly risen, and she pointed out the way over the bridge. I at length reached Gadsden, and after a great deal of trouble I found the Post Commissary, who informed me that the soap I had come for had already been sent out. The night was a frosty one, and the cold or something else brought on a pain in my left side. I got into camp about daylight suffering very much from the pain. Sometime after daylight I consulted a physician. He told me to apply a mustard plaster; that it was rheumatism and was caused by the cold.

After the surgeon and his staff, who had their headquarters in the house, had gone, I went over to the house where a pretty girl was. When I went in " I seen her at the window " and went up and reported my case and asked for some mustard. She very politely invited me in and accordingly I went in, where I found a very old man sick in bed. She was a very pretty girl indeed, and I think she was the prettiest that I have seen in a long time. She was sitting on the bed with her face to the window and her back towards me. She got off the bed, which I could see under and turned in order to come into the middle of the room. As she did so her dress clung to her body and I saw her leg as high up as the knee and a very pretty one it was too. The old lady, her mother, made a mustard plaster for me and a young man, who was in the room, put it on my side for me and I went back to my camp, rolled up in my blankets and went to sleep. When I awakened the pain was much easier and I felt much refreshed.

We left this camp about 3 p.m. I rode in a wagon but the jolting caused me great pain in my side. We didn't go into camp until late at night. Made about 10 miles over a bad road.[9]

[9] At Gadsden Hood was joined by General Beauregard. The latter was in command

Sunday, October 23: My side is something easier today. Collins and I went up a mountain side and gathered our pockets full of chinkapins. They grow in great quantities here. We passed through the dingy little village of Ashville to-day. It is a little, dirty, smokey, one-horse town containing very few houses.

Monday, October 24: Foot of Racoon Mountain. Being quite unwell I took some Blue Massrilla last night, which I think benefited me some. Thinking that a walk would do me some good I went on ahead of the train this morning immediately after daylight and I have walked to this point, a distance of three miles. It is very hard work for the teams to climb this steep ascent and every wagon must have several men to aid the mules or they would never succeed in getting to the top. The distance is nearly a mile, and it is the most precipitous road that I ever saw wagons travel over. I went to the summit and waited for a long time for the wagons to make their appearance, but as everything was going along so slow I came to the conclusion that they would not be able to make it that day, so I returned to the train. From

---

of a newly created department which stretched all the way from the South Carolina coast to the Mississippi River. The Army of Tennessee was the only considerable body of troops in this command, thus Hood was subject to some supervision from Beauregard. After much deliberation Beauregard agreed to Hood's proposed Tennessee campaign. In describing his plans for the invasion of Tennessee, Hood declared: "I decided to make provision for twenty days' supply of rations in the haversacks and wagons; to order a heavy reserve of artillery to accompany the army, in order to overcome any serious opposition by the Federal gun-boats; to cross the Tennessee at or near Guntersville, and again destroy Sherman's communications at Stevenson and Bridgeport; to move upon Thomas and Schofield, and to attempt to rout and capture their army before it could reach Nashville. I intended them to march upon that city, where I would supply the army and reinforce it, if possible, by accessions from Tennessee." *Battles and Leaders,* IV, 426.

With this accomplished, Hood next planned to march into Kentucky where he could threaten Cincinnati. If Sherman should follow and attack, Hood felt by that time he would be strong enough to win a victory for the Confederacy. This accomplished, he would then send reinforcements to Lee in Virginia or, better yet, march the Army of Tennessee across the mountains and attack Grant in the rear. If Sherman did not follow him, but marched north through Georgia and North Carolina to Virginia, Hood felt that he could reach Virginia before Sherman and attack Grant in conjunction with Lee. This attack, he believed, would crush Grant and allow the combined Confederate armies under Lee to march upon Washington, or turn and destroy Sherman. As one authority has stated: "It was an entrancing dream—and it was by no means impossible." Horn, *Army of Tennessee,* 379.

the summit of this mountain I could see miles and miles away in every direction and mountain after mountain arose to the view, and the valley below lay like a picture before me. It was a very pretty scene.

As I surmised we were not able to work our way over the mountain yesterday, but we have a fair start for it to-day. I had to go along behind the wagon with a rail and hold the wheel every half foot during the ascent, and it was very hard work. We finally made it alright.

We arrived late in the night at our camp about 20 miles from where we started having crossed two mountains on the route. This I think was doing pretty well, but the way it is using up the mules is a caution.

Tuesday, October 25: We left camp very early as usual this morning. The roads are the roughest that I ever saw. We travelled today about 27 miles and went into camp about 14 miles west of Blountsville, Alabama. We passed through Blountsville. It is the dirtiest little place that I have seen yet. We heard a good deal of firing after we went into camp. This firing is supposed to be at Decatur.[10]

Friday, October 28: We did not go into camp last night until after dark and the old nigger that I have to cook for me is so worthless that I have nearly all the work to do myself. I make him bring some water occasionally which is some help.

Saturday, October 29: We were off this morning before it was getting light. We have had a better road than usual to-day.

This kind of service is enough to wear any man out. We travelled hard to-day until after night, and then we must grope around in the darkness and find wood and water and by the time we cook our suppers it is 12:00 o'clock and we must be up about three hours before day. If this was only for a day or two I would not mind it, but it is a constant thing and it is using me up.

Sunday, October 30: We did not leave camp until after day-

---

[10] Decatur was found too strongly defended by the Federals to be taken by storm and since time did not permit a siege, Hood's army continued westward hoping to find a suitable point to cross the Tennessee River. *Ibid.,* 380.

light this morning. We have bad roads again. We are to go to Tuscumbia, Alabama.[11]

From the account I can learn there is very little doubt that Lincoln will be reelected and if he is we may prepare for another four years of it. Well, *let her rip*, I say. It is better to fight always than to give it up.

Monday, October 31: We reached Tuscumbia about 3 p. m. where we found the army had just arrived and was going into camp. It is reported that Hood has crossed the river.[12]

Tuesday, November 1: We moved our train from the South side to the West side of Tuscumbia this morning immediately after daylight. There is the largest spring here that I ever saw anywhere. It is a regular river boiling out of the rocks and the stream is full and very clear. It is nearly deep enough where it comes out of the rocks to swim a horse.

Saturday, November 5: This is as fair a day we have had since last Tuesday. The weather has been very cold, wet and disagreeable, and I have not slept any ways comfortable for a week.

There were some Yankees on the other side of the river, about 2,000 and when our forces first came up, they thought they were some of our cavalry and shouted to them to come over and get some sugar and coffee. We planted some 18 pieces of artillery on the bank of the river, and placing 18 men in each pontoon boat, of which there were 25, we let loose one round at them—and started the boats across. The way the Yankees traveled was a caution.

Everyone's getting ready to move. They have taken all good mules from the Brigade train and placed them in the Supply Train and given us their old worn out stock. We are to go to Aberdeen, Mississippi and the forces are going God knows where.[13]

[11] There was a good crossing at Tuscumbia and Hood felt that its location would facilitate his getting much needed supplies. *Ibid.*

[12] Hood endured many irritating delays at Tuscumbia and it was not until November 21 that the Confederate army finally got into motion north of the river bound for middle Tennessee. *Battles and Leaders*, IV, 428-29.

[13] While Hood and his army launched the ill-fated invasion of Tennessee, Patrick and other noncombatants in the brigade train were ordered into Mississippi. Working there in relative safety, all returns could be brought up to date.

Col. Hunter was here yesterday. He looks very well indeed, and says he is in fine health. He was out of tobacco and could not get any, so I gave him a couple of bags.

Sunday, November 6:   I have just received letters from Mother and Sis dated Oct. 13, 1864, and I am very glad indeed to receive these as it relieves me very much. I feared the Yankees would do a great deal of damage. The only loss that the family sustained was Little Frank's pony. They took Frank prisoner but released him, keeping his pony. The Yankees came there on the 6th inst. disguised as Confederate cavalry but they did very little damage. Among the prisoners was Bill Stone.

Sis says she intends to get married after the war is over. She says she has found the nicest sort of a young fellow but she doesn't give his name.

Wednesday, November 9:   We left Tuscumbia about 12n. The weather is very pretty and has been for several days and to-day the rain came down in torrents. I think it rained as hard to-day as ever I saw it fall. The roads were full of water and the mud was up to the axels all day. There was an order issued by General Hood that all worn out stock should be taken out of the Supply Train and replaced with the best mules from the Brigade Train. This was done but we had our teams sent away under pretense of going for forage and thus escaped having my good team taken away and replaced by worthless stock from the Supply Train. They proved a little too sharp for us after all, for as we came out on the road after the train was under way they examined every team as it came by and took one of my mules and put in an old worthless thing that did not have strength to tighten the traces. This made our progress very slow.

About five miles from Tuscumbia we crossed a mountain. This was the worse piece of road that we had ever had yet. There were regular rock steps in the solid rocks as square and even as though they had been cut out, and each one of these steps was at least two feet high. We reached the foot of the mountain about dark but we were not able to cross it until nearly midnight, and we only succeeded then by putting seven mules to each wagon. I toiled up the long rocky hills with a weary heart and a worn out body.

243

Thursday, November 10: We were off at daylight and the road is very bad. We passed through the little town of Frankfort to-day. It is a dirty little hole consisting of a courthouse, jail, two or three little stores and two blacksmith shops.

We reached Cedar Creek about 2:00 p.m. where we were compelled to wait until the next day for the water to fall so that we could cross.

Friday, November 11: This has been a beautiful day and we have laid up all day in order that Hood's Headquarter Train may overtake and pass us. A devil of an idea to keep a whole train waiting during such beautiful weather for two or three Headquarter wagons to pass.

Had a conversation with an old citizen, the Judge of the county court, to-day and in the course of the conversation he said that the citizens in this part of the country were destitute of almost everything. They did not even have bread enough he said, and all that they had used this year was hauled from Mississippi, a distance of 75 miles.

One citizen said that he had not eaten any meat this year. He had some cows, he said, and he lived on the milk and bread and cooked his vegetables with butter.

Between the Yankees and our cavalry they are without anything.

Saturday, November 12: Still traveling. The roads are much better. The weather continues fair and frosty. I manage to sleep very well by keeping a large fire in front of my tent.

Monday, November 14: We are now within 40 miles of Aberdeen, [Mississippi] which I understand is our destination.

Tuesday, November 15: It rained hard last night and it is a cold, drizzly, unpleasant day. We are in camp near Smithville, Mississippi, which is a one-horse concern.

Wednesday, November 16: We are still in camp near Smithville. I am annoyed by several little things and I am out of humor. The weather is so bad that it is enough to give any man the blues; my tent is knee deep in mud and water and the smoke almost put my eyes out; I am hungry, for I have not had anything to eat since morning and when night comes I must roll down in the mud.

On top of the whole of it I have just learned that old Lincoln has been re-elected to the presidency. Well I suppose that we are in for four years more. Damn the day, fight it out I say as long as there is a man to fight with. I am devilish tired of Jeff Davis and his crew but I am not in favor of stopping the war until we are independent.

As the man says this is *heavy* weather. Everything we have is *heavy*. If a man can do anything very well, they say he is very *heavy* on it. If the weather is cold or hot, very dry and very wet, it is quite *heavy*. If they see an article in the papers they deem pretty good, they pronounce it a *heavy* document, if they see a pretty woman, she is very *heavy* one.

Sunday, November 20: We arrived at this camp day before yesterday. We are some eight or ten miles from Aberdeen. I have secured a room at a farmer's house nearby to write in. There are two lovely young ladies there.

Saturday, December 3: I have been so very busy with my returns that I have not written in my journal for several weeks.

The weather has been exceedingly mild during all this week, almost as warm as summer weather. I have a comfortable, pleasant room, but it has no fireplace, though I am close to the parlor where there is always a good fire, and when I go in to the fire I always see the girls. I am making love to the eldest one right *heavy*. Her name is Margaret, or as they call her Maggie. The younger one is named Isabelle. They are both passably good looking and tolerably intelligent, though they are very dark skinned. Maggie comes to my room every half hour to see me and I don't know but what she has really taken a fancy to me, at least she acts a little like it.

There is a very handsome girl, a Miss Stuart, who is a very stylish young lady indeed that comes here frequently. I am acquainted with her and I believe that if I had an opportunity I could make pretty good headway with her but I suppose that it is better to take one at a time, because between two stools I may fall to the floor.

Miss Stuart was here this morning to see Maggie about taking part in some tableaus they are getting up, but she declined. I am getting along slowly with my returns and now I have come to a full stop for the want of vouchers.

Saturday, December 24: This year is nearly gone and the fourth Christmas that I have been in the army is now at hand. I am 29 years old today, though I tell the girls that I am only 26.

We are expecting every day to receive orders to leave for Columbus, Mississippi to store our papers there.

I have had a good time since I have been at this camp. I have had a good comfortable bed to sleep in every cold night that has come and I have had a pleasant time with the girls in the neighborhood. I have carried on a heavy flirtation with Maggie and she and I are as loving as any two beings can be. I believe she loves me though it is hard to tell. One thing is that she allows me to take a great many liberties with her which I do not think she would allow anyone else to take.

Sunday, December 25: This is destined to be a dull Christmas to all hands in camp though I have passed the time pleasantly enough with the girls.

Monday, December 26: It is rumored that we are to leave this place before a great while. I will be loath to go because I have the best kind of quarters and besides that, Maggie and I are getting along very well indeed the particulars of which I shall give at some future time.

I have sent out several times for some whiskey but have failed to get it, and I presume that it will be better if I don't get it. The day is dreadfully cold and gloomy.

I am teaching Maggie Phonography so that she can correspond with me in that style when I go away.

I have bid farewell to Miss Stuart in the way of a flirtation, because I have already as much as I can attend to with Maggie and it is impossible to carry on both at once. Maggie is very affectionate and I have a good deal of pleasure in her society.

Tuesday, December 27: We were ordered to Columbus, Mississippi this morning, and about 2 p. m. we left camp. I went up to Mr. Ross's and bid the family farewell, and Maggie let me hug her and kiss her for perhaps the last time. Maggie says that she never will forget me and I do not believe that she will for I never talked to any woman in my life as I did to her. She says that she never had any man to presume to say such things to her as I did, and that what astonished her so much was that she should take it up and carry it on with me. I told her that the reason was because she loved me and had the same confidence in me that she would have if I were her husband. I know that if she did not love me that she would not have let things go on as they did.

One night I had a great notion to seduce her, but I didn't do it. There is one thing that I have resolved never to do, and that is to seduce a girl and if I should allow my passions to get the better of my judgment, I will marry the girl that I slept with. I could have .seduced Maggie for I had gained her entire confidence and she had come to think that everything I said and did was all right and looked up to me in everything. It was with a heavy heart that I left her, for I had formed quite an attachment for her and I was sorry to leave her and she was sorry to see me go. Perhaps I may meet her again before the war is over. She is a smart, active intelligent girl, and will make some man an excellent wife, but I could not think of marrying her. She gave me a lock of her hair before we parted.

Wednesday, December 28: We arrived at Columbus about 2 p.m. and had a great deal of trouble in finding room for our brigade.

After hunting around a long time and going from one citizen to another we at length obtained room, by storing part in one place and part in another. John Niolon and I are in the same room together and a very comfortable place it is too. It is a small room but there is room enough for his baggage and mine and there is a fire place. Our greatest trouble has been to get wood. All we use now we get by hiring a nigger to steal it for us, but we expect to buy some in a day or two.

I sent Maggie and Ebbie a thimble each and I also sent Maggie a paper of snuff which I ascertained that she was in the habit of using. If I only had some money I would make her a present of some value. I wrote her a short note also. The weather's turning quite cold.

Thursday, December 29: I sent a long letter to Maggie to-day by a man who is going out there. Fay Stuart, although much the handsomest, I have dropped from the fact that it is impossible to carry on a flirtation with two girls at the same time.

Friday, December 30: Weather very cold and freezing. We bought a load of wood to-day, a little over ¼ of a cord, for which we paid $13.00.

It is reported that Jeff Davis is dead; that Hood has been very badly whipped in front of Nashville and is in full retreat with the enemy hotly pursuing, and that Forest is gallantly covering the retreat. Hood, they say, has lost 65 pieces of artillery besides about 10,000 men. He is now at or near the Tennessee River in North Alabama.

Taken all together the aspect of affairs is anything but encouraging to say the least. If the government allows Hood full swing, he will soon terminate his army.[14]

I took a walk over Columbus to-day and I find it a very pretty place indeed. It is some-what larger than Baton Rouge and there are quite a number of elegant residences. I like the place very much.

Sunday, January 1: This is the first time I have written 1865 to put the date. The weather is fair and very cold.

John and I are doing our own cooking but we are both so lazy that we never cook anything until starvation drives us to it. We sleep very comfortably because we keep a fire burning all night.

Tuesday, January 10: Have just learned of the capture of our regiment at or near Franklin, Tennessee. Col. Hunter and the whole squad went up together.[15]

---

[14] After appalling losses at Franklin, Hood marched to Nashville where on December 15 the Confederate army was shattered in one of the most complete victories won by a Union army during the war. Following this great disaster the forlorn remnant of the Army of Tennessee retreated to Tuscumbia, through Iuka to Corinth and thence to Tupelo, Mississippi where they went into camp on January 10, 1865. Generals Forrest and Walthall gallantly shouldered the difficult task of holding off the pursuit and thus permitting what was left of Hood's army to escape. Horn, *Army of Tennessee*, 394-421.

[15] So many men in the Fourth Louisiana were killed or captured in the fighting around Nashville that the few survivors were added to the Sixteenth Louisiana. They continued to serve with this unit until January 12, 1865, when the Fourth

I have to-day just returned from a visit to my darling Maggie and a devil of a time I have had of it, too. I went out last Saturday and spent one day and two nights there. She seems to love me better than ever and she talks to me now as freely as ever woman spoke to man. I kissed her and hugged her for two hours the morning I left. I am certain she will not forget me soon.

I started back yesterday but it rained so very hard that I was forced to stop at a house about nine miles from town where I had first-rate quarters though the old lady charged me $8.00.

Sunday, January 15: I am bothered like the devil by some men belonging to French's Division who are in the next room. They are entirely too free with everything John and I have, and they took the liberty of appropriating anything they see. And they do it too. They take my wood, and candles, and ink and paper and one day I had some rations cooked and they came in when I was eating and ate the most of it up. Damn such familiarity I say. I don't like it at all.

I received another letter from Maggie day before yesterday. She seems to be very uneasy and thinks that I will speak about what has been said between herself and me. She says that the thoughts of me speaking about it makes her particularly miserable. I wrote her a letter in reply assuring her that I never would mention it. She says that in her cool moments when I am not about she trembles for the manner in which she has talked to me.

Jack Bell and I are both quite homesick and very anxious to get home. The troops are being furloughed now by the regiment and brigade and if Jack and I do not go to the front I am afraid that we will be entirely overlooked.

It is pretty heavy on us to pay about $8.00 per month for fuel. Damn a government that can not furnish us a little wood.

Wednesday, January 18: I received a letter from Maggie last

Regiment was partially reorganized and ordered to Mobile. On February 3, 1865, the war-worn remnant arrived at Camp Moore and a few days later helped to defend Spanish Fort in one of the last actions of the war. Less than forty men answered the final muster. Kendall, "Diary of Surgeon Craig," *loc. cit.*, 53-70.

night. She speaks about a party they had at her house last week and she says she wishes I had been there.

It is rumored that the Army is to be sent to South Carolina and some of us to Georgia and some of us to Alabama, but the truth is that no one knows anything about it.[16]

There are reports floating also that we are about to make a proposition to France and England that if they will recognize us that we will emancipate the slaves within 25 years, and that this thing is now before our Congress. For my part I am in favor of it and so is every man I have heard speak about it. If we continue to lose ground as we have for the last 12 months, we will soon be defeated, and then slavery will be gone any way, and I think it is better that we should give up slavery and gain our independence. There is no doubt in my opinion that we are gone unless something is done for our welfare and that very quick.[17]

Jack Bell and I are both very anxious to obtain a furlough but there seems to be no prospect of it at present. I spend my time reading, writing and playing chess.

Sunday, January 22: I have received orders from Mulherin to report to the Army at once and I will be off in the morning if I can procure transportation. I have the order and all is ready but there is some difficulty in obtaining transportation.

There are base rumors, *heavy* rumors, as the boys say, floating this morning. England and France are to recognize the Confederacy on the 4th of March next.

Hood's Army is completely cleaned out and demoralized. This campaign has been the most disastrous of the war, and is certainly a very severe blow to us.

What is left of our regiment has been consolidated with the 16th regiment and Gibson's Brigade has been ordered to Mobile.

[16] After a short rest the Army of Tennessee was off to the wars again. They were sent to the Carolinas to join their beloved General Joseph E. Johnston in a frantic effort to halt Sherman as he marched northward from the sea. Stewart's corps, including Patrick's regiment, left Tupelo on January 30. Horn, *Army of Tennessee*, 423.

[17] In one final effort to gain European aid the Confederate government proposed to England and France emancipation of the Negroes if slavery was the "obstacle" to recognition. This proposal ended in futility and thus the last hopes of the Confederacy faded. Owsley, *King Cotton Diplomacy*, 550-61.

I learned that the brigade is permanently detached from the Army of Tennessee and will remain at Mobile all the time. Gibson says that he intends to order every detailed man back to the command.

Wednesday, January 25: I have not been able to get away yet for the want of transportation. The train has been ordered on the other road for the purpose of transporting troops down the road and will not be back for some days. I am very anxious to get away for I have very little money and I am here on expense. I would like to be with the Army any how because I would stand some chance of obtaining a furlough and I think it is about time that I was going home for it has been over 12 months since I was there.

I believe that I mentioned having received eight letters from home. Mother wrote me a letter in which she says that she received my letter and that Ann received the one that I wrote her. Ann has not answered it yet and I wrote to Mother that if Ann did not write to me, why God bless her, she might go. That I was much obliged to Ann for sympathizing with me in my troubles, but that if she did not deem my letters worth an answer, that I would rather she would bestow her sympathies where they would be more appreciated. Damn the day she asked me and insisted upon my writing to her and this makes the third time that I have written to her, and if she does not answer this she may just go to hell. That is all I have to say.

Friday, January 27: I was informed this morning that there would not be any train here for two weeks. I am very anxious to leave this place but I must succumb to circumstances. It costs me a great deal to purchase wood and as the weather is very cold I am bound to have a fire all the time, and unless I keep a fire burning all night I sleep cold. The ground is frozen.

I have been quite unwell for ten days past with rheumatism in my chest which is very painful and I fear very dangerous though I am much better now. I sent Mulherin a telegram asking him what I must do but I have received no reply. Our corps is about to leave for Meridian where I hope it will remain for the balance of the winter, though some seem to think it will be sent to South Carolina, with the other two corps.

I see very little prospect of our gaining our independence soon, and in fact I have lost all hope of our working our way through unaided. In my opinion France and England will never allow the old union to be as it was before the war and I believe that they will recognize us if they feel assured that we are about to go under.

I received a letter from Maggie yesterday. I pronounced the question in shorthand to her. It was whether or not she loved me well enough to marry me. She wrote back that she could not read it. I have written another letter saying that I should never ask the question again, and that for the future I should not ask any questions. I have written her a pretty sharp letter and if she does not like it I cannot help it. She is a nice girl and she has always treated me very well indeed, but as I never expect to marry her, I had just as well raise the devil about that as anything else, and bid farewell to her afterward.

I have spent many happy days with her, and she says they were very pleasant to her. I believe that she loves me, but she is afraid to acknowledge it because she thinks that I may deceive her. I am surprised now that I went as far as I did though I do not think she is a girl to take anything much to heart, so there is no harm done anyway. She will soon forget me and I will soon forget her, and that will be the last of the matter. She would have let me do anything that I pleased if I had remained there a little longer, and in fact I could have done it any way, but I did not feel disposed to take advantage of her. She confided wholly in me, and she kept no secrets from me. I almost fell in love with her on account of her unreserved confidence in me. She talked to me about everything just as though I had been a girl as well as herself. My letter is very cold and formal and in fact I am almost in doubt whether to send it or not, but then I had as well break the matter off now as at any other time.

There is nothing new from anywhere. I pass my time reading when I can get anything to read, and in playing chess with any player that happens to drop in. I have improved considerably since last summer though I play a very poor game yet. Playing with inferior players doesn't improve me much.

Saturday, January 28: I sent my letter to Maggie this morning by a man who is going there. I shall wait an answer to this with more impatience than any that I have written her yet. It is a pretty sharp letter and one that must certainly call forth a decisive answer. She has always seemed to be very fearful of offending me. Now it will be the very devil if she is really in earnest about the matter and should take the matter to heart. A woman is a fool anyhow and there is no telling anything about them. She may be in earnest and she may not. I hope she will think nothing more of the matter though it would be a little flattering to my pride to be assured that she did love me but it seems to me I had rather she didn't on her own account. I believe it to be wrong and in fact mean for any man to trifle with the affections of a young girl especially when she has not seen any more of the world than Maggie has and for this reason I wish that she would think no more of me. I can leave her without a single pang, though she doesn't think so. I wish now that nothing more than words of friendship had passed between us.

In my opinion we are nearly at the end of our row. I feel pretty sure that Richmond will go next after the fall of Savannah, and that will be the forerunner of our downfall. When Sherman is prepared he will capture Savannah and Charleston and then away everything goes. I think that I have been one of the most sanguine men in the Confederacy until the last two months or rather until the fall of Atlanta and now I cannot see any salvation for us except in foreign intervention, which I have no doubt will come before we are entirely subdued. France must recognize us because if she doesn't and the Confederacy is brought back into the Union I would not give a cent for Maximilian's City in Mexico. The United States did not know its strength until the war began, and now they have a very powerful fleet ready to cope with any nation on the globe, provided that nation makes the attack. They are abundantly able to drive away any invader from the soil for their armies are already equipped and now in the field.

I received a telegram from Mulherin just now instructing me

to take the baggage to Artesia, that they were to start yesterday.

Sunday, January 29: This is a beautiful day and the weather has moderated considerably.

There are more peace rumors this morning. A telegram from Richmond dated yesterday states that Vice-President Stephens, Hunter of Virginia and Judge Campbell are to be sent to Washington empowered to treaty with the United States for peace.[18]

The weather has moderated considerably and the ground has thawed and the sun once more shines out warm and pleasant though the earth is a little damp under foot. It being so genial, Joshua Smith and I took a long walk over the city and among other places we visited the city cemetery. There are a great many tombstones and monuments in it some of which are very pretty. I presume the place has been used as a graveyard for a great number of years but it has the appearance somehow of being of very recent date. The tombstones and monuments look as though they had been newly put up in the last two or three years, and it reminds one very much of a new house just erected in the midst of a forest. A great many of the graves had fresh evergreens placed upon them, showing that those who lay quietly resting beneath are not forgotten by their loving friends and relations. I saw one old portly fine looking gentleman standing near a monument leaning upon his cane, seemingly in deep thought. He looked quite lonely and disconsolate. Joshua knew him and informed me that his wife was buried beneath the marble that was near the old man.

There was one marble tomb that had a door which seemed to be left so that anyone could open it, and Joshua and I by means of a little stick opened it and looked in. We saw a large metal case, very rusty, another one which was done up in zink or lead and the remains of a wooden one that had almost entirely decayed, as well as the body that was originally in it. There were

---

[18] Reference is to the approaching Hampton Roads Conference where three Confederate commissioners—Alexander H. Stephens, Robert M. T. Hunter, and John A. Campbell met with President Lincoln and Secretary of State William H. Seward on February 3, 1865. The upshot was no agreement since Lincoln would hear of nothing but Union, emancipation, and no armistice while the Confederates would be satisfied with nothing less than independence. Coulter, *Confederate States of America,* 552-53.

some half bones lying near it, a part of a skull. The tomb emitted no smell whatever. It always makes me feel sad to look at such things.

There are plenty of peace rumors floating now and I have no doubt that matters will be brought to a close before a great while.

Monday, January 30: Weather very fair and pleasant. It is probable that we will not be able to get away before next week because the whole army must be moved to Meridian before we are allowed to start.

I wrote another letter to Maggie to-day, but there was nothing particular in it. It was quite a cold one and does not breathe that spirit of love that all my former letters have. I am making my arrangements to gradually drop out now. I sent the letter by Collins who says he will deliver it.

I have just received orders from Mulherin to report with everything to him at West Point. He sent two wagons to bring his baggage and I will leave in the morning at daylight if I can get all things ready. I am glad to get away though I would like to have received a letter from Maggie before I left.

Appendix[1]

INDIVIDUALS MENTIONED IN PATRICK'S DIARY

Allain, Louis, corpl., Co. I; paroled at Natchitoches, Louisiana, June 6, 1865.

Andrew, James, private, Co. G, captured at Canton, Mississippi, July 10, 1863; discharged from military prison, St. Louis, Missouri, July 31, 1863.

Attler, Carl, private, Co. A.

Ball, Jack, Mrs., a resident of Clinton.

Batchelor, T. J. C., private, Co. G; transferred to a Clinton hospital, December, 1862.

Bell, Clarence, sergt., Co. G; taken prisoner of war and paroled at Meridian, Mississippi, May 14, 1865.

Bell, Jack, private, Co. G.

Bell, R. P., private, Co. G; listed by Patrick as being wounded in the leg at the battle of Ezra Church near Atlanta, Georgia, July 28, 1864.

Blow, James M., sergt., commissary, Cos. I, F, S; paroled at Meridian, Mississippi, May 14, 1865.

Boone, R. M., capt., 2nd Field Battery, Louisiana Artillery; died of wounds June 15, 1863, at Port Hudson.

Bradford, Barnets G., private, Co. F.

Bradford, John, private, Co. A; captured and paroled at Port Hudson, July 4, 1863; wounded August 31, 1864, at Jonesboro, Georgia; recaptured. He was Robert Patrick's closest friend during the course of the war.

Brown, Rees, private, Co. K; listed by Patrick as being wounded in both legs at the battle of Ezra Church near Atlanta, July 28, 1864; granted disability furlough August 3, 1864.

Burns, John H., private, Co. G; taken prisoner of war and released on oath of allegiance to the United States, May 18, 1865.

Cain, Richard, a resident of Clinton.

Carter, William P., private, Co. A; present on all rolls to February, 1862.

---

[1] Unless otherwise indicated all Confederate soldiers identified are from Robert Patrick's own regiment—the Fourth Louisiana Infantry.

Chapman, Boatner, private, 4th Co. Battery, Washington (Louisiana) Artillery; promoted to chaplain, December 30, 1864. He was a young Clinton minister who enlisted at the age of 17.

Chapman, W. J., private, Co. A; killed in action July 28, 1864, at the battle of Ezra Church near Atlanta, Georgia.

Collins, Hart, a clerk in Patrick's office from Clayton, Alabama.

Collins, R. E., private, Co. A; killed in a skirmish at New Hope Church, Georgia, June 4, 1864.

Comstock, George C., Mrs., a resident of Clinton.

Cook, Albert G., sergt., Co. K; listed by Patrick as having been killed on July 28, 1864, at the battle of Ezra Church near Atlanta, Georgia.

Craig, E. D., private, Co. K.

Craig, J. M., surgeon.

Crawford, Arthur, private, Co. A; detailed to commissary duty.

Crocket, Garnell, a resident of Clinton.

Daniels, B. S., sergt. major, Co. G; wounded near Atlanta August 31, 1864; died September 3, 1864.

D'Armond, Frank, private, Co. G; listed by Patrick as having been wounded in the hip on July 28, 1864, at the battle of Ezra Church near Atlanta, Georgia; taken prisoner of war.

D'Armond, J. G., 1818-1892, proprietor of a boarding house in Clinton.

D'Armond, John, sergt., Co. G; listed by Patrick as having been killed on July 28, 1864, at the battle of Ezra Church near Atlanta, Georgia.

Davis, Clay, a close friend of Patrick and former resident of Clinton who served as telegraph operator at Magnolia, Mississippi. The two frequently corresponded during the war.

Davis, Lewis, a civilian employee working at Port Hudson and a friend of Patrick.

Davis, Morris B., private, Co. G; member of the regimental band; captured near Nashville, Tennessee, December 16, 1864; exchanged February 17, 1865.

Delee, Felix, private, Co. E, 1st Louisiana Cavalry.

Depriest, James, private, Co. A; killed April 6, 1862, at the battle of Shiloh.

Doughty, W. E., private, Co. G; listed by Patrick as having been wounded in the face July 28, 1864, at the battle of Ezra Church near Atlanta, Georgia.

Doyle, John, private, Co. G; wounded near Jonesboro, Georgia, August, 1864. He was one of Patrick's closest friends during the war.

Easley, W. A., private, Co. I; detailed as teamster.

Falconer, Kinlock, Adj. Gen., Army of Tennessee.

Fenner, C. E., capt., commanding officer, Fenner's Battery.

Fiester, A. T., capt., Co. A; killed August 31, 1864, near Atlanta, Georgia.

Fiester, Thomas, private, Co. G. He was one of Patrick's closest friends during the war.

Fogg, Howell J., a commissary officer at Port Hudson.

Gail, Caleb, jailkeeper in Clinton.

Garner, George G., lt. col., Adj. General's Department, Army of Tennessee.

Godfrey, J. A., chaplain, Cos. F, S; resigned in September, 1863.

Green, P. A., private, Co. G; listed by Patrick as having been wounded in the thigh July 28, 1864, at the battle of Ezra Church near Atlanta, Georgia.

Gurney, William J., private, Co. K; proprietor of a confectionary, bakery, and grocery establishment in prewar Clinton.

Hardesty, Lee, Mrs., a resident of Clinton.

Haynes, J. H., private, Co. C.

Hays, R. W., private, Co. A; listed by Patrick as having been wounded in the hand and arm July 28, 1864, at the battle of Ezra Church near Atlanta, Georgia.

Heckler, Gus, private, Co. G; drummer in the regimental band.

Hereford, L. S., 1st lt., Co. F.

Hilliard, John T., capt., Co. G; killed April 6, 1862, at the battle of Shiloh.

Hobgood, E. W., private, Co. A; listed by Patrick as being wounded in the face July 28, 1864, at the battle of Ezra Church near Atlanta, Georgia.

Hobgood, Harvin, private, Co. G; listed by Patrick as being killed July 28, 1864, at the battle of Ezra Church near Atlanta, Georgia, but he was only wounded and taken prisoner; died in Federal military prison, March 28, 1865.

Hunter, Samuel Eugene, col., commander, 4th Louisiana Infantry Regiment; captured near Franklin, Tennessee, December 17, 1864; released on oath July 25, 1865. Hunter died June 19, 1870, just a few months prior to his thirty-eighth birthday. On June 28, 1870, the surviving members of his old regiment met at the East Feliciana Parish courthouse in Clinton to honor their former commander by organizing a Hunter and East Feliciana Soldier's Monument Society. A brief biography of Hunter, written by his old friend Capt. J. G. Kilbourne, may be found in the *East Feliciana Patriot* (Clinton), July 2, 1870.

Huston, Henry, corpl., Co. G; listed by Patrick as being wounded in the arm July 28, 1864, at the battle of Ezra Church near Atlanta, Georgia; captured August 5, 1864; paroled at Meridian, Mississippi, May 14, 1865.

Hyde, Charles H., private, Co. I; detailed as hospital steward.

Jackson, James, col., 35th Alabama Infantry Regiment.

Jackson, William, private, Co. A; listed by Patrick as being wounded in the face July 28, 1864, at the battle of Ezra Church near Atlanta, Georgia.

Johnson, B. C., corpl., Co. G; paroled June 3, 1865, at Alexandria, Louisiana.

Jones, W. B., private, Co. G; listed by Patrick as being wounded in the arm July 28, 1864, at the battle of Ezra Church near Atlanta, Georgia; captured near Franklin, Tennessee, December 20, 1864; exchanged at New Orleans, May 25, 1865.

Kendrick J. S., private, Co. F.

Kilbourne, J. G., capt., quartermaster.

Knox, W. A., private, Co. A; leg amputated after wounds received July 28, 1864, at the battle of Ezra Church near Atlanta, Georgia.

Lane, William A., 1st lt., Co. A, 16th Louisiana Infantry Regiment.

Lea, W. D. corpl., Co. A; killed July 12, 1863, near Jackson, Mississippi.

Lee, P. H., lt. col., commandant of the post in Clinton.

Lewis, Alonzo, a resident of Clinton.

Lewis, Charles D., sergt., surgeon, Cos. C, F, S.

McAdams, J. P., private, Co. A; listed by Patrick as having been wounded on July 28, 1864, at the battle of Ezra Church near Atlanta, Georgia; died August 5, 1864.

McCarthy, Daniel, lt., Co. D; died of wounds received August 9, 1864, near Atlanta, Georgia.

McGuire, Thomas, capt., Cos. B, F, S, 12th Louisiana Infantry Regiment.

Mackey, Wade, a resident of the Clinton area.

McKie, Robert, private, Co. A; killed at the battle of Shiloh, April 6, 1862.

Mansker, James, telegraph operator and photographer in Clinton.

Marchant, James A., sergt., Co. K; wounded near Atlanta, Georgia, August 31, 1864; left arm amputated.

Mark, Ann, a resident of Clinton.

Marston, James, sergt., Co. A; listed by Patrick as having been wounded in the head July 28, 1864, at the battle of Ezra Church near Atlanta, Georgia.

Matthews, Wallace W., private, Co. A; captured at Nashville, December 16, 1864, exchanged February 17, 1865.

Miles, William R., col., captured July 9, 1864, at Port Hudson; exchanged October 15, 1864.

Mills, Eliza, Miss, prominent in Clinton educational circles. From 1842-1853 she served as principal of the Clinton Female Academy. In 1855 she organized the Hope Terrace School in Clinton which continued to operate until the Civil War. See William Mobley, "The Academy Movement in Louisiana," *Louisiana Historical Quarterly*, XXX (July, 1947), 823.

Montan, William, private, Co. B; clerk, commissary department.

Morgan, J. H., private, Co. K; deserted and captured at Clinton, October 9, 1864; released on oath May 29, 1865.

Moses, Bernard, chief musician, regimental band.

Nash, J. E., private, Co. G.

Norwood, Alexander S., col., 27th Louisiana Infantry Regiment; captured at Vicksburg, July 4, 1863; paroled at New Orleans, January 9, 1865; served as sheriff in East Feliciana Parish prior to the war.

Overton, J. F., private, Co. K.

Pennington, William F., lt. col.; captured at Nashville, December 16, 1864, released from Johnson's Island, Ohio, July 25, 1865.

Pond, Preston, Jr., col., 16th Louisiana Infantry Regiment.

Pope, Marshall, private, surgeon, Cos. F. S; resigned May 19, 1862.

Postlewaite, J. J., private, Co. D, 18th Louisiana Infantry Regiment; taken prisoner of war and paroled at Meridian, Mississippi, May 11, 1865.

Pullen, E. J., major, captured at Nashville, December 16, 1864; released on oath of allegiance July 25, 1865, at Johnson's Island, Ohio.

Purdy, V. M., private, Co. C; taken prisoner of war and paroled at Meridian, Mississippi, May 14, 1865.

Raphael, H., capt., quartermaster at Port Hudson.

Reid, James, Jr., capt., Co. D; captured near Franklin, Tennessee, December 17, 1864, released on oath of allegiance from Johnson's Island, Ohio, June 17, 1865.

Richarts, John, private, musician, Co. A; captured near Columbia, Tennessee, December 16, 1864; exchanged at Pt. Lookout, Maryland, February 17, 1865.

Roach, Hannah, Miss, a resident of Clinton.

Roberts, D. B., an elderly Baptist preacher who was the father of John M. and William J. A. Roberts, prominent residents of Clinton.

Rowe, John S., private, Co. A.

Scharch, Charles, private, Co. D; detailed as a teamster. Apparently Private Scharch did not relish the life of an infantryman for in April, 1864, he requested and received a transfer to the Confederate Navy.

Scott, T. J., 3rd lt., Co. G; detailed to serve as Chief of Police in Clinton; killed in action August 31, 1864, near Atlanta, Georgia.

Shropshire, W. C., private, Co. A.

Skipwith, Henry, sergt., Cos. E, A; taken prisoner of war and paroled at Meridian, Mississippi, May 14, 1865.

Skipwith, Thomas, private, Co. A.

Steadman, George A. W., 2nd lt., Co. K; listed by Patrick as having been wounded in the head July 28, 1864, at the battle of Ezra Church near Atlanta, Georgia.

Stoke, Jane, Miss, a resident of Clinton.

Stone, William M., private, Co. A; taken prisoner of war at Port Hudson, July 9, 1863.

Thompson, David C., sergt., Co. A; wounded in the battle of Atlanta; paroled at Meridian, Mississippi, May 14, 1865.

Wall, Benjamin D., private, Co. B., 18th Louisiana Infantry Regiment; died in action at the battle of Mansfield, April 8, 1864.

Wall, Wesley W., private, Co. G, 19th Louisiana Infantry Regiment; captured at Chickamauga, Georgia, September 20, 1864; discharged at Camp Douglas, Illinois, June 14, 1865.

Weathersbee, Sam, private, Co. F; detailed as ambulance driver.

Wedge, D. J., private, Co. G; a prominent Clinton attorney both before and after the war.

Whitehead, Joseph, private, Co. A; detailed as hospital steward.

Whiteman, Charles P., capt., Co. D; captured at Port Hudson, July 9, 1863; released at Johnson's Island, Ohio, June 11, 1865.

Williams, S. B., private, Co. A; killed in action near Atlanta, Georgia, July 21, 1864.

Winens, Charles R., major, 19th Louisiana Infantry Regiment.

Woolfolk, James D., major, quartermaster, Cantey's division, Army of Tennessee.

Wooster, J. S., 1st lt., Co. D, commissary officer, captured near Morganza Bend, Louisiana, October 6, 1863.

Worsham, J. D., sergt., Co. A, wounded on August 31, 1864, near Atlanta, Georgia.

Worthy, Scott J., private, Co. A; taken prisoner of war and paroled at Shreveport, Louisiana, June 20, 1865.

Zimmerman, Dominique, a resident of Clinton.

Index